Creating the Practical Man of Modernity

Focused on the appropriation of John Dewey's ideas on progressive education in revolutionary Mexico, this book reconsiders the interpretation and application of Dewey's ideas in the world. Rodriguez examines the use of Dewey in Mexico's state-building projects as a vantage point to assess the global impact of Dewey's pedagogy. As these projects converged with Dewey's desire to employ education as a tool for effective social change, Rodriguez understands Dewey not just as a philosopher but as an integral part of the Americas' progressive movement and era.

Victor J. Rodriguez is lecturer in history at Wenzhou-Kean University, China.

Routledge International Studies in the Philosophy of Education

For a full list of titles in this series, please visit www.routledge.com

34 **Education Reform and the Concept of Good Teaching**
   Derek Gottlieb

35 **Posthumanism and Educational Research**
   Edited by Nathan Snaza and John A. Weaver

36 **Parallels and Responses to Curricular Innovation**
   The Possibilities of Posthumanistic Education
   Brad Petitfils

37 **The Educational Prophecies of Aldous Huxley**
   The Visionary Legacy of Brave New World, Ape and Essence, and Island
   Ronald Lee Zigler

38 **Popper's Approach to Education**
   A Cornerstone of Teaching and Learning
   Stephanie Chitpin

39 **Neuroscience and Education**
   A Philosophical Appraisal
   Edited by Clarence W. Joldersma

40 **Teachability and Learnability**
   Can Thinking Be Taught?
   Paul Fairfield

41 **Reinventing Intercultural Education**
   A Metaphysical Manifest for Rethinking Cultural Diversity
   Neal Dreamson

42 **Creating the Practical Man of Modernity**
   The Reception of John Dewey's Pedagogy in Mexico
   Victor J. Rodriguez

Creating the Practical Man of Modernity

The Reception of John Dewey's Pedagogy in Mexico

Victor J. Rodriguez

NEW YORK AND LONDON

First published 2017
by Routledge
711 Third Avenue, New York, NY 10017

and by Routledge
2 Park Square, Milton Park, Abingdon, Oxon, OX14 4RN

Routledge is an imprint of the Taylor & Francis Group, an informa business

© 2017 Taylor & Francis

The right of Victor J. Rodriguez to be identified as author of this work has been asserted by him in accordance with sections 77 and 78 of the Copyright, Designs and Patents Act 1988.

All rights reserved. No part of this book may be reprinted or reproduced or utilised in any form or by any electronic, mechanical, or other means, now known or hereafter invented, including photocopying and recording, or in any information storage or retrieval system, without permission in writing from the publishers.

Trademark notice: Product or corporate names may be trademarks or registered trademarks, and are used only for identification and explanation without intent to infringe.

Library of Congress Cataloguing in Publication Data
A catalog record for this book has been requested

ISBN: 978-1-138-19460-1 (hbk)
ISBN: 978-1-315-63878-2 (ebk)

Typeset in Sabon
by Apex CoVantage, LLC

I owned an infinite gratitude to my family for their support and appreciation of the sacrifices in pursuing my doctoral career. To my late father, Victoriano, my mother, Corina, and my brother Daniel, I dedicate this achievement, for it is the fruit of our collective effort to survive and prevail in what have often been trying circumstances. My brother has been untiring in his support of my decision to enter graduate school, and few know how much it meant to me to complete my education. I also owed a debt of gratitude to my grandparents, José, Felicitas, and María. Their determination to succeed and leave their places of birth to pursue a new future always informed my orientation to life. I have finally fulfilled my promise to you.

Contents

	Preface	ix
	Acknowledgments	xxi
1	Introduction: Race, Modernity and Nation in the Reception of Dewey's Pedagogy in Mexico	1
2	Radical Dewey: Deweyan Pedagogy in Mexico, 1915–1923	7
3	Practical Dewey: Mexican Protestants and the Promise of America	29
4	Moisés Saénz and the Revolutionary Project of the *Escuelas Activas*	57
5	Dangerous Dewey: The Critique of the Dewey Project in Mexico (and Dewey's Critique of Mexico)	100
	Bibliography	135
	Index	147

Preface
Dewey and the Meanings of Modernity in Mexico

Introduction

This book historicizes the purposes and projects served by the invocation of universal education through an examination of the dissemination of John Dewey's pedagogy in Mexico, the core of one of the twentieth century's most important projects in mass education. As it was the case in China,[1] Soviet Russia,[2] Turkey[3] and Brazil,[4] Mexico became a crucial ground for the appropriation of American notions of progress, where Dewey's philosophy of education played a central role in the efforts of these nations to become modern. Through Deweyan education, Mexican intellectuals, such as his self-professed disciple, Moisés Sáenz, endeavored to create new subjects of modernity who could generate the modern within the nation. Intended both to create a modern nation as well as to save the Mexican state from the very own forces unleashed by modernity, the uses of Dewey in Mexico also responded to the imperative of constructing a homogeneous nation out of innumerable local and regional particularities as a path to produce social efficiency at a national level.[5] Thus two dimensions of modernity emerged at every stage: first, creating a subject with a distinct form of consciousness and practical orientation to life; second, producing a social foundation amenable to the social efficiency that subject would need to produce modern forms. As these two objectives indicate, none of Dewey's interlocutors intended to purely imitate American forms, but aspired to generate the modern as an indigenous form of development.

This book aims to reconsider an important problem in the translation of Dewey's ideas in the world. Recent historical work on Dewey's influence in the early twentieth century has shown how Dewey's followers consistently debated and oftentimes rejected Dewey's warning that democracy could only be begotten through democratic means. These scholars have also identified contradictions in Dewey's own thought. David C. Engerman, for example, has noted how Dewey coupled his "endorsement of Soviet practices in Russia" with a rejection of Soviet means "for his own country"[6]—that is, the United States. Jessica Wang, although a more sympathetic observer of Dewey in China, has outlined tensions between Dewey's fondness for preserving the rich pluralities of the Chinese village world and his simultaneous desire for a social foundation that could ensure the necessary basis for the industrialization and secularization of China.[7] The collective of writers in Thomas S. Popkewitz's *Inventing the Modern Self and John Dewey* and in Rosa Bruno-Jofré and Jürgen Schriewer's *The Global Reception of John Dewey's Thought* have opened new paths of interpretation, uncovering contradictions between means and ends in Deweyan projects worldwide to create individuals as agents of change.[8] These books have linked the appropriation of Dewey in Mexico to the nation-building projects of the revolutionary government. Rosa N. Buenfil Burgos has uncovered how Dewey's interlocutors in Mexico altered his ideas, thus fabricating Dewey even when preserving elements of his thought: Dewey as an indigenous foreigner.[9] Rosa Bruno-Jofreé and Carlos Martínez Valle have detailed the uses of Dewey in in Mexico during the 1920s for purposes of nation-building and the various ways the project adopted the structures of an internal colonialism.[10]

In the same vein, this book will discuss the tensions that plagued the uses and invocations of Dewey in Mexico as the process to create a common purpose and an underlying unity to the classroom eventually contradicted the means-ends philosophy that animated the democratic and egalitarian aspirations of Dewey's pedagogy. It aims to expand on current scholarship by moving away from the model of originals and deviations, in the process uncovering new relationships between Mexican interlocutors of Dewey and Dewey's own thought. It looks at Dewey not just as a philosopher but as an integral part of the Americas' progressive movement and era. It takes seriously Dewey's pragmatist assumptions concerning the nature of American society and its underlying unity embodied, as Westbrook notes, in the "rational public."[11] As this book will argue, the reading of this assumption in Dewey and in Dewey's America structured in important ways the meanings of Dewey (and modernity) in Mexico. Thus an assumption in the work of Dewey became a regulating aspect of the interpretation of his thought in Mexico. Appropriations of Deweyan pedagogy in Mexico for the most part held in common that the diversity of Mexico's life-worlds constituted essentially a roadblock to modernity,[12] an expression of the concern with the resolution of what Mexican social scientist Andrés Molina Enríquez denominated Mexico's "Great National Problems," oftentimes conceived in racial terms: how the plurality of Indian worlds and the miscegenated character of the Mexican constituted an encumbrance to modernity.[13] Thus limiting, if not eradicating, cultural expressions that contradicted the project were not only tolerated, but also actively encouraged.

The Mexican uses of Deweyan pedagogy covered in this book, most of whom preceded experiments with revolutionary experiments with Deweyan education in China, Russia, Brazil and Turkey, suggest that these tensions stemmed not simply from misinterpretations or misappropriations of Dewey but from a more complex reading of American progressive society in general and Dewey's instrumentalism in particular. If we could define progressivism according to Cornell West's characterization of pragmatism as "a continuous cultural commentary or set of interpretations that attempt to explain America to itself," then Mexican readings of Dewey and American progressivism involved an interpretation of that interpretation and of its ambiguities and contradictions.[14] In the case of Mexico, that interpretation expressed itself in the conviction that the social efficiency of the Deweyan classroom—and thus American society—could only be explained by the shared values that upheld a community of like-minded individuals. Therefore establishing a homogenous base for the nation became a central goal of all projects in Mexico, invoking Dewey as a prophet of modernity, and worked, as I will explain later, as a supplement to Dewey's own ideas about American society. Thus modernity came to be defined in terms of the nation-state: an entity where culture and borders were congruent and where individuals could act in creative and productive ways because the underlying unity of the social world allowed it without disrupting social order: order and progress reconciled.

Mexico's Deweyan project arose out of contrasting and historically evolving interpretations of the meaning of the modern. This book will explain how Dewey's various interlocutors constructed the subject of Deweyan pedagogy and how the diversity of Mexico—both indigenous and non-indigenous—figured as the major obstacle to the construction of a "national soul," by which they meant the shared set of values that would guarantee a foundation of social efficiency for the practical man of modernity. In this preface, I will provide an outline of the contradictions of a from-the-top nationalist project of education based on earlier appropriations of Dewey in Mexico, which had intended to defend the local community versus the encroaching power of the national state and thus preserve local forms of power and cultural expression, while also laying bare the exclusions that became necessary to make the project viable. In the process, it will identify tensions within Dewey's pedagogy itself, which emerged during its implementation and critique in Mexico, and which integrated Dewey's ideas into the narratives of race and empire that suffused Mexican nationalists' narratives and their own vision of the America that upheld Dewey's vision of education and philosophy of the common man in general. I will conclude by offering a framework that may allow us to theorize the Dewey project in Mexico and set the basis for future investigations of Dewey and the world.

Dewey and the Meanings of Modernity in Mexico

Anarchists, Socialists and the "Escuelas Activas" Movement

On chapter 2, *Radical Dewey: Deweyan Pedagogy in Mexico, 1915–1923*, I focus on how Deweyan educational ideas first circulated in Mexico among radical groups of anarchists and socialists along with the works of Mikhail Bakunin and Francesc Ferrer i Guàrdia. Seeking to create a future democratic, egalitarian and secular nation of productive and practical individuals, Deweyan schooling provided a powerful model of how to recreate the life of the community within the school by inserting production at the heart of the learning process. This technique dovetailed especially with the anarchist goal of making the world transparent and available for change and liberating society from the shackles of the artifice of religious dogma. By placing production at the core of the process of education, anarchists and socialists promoted a universal version of modern education that prioritized the practical and the useful motivated by the conviction that only labor created value. They integrated Deweyan principles in an educational enterprise where democracy constituted the end point of a future revolution they deemed reflected universal goals. Given their understanding of the secular underpinnings of Deweyan philosophy, Dewey became associated also with the effort to create a collective and homogeneous social foundation for Mexico through two important objectives: a civilizational mission to Native Mexicans and a project to displace religious life—Catholicism—from a central place in Mexican society. These two limits to freedom structured the boundaries of anarchist and socialist liberation, making freedom and exclusion mutually related aims. This history of appropriation associated Dewey early on with a philosophy of liberation that intended to assimilate indigenous people into a future industrialized society that stood for the Mexican nation itself.

One crucial aspect of this translation of Dewey in Mexico was the way that the "community in miniature" that organized school activities in Dewey underwent a significant transformation. Rather than serving to suture the alienation of individuals from industrial society (especially from the modes of production that had been torn asunder from the traditional home and thus were not visible anymore), the "community in miniature" served more of an imaginative function: to visualize the future modern and industrial society, one radically different from the student's own agricultural communities. As a consequence, it tended early on to acquire purely utopian characteristics. These qualities became more pronounced in the uses of Dewey by the proponents of the *escuelas activas* movement who, during the early decades of the twentieth century, promoted Deweyan education to create a modern Mexican nation. Rather than endorsing a future universal brotherhood of workers, the *escuelas activas* supporters imagined a future Mexico as a unified nation with a unified social consciousness struggling for specific ideals of social justice that grew out of the particularities of Mexican history, such as land redistribution and respect for all individuals. The social community of the school then represented a future nation-state where a socialized world provided meaning to the individual who would cease to be an "isolated individual" and instead become a productive and enterprising subject. The dual purpose of education—a national community and a national consciousness—conformed to the nationalist aspiration to create social justice and a world of "harmonious disorder" where productivity and creativity generated rather than conspired against social order and unity.

Like the anarchists, the *escuelas activas* proponents fully accepted as a fact that industrial life signified the modernity of a future nation of individuals engaged in experiments and projects or as they describe it, of individuals oriented toward life and not the false and mystified reality created for them by the Catholic Church. In a similar manner also, they placed their faith in the possibilities of a social order arising purely out of human interaction, thus rejecting a strong central state. As opposed to the anarchists, the promoters of the *escuelas activas* placed the United States at the center of their educational efforts with the conviction that Deweyan education would reconcile order and progress. This interpretation of the role of Deweyean education tended to reverse the causal relationship between disciplinary orders and education, with discipline being the cause and not the consequence of America's industrial order. Thus Deweyan education offered not just a model of education but also reflected ideal aspects of American society itself. They therefore intensified the various ways whereby idealized aspects American culture served as model for a future Mexico. A final product of their interpretation of Deweyan education was the way that education would serve in Mexico to connect individuals and through a process of socialization create an underlying foundation for a creative and productive subject rather than create consciousness of how industrial society had connected individuals and interrelated their fates, which was the case for American progressives.

The more nationalist discourses of education became, the more Dewey featured as the locus of a modern future for Mexicans. Mexican teachers during the first two decades of the twentieth century defended Deweyan education, especially because it promised to create a national character unifying a diversity of human groups in Mexico as a necessary condition to strengthen Mexico against foreign aggression. Pedagogues and intellectuals writing for the journal *Educación*—where Dewey figured as a member of the editorial board—moved away in various ways from structural concerns, such as land redistribution and equality before the law, and toward the creation of a practical subject oriented toward experience as the main task for a new education—one that would produce an indigenous modernity for Mexico. This shift meant that racial issues became inextricably connected to the invocation of Dewey as a prophet of the modern. Imagining Native Mexican autonomy—both cultural and economic—as an obstacle to progress national unity, the writers of the journal *Educación* favoring Dewey also championed racial homogeneity as a solution. Essays published in this journal constantly reminded readers of the stark contrast between the power of Anglo-Saxon societies and the poverty of Latin American nations, attributing the reasons for the wonderful progress of America to the practical and pragmatic spirit of the Anglo-Saxon operating in a nation of like-minded individuals.

Moisés Sáenz and Mexican Protestantism

The essays in *Educación* exemplify how discourses on Dewey became intertwined with interpretations of American history. In chapter 3, *Practical*

Dewey: Moisés Sáenz and the Promise of America, I focus on how Mexican Protestants of the early twentieth century exemplified these aspects of the reception of American progressive ideas on education. Moisés Sáenz, the Protestant minister who established Dewey as the patron saint of Mexico's revolutionary education in the 1920s, viewed the American corporate order as the referent for understanding American modernity. More specifically, he lionized the American entrepreneur as the practical subject that had made the United States powerful and wealthy. Protestants in general extended that ideal to their preachers and teachers as the epitome of the practical man. Whereas they valued American democracy, they focused on practical values as a moral goal both proper and productive for the individual and the community. In ways similar to anarchists, socialists and the defenders of the *escuelas activas*, the desire for American forms did not mean imitation of American mores and values, but the acquisition of technologies that could sustain an indigenous modernity. In the case of Protestants, technologies of association, ways of organizing the social world where the school occupied the central place, all imported from American missionaries, served to support values that they affirmed in their local life and that had led them to accept conversion in the first place. Education could similarly reproduce within the community the ways of seeing of the enterprising subject who worked for the common good while seeking to satisfy his own objectives. Thus modern forms of thinking—an orientation toward life—corresponded to modern forms of association. Protestants reified their vision of the good life in the Protestant complex where churches, along with hospitals and schools, established a continuous and socialized space within which the practical character of the individual could become effective. Practical inquiry was made possible by the social efficiency produced by like-minded individuals engaged in the world. They defended their vision of the world as the opposite of Catholic society in general, which they labeled artificial. A self-regulating democratic community based on horizontal bonds of equality constituted the endpoint of social relations.

These priorities shifted dramatically as Sáenz entered public service. The nation-state replaced the community so that education acquired that task of unifying (by eradicating) the diversity of Mexican people's cultures so that the unique borders of the nation were congruent with a unified historical consciousness. Sáenz's sojourn at Teachers College at Columbia University in New York acquainted him with the philosophy of John Dewey, and upon his return to Mexico, he supported the introduction of the project method and techniques of education that, in his mind, would foster a practical orientation to life similar to the ones he encouraged in Protestant education, but with a substantial difference: that the ways of the practical man would advance the welfare of the nation, which now clearly displaced the local community in the rhetoric of nationalist education as the end point of education. The special worth of Dewey rested on how education could nurture a practical character for future citizens of the nation, the practical subject of modernity who would generate the modern from within the nation and thus strengthen national sovereignty. In 1923, Sáenz ascended to the post of sub-secretary of education, establishing Deweyan pedagogy as the pedagogy of the Mexican revolution.

It has been well established that Sáenz did not meet Dewey personally and did not attend classes dictated by him at any time. Yet, the invocation of Dewey as patron of modernity conformed to basic conceptual convergences between Dewey and Sáenz. Let's begin with the project method. First, we have the implicit analogy between Sáenz's Mexican Indian (beholden to the Catholic artificial order) and Kilpatrick's American slave. Kilpatrick defined the civilized free subject of Deweyan education as the opposite of the American slave: the free subject could act according to his or her own purposes, whereas the slave executed the purposes of the master. Sáenz, along with most if not all Mexican Protestants, firmly believed that Mexico's Catholic people functioned in a world defined for them by the Catholic Church, an "artificial order." Second, we have an implicit analogy between the open-ended world of free and productive inquiry of Deweyan philosophy and to employ Dewey's own words, the "magical inquiry" that Sáenz found prevalent in Catholic Mexico. To one corresponded democratized forms of inquiry, whereas the other relied on practical and pragmatic ways of thinking reserved for an elite, whereas the majority relied on magic and spectacle. These analogies firmly bound Sáenz to Dewey both explicitly and implicitly so that the adoption of Deweyan education obeyed an imperative to foster practical thought. Practical inquiry linked Dewey to Sáenz and defined for Sáenz what Dewey could bring to Mexico. Although the goals of state education entailed dual goals—both creating a "national soul" and a practical man of modernity—the key to Sáenz's adoption of Dewey rested on the fostering of practical ways of thinking so that practicality could become the "national character" of a future "coherent" Mexican society. Thus a new expression to the dual task of education emerged whereby education would create a national soul and a national subject that was practical and entrepreneurial.

The National Deweyan Project: From a Pedagogy for a Modern Society to a Pedagogy to Generate Modernity

In chapter 4, *Mexico's Escuelas Activas Project: Dewey's Theory of Inquiry in Mexico's Rural Schools, 1923–1929*, I begin by focusing on how the Mexican state gave official recognition to the national project through legislation that enshrined Deweyan active-learning schooling as the pedagogy of the Mexican revolution. Sáenz, now self-described as disciple of Dewey, established model schools—*escuelas tipos*—that would serve as experimental bases and prototypes for the total transformation of Mexican rural schools and thus national education. The prototype rural schools contained within all aspects of rural society: an annex to raise animals, a cultivation plot or orchard (*huerto*) and flower garden for agricultural work, and a classroom wherein to coordinate the school activities structured by the student labor. Each school would establish connections to the outside community to provide a continuum between the labor performed inside and the labor performed outside the school. Explicitly rejecting vocational education as the goal of the *escuelas activas*, Sáenz intended students to visualize their peasant world as outside themselves so they could entertain its productive capabilities and thus develop the cognitive skills of practicality and entrepreneurial spirit that he so wished them to have. Convinced that the traditional religious social order had made Mexicans into "isolated," "apathetic" and "passive" subjects, the new schools would spawn a new subject of modernity: the practical man. Thus Deweyan education acquired clearly a causal relationship to modernity: rather than an education to raise students' consciousness of how industrial life had interrelated them as members of the nation, the *escuelas activas* were meant to create modernity by forging literally impresarios of modernity who, through their projects, would integrate Mexico into an industrial nation: the modern Mexican nation-state.

Thus the rural schools became from 1923 to 1929 the main conduit for the dissemination of Deweyan pedagogy throughout Mexico with the project method as the centerpiece of their curriculum. Through their agency, Sáenz intended to socialize the child's world and to unify social contexts: home, town, nation; ground all learning in the material world that surrounded the child through labor, communicative practices, and investigation; all leading to a new relationship with the world that was immediate and productive. Schools invested time and effort in the implementation of techniques such as the "center of interest" and the "system of correlations" whereby school activities would give rise to the curriculum and lead students to understand the connectedness of the world through their own set of associations. Sáenz deterred teachers from relying on memorization and the reading of books, and the use of tests and examinations, and instead to evaluate projects solely on their instrumental quality: their ability to produce more problematic situations for further learning. Libraries would then also fulfill an instrumental mission since books were to be used to solve problems and not merely to memorize contents: there were no sacred books and thus no sacred texts. Schools instructed students to jot down observations, discuss findings with classmates, and suggest new projects to connect the school to the community, so that schools were to become "projectories," almost a factory of projects.

Sáenz's Deweyan venture consolidated the role of race in the dissemination of Deweyan education. First, the project reproduced aspects of the European *mision civilisatrice*. The purpose of creating a nation of entrepreneurial individuals meant that a separate Indian identity had to disappear by a process of socialization meant to unify human contexts so that a national experience would arise and local native loyalties disappear. Thus the project benefitted and shared a historical space with the violent and coercive attempts by the presidential administration to assimilate Native people and destroy their autonomies. Second, the project intended to displace religion, and the Catholic Church specifically, from any central role in social relations. The school would replace the church and a secular education would uproot any form of religious instruction and ideologies. The Spanish language would displace native tongues. It is important to note that state power was not omnipotent: peasant and Indian communities limited the spread of state power through the education system. Communities did not reject the education initiative per se but attempted to negotiate with the state in defense of their local autonomy. Third, a final limit to Deweyan schools involved a specific role played by *socialización* or socialization. Whereas the entrepreneurial subject occupied a central place in the goals of Deweyan schools in revolutionary Mexico, *socialización* intended not only to homogenize material and human contexts but also ensure that the future entrepreneur would not flock to the cities. Where else in an agricultural nation can one live as modern? Thus forging a "rural spirit"—that is, instilling a sense of loyalty to the countryside so that educated peasants and indigenous people would remain in their communities to make them modern—became an important feature of the system even if it violated individual (and family)'s choice. Other outcomes were not acceptable. This certainly constituted an effect of the introduction of educational techniques born out of industrial conditions into a peasant nation seeking to become industrialized.

One could speculate that Sáenz, who had visited the laboratory schools at Columbia and certainly had known about the Chicago laboratory school that Dewey founded, could not have ignored how these from-the-top goals violated Dewey's means-ends philosophy and democratic spirit since the laboratory schools themselves had been established by a careful process of selection that ensured the social efficiency that Mexicans wished their nation possessed. In many ways, Sáenz seemed to respond to an assumption in Dewey's philosophy: that American society already enjoyed an underlying unity and shared set of values. In Mexico, this social homogeneous foundation would need to be created in the first place. Since his days as a Protestant minister, Sáenz had wondered how Mexico could generate the wonderful social efficiency that in his mind explained American power and productivity. The belief that American homogeneity had underwritten American material success ran strongly in Mexican and Latin American intellectual circles since the publication of the essay *Ariel* by José Antonio Rodó. For Rodó, writing as the United States defeated Spain in the war of 1898, the fact that the English utilitarian spirit had spread uninterrupted in the North American continent (and without the balance provided by countervailing traits of the English people) explained how the American practical character had defined American power in commerce and science. It explained their power. Thus discourses on practicality and race became pivotal to understand Latin American poverty and weakness vis-à-vis the United States. Given the centrality of the concept of the practical to define the foreign in Mexican history, it would not come as a surprise that the critique of the

Dewey project precisely targeted this aspect of Sáenz's pedagogy as not just misguided, but as antithetical to the meaning of Latin American culture and in blatant defiance of the particularities of Mexican history.

In chapter 5, *Dangerous Dewey: The Critique of the Dewey Project in Mexico (and Dewey's Critique of Mexico)*, I begin by looking at how Sáenz's most acerbic critic, José Vasconcelos, termed the insertion of Dewey in Mexico as a form of "spiritual colonialism" made possible by internal enemies of the nation such as Sáenz. In *El Peligro Dewey*, a chapter of his book *De Robinson a Odiseo—From Robinson to Odysseus*—Vasconcelos elaborated on what Edmundo O'Gorman denominates "the great dichotomy," a narrative of identity that opposed Mexican identity (and history) to Anglo-Saxon identity (and American history). Vasconcelos reaffirmed the European origins of Mexico in a genealogy that linked Greece and Rome to Latin Europe, identifying Mexico with the Western values of logic and reasoning and transforming American culture into a non-Western domain of simple, astute, improvising and strictly technical subjects that lacked the signifier of Western identity: reason. Thus practical Americans, all Americans, lacked "any true culture" and the abilities to systematize, theorize and produce knowledge: the dissemination of Anglo-Saxon values in Mexico amounted to a violation of the national essence. Values deemed practical, even when performing a positive role in society, were of a lower register and subordinate to higher principles. Vasconcelos' critique stood for a critique of American culture and the values of commerce and the market.

Two distinct voices against Sáenz's Deweyan project arose from intellectuals that rejected the triumphalism of Vasconcelos and instead embraced a tragic view of Mexican history. Vicente Lombardo Toledano, a major voice for labor and Marxist intellectual thought, formulated a critique of Sáenz that nevertheless expressed admiration for the liberating aspects of Deweyan pedagogy. In *El problema de la educación*, Lombardo Toledano argued that Sáenz had appropriated the technocratic aspects of Dewey's education, proper to an industrialized nation, and transplanted them to Mexico. In doing so, he had ignored the "tragedy of Mexican history." Whereas Dewey's industrial America possessed the necessary social cohesion that could leave individuals free for "*libre examen*" or the freedom of self-examination and thought that characterized the Protestant foundations of the project (and serve as foundation for Deweyan inquiry), Mexico needed dogma. He argued that the imperial ideology of Vasco de Quiroga, a Spanish colonial cleric, could serve as a better foundation to create that social foundation and to civilize the Indian into "a factor of production." Lombardo Toledano, as most Mexican intellectuals, worked under the assumption that the Spanish colonial mission to save the Indian had failed or been incomplete and only the practical education of Quiroga's mission could complete it. Thus he aligned Dewey's pedagogy with imperial education, but distinguished it from colonial practices by that very fact: Dewey's philosophy assumes a homogeneous social foundation; Mexico did not have one. Implicit was the assumption that America did not possess a tragic history of Indian destruction, of irremediable heterogeneity.

Antonio Caso, a philosopher, educator and member of an influential intellectual group called *Ateneo de la Juventud*, formulated a critique of Dewey as a critique of American progress. Although he did not reject progress *in toto*, Caso repudiated its application to a nation marked by the tragedy of empire: on the one hand, the beneficiary of European civilization; on the other that same European spirit had been compromised in its dissemination by the destruction of Native life that attended it. Thus Mexico had become an incomplete nation from its inception, and its heterogeneity structured Mexican identity. Dewey's ideas and Sáenz's projects, based as they were on the scientific and practical values that made the United States the ruler of contemporary industrial civilization, offered Mexico a lesser route to the future. Mexican modernity could only be valuable when "disinterested action" and not practical inquiry formed the basis of state action and good will. Caso did not deny the validity of Dewey's common man but demoted it as an ideal for Mexico. Caso's dogma was a Mexican history where heterogeneity had tragically become an impediment to the kind of development that characterized Anglo-Saxon societies of his time. Like Lombardo Toledano, he subscribed to the idea that the tragedy of history—human heterogeneity and Indian dispossession—made Mexico different than the United States. These critiques illustrate how the insertion of Dewey in Mexico shook the intellectual foundations of that nation, challenging sacrosanct notions of the nation and intellectual legitimacy.

In many ways, they doomed Sáenz's project, which collapsed when it became evident by 1929, when Sáenz left the sub-secretary of education, that it had failed to create the modern subject. Mexican teachers never fully understood how to apply the method in class; students instead idled or in other instances took control of the school. Parents complained that students did in school the same work they did on the farms. Why should they send students to study in the first place? In many rural areas, teachers mocked the new principles of education, whereas parents worried that their children were being converted to Protestantism. Perhaps most importantly, the state's project to assimilate Native Mexicans to a secularized culture and the violent assault on their mores, language and Catholic loyalties only served to associate Dewey with a top-down state project that fundamentally looked down upon Native and peasant culture. Thus the project relied on a set of limitations and exclusions that structured its implementation and were never the subject of contestation. When communities forced negotiations with the state for better conditions, they occurred in response to the expansion of state power in education and not because of the democratic qualities of the new education.

The end of the Dewey project brought to light tensions and contradictions in the appropriation of Dewey's ideas. First, a project historically rooted in the desire of Mexicans to protect their local communities and ground progress in democratic autonomous polities instead sought to replace community with the nation-state to the detriment of local autonomy. Second, the racial underpinnings of the project violated the principles of democratic self-expression that Deweyans had sought to foster in the individual in the first place. Third, various positive aspects of the project—for example, families building communities across the border to enrich their students' education and to encompass both American and Mexican cultures or students "taking control" of the classroom—were interpreted as violations of the Deweyan spirit, not as expressions of freedom and creativity.

Sáenz's last project for the state in 1932, the experimental station at Carapan in the state of Michoacán, exposed further ironies. Conceived partly as a laboratory school and partly a social settlement for the integration of Mexican Indians into the nation, it folded in less than a year. In his memoirs of this project, Sáenz critiqued the civilizational mission of the Deweyan schools as a one-way street, instead positing that cultural change must always imply mutual transformations. He critiqued the objectification of the Indian in Mexico, arguing that the Indian dwelled within all Mexicans—culturally and racially. He criticized state education as a colonial enterprise, proposing instead that civilization—by which he meant the European aspects of Mexican society—should be offered to the Indian. Conscious of his own inclinations, he reaffirmed his commitment to European values and the necessity of integrating Indians through education as the only way to create a nation-state and survive in the industrializing world, but he did so in the tragic mode of Lombardo Toledano and Caso. There was a sense of deep irony in Sáenz, invoking values (interdependence, transparency, community) that scholars would deem very much part of Dewey's vision of the world in the very process of critiquing the Deweyan experiment in Mexico. Yet, on the other hand, it seemed that daily contact with Indian and peasant communities in the experimental station at Carapan had made of Sáenz a practical man.

Acknowledgments

This book would not have been possible without the advice, commitment, and support of the members of my graduate dissertation committee, Jessica Wang and Valerie Matsumoto. Their intellectual compass, sharp commentary and personal commitment to my project provided me with the necessary leadership, guidance and inspiration to complete my doctoral work, which served as the basis for this book. I also wish to thank my colleagues Dr. Islam Nazrul and Kris Ho at United International College in China, where I worked after graduation and with whom I discussed this project and exchanged valuable ideas.

I would like to thank the editors of the journal *Education and Culture* for making possible the use of my article "Radical Deweyan Pedagogy in Mexico, 1915–1923," published in 2013. I also owe a debt of gratitude to the scholars and archivists who made the research for this project possible. I am grateful for the assistance given to me by Professor Larry H. Hickman at the Center for Dewey Studies and to James Downhour, Michael McNally and Jean Ohms at the center for their assistance during the dissertation stage of this research. I also wish to extend my gratitude to the staff at the Special Collections Research Center of the Joseph Regenstein Library at the University of Chicago, especially to Christine Colburn, Julia Gardner, Barbara Gilbert, David Pavelich and Reina Williams. In New York, I am indebted to the research staff of Special Collections at the Milkman Library of Teachers College, as well as the research staff of Berkeley's Bancroft Library, and UCLA's Charles E. Young's Research Library, for their help in locating published primary sources in my area of research.

I am also deeply indebted to the archivists who assisted me in my research in México. First of all, my eternal gratitude to *El Profesor*, who guided me through the *Archivo Histórico de la Secretaría de Educación Pública* in Mexico City and without whom I would not have been able to navigate and find precious sources in the history of Mexican education. I respect your wishes to be known simply as *El Profesor*, which is the way all of us knew you when you worked in the archives of the Secretariat of Education. I also wish to thank the archival clerks at the *Archivos de la Nación*, especially those of the *Fondo Obregón-Calles*, where most sources for the period are

xxii *Acknowledgments*

archived. My gratitude to Aurora Gómez Galvarriato Freer, the *Directora General* of the *Archivos*, and Lourdes Gabriela Ramírez Sotelo, the *Jefe del Departamento de Archivos del Gobierno Federal*, for their contributions to my investigation. At the *Biblioteca Nacional*, I wish to express my debts to Dr. Guadalupe Curiel Defossé, the *Directora* of the *Biblioteca*, Arnulfo Inessa Ortega and Lorena Gutiérrez Schott in the *Hemeroteca Nacional*, and Benigno Rafael Sosa Cárdenas at the *Centro de Investigaciones Bibliográficas* of the *Biblioteca*.

Notes

1. Major works on Dewey and China have focused to varying degrees on how Dewey's ideas in China encountered conceptual obstacles in the formation of a social foundation in an area of the world not formed as a nation-state. See, Barry Keenan, *The Dewey Experiment in China: Educational Reform and Political Power in the Early Republic* (Cambridge, MA: Harvard University Press, 1977); Maurice Meisner, *Li Ta-Chao and the Origins of Chinese Marxism* (New York: Atheneum, 1974), especially chapter V; Zhixin Su, "A Critical Evaluation of John Dewey's Influence on Chinese Education," *American Journal of Education*, 103, no. 3 (May 1995); Sor-Hoon Tan, "China's Pragmatist Experiment in Democracy: Hi Shih's Pragmatism and Dewey's Influence in China," *Metaphilosophy*, 35, no. 1 & 2 (January 2004); Jessica Ching-Sze Wang, "John Dewey as a Learner in China," *Education and Culture*, 21, no. 1 (2006); Jessica Ching-Sze Wang, *John Dewey in China: To Teach and to Learn* (Albany: State University of New York Press, 2008); Zeng Zida, "A Chinese View of the Educational Ideas of John Dewey," *Interchange*, 19, no. 3 and 4 (Fall/Winter, 1988). Other works not written by historians that discuss Dewey and China see, Joseph Grange, *John Dewey, Confucius, and Global Philosophy* (Albany: State University of New York Press, 2004); David A. Hall, *The Democracy of the Dead: Dewey, Confucius, and the Hope of Democracy for China* (New York: Open Court Publishing Company, 1999); Sor-Hoon Tan, *Confucian Democracy: A Deweyan Reconstruction* (Albany: State University of New York, 2004). China is not the only East Asian nation that experimented with Deweyan ideas. On the case of Dewey's pedagogy in in Japan see, Victor N. Kobayashi, *John Dewey in Japanese Educational Thought* (Ann Arbor: University of Michigan, Comparative Education Series, Number 2, 1964); Sharon H. Nolte, "Industrial Democracy for Japan: Tanaka Odo and John Dewey," *Journal of the History of Ideas*, 45, no. 2 (April–June 1984); Naoko Saito, "Education for Global Understanding: Learning from Dewey's Visit to Japan," *Teachers College Record*, 105, no. 9 (December 2003); Naoko Saito, *Globalization and the Understanding of Other Cultures: Beyond the Limits of Deweyan Democracy*, manuscript in my possession. Historians of Chinese education have focused more on actual experiments with education in China whereby Deweyan school discipline was extended to the social world, thus making society a school rather than creating a social world within the school. See for example, Yusheng Yao, "The Making of a National Hero: Tao Xingzhi's Legacies in the People's Republic of China," *Pedagogy and Cultural Studies*, 24, no. 3 (2002); Yusheng Yao, "National Reconstruction through Education: Tao Xingzhi's Search for Individual and National Identity," *East-West Connections. Review of Asian Studies*, 1, no. 2 (2002); Yusheng Yao, "Rediscovering Tao Xingzhi as an Educational and Social Revolutionary," *Twentieth Century China*, 27, no. 2 (2002).

2. See David C. Engerman, "John Dewey and the Soviet Union: Pragmatism meets Revolution," *Modern Intellectual History*, 3, no. 1 (2006). Also on Russia, William W. Brickman, "Soviet Attitudes toward John Dewey as an Educator," *John Dewey and the World View*, edited by Douglas E. Lawson and Arthur E. Lean (Carbondale: Southern Illinois University Press, 1964).
3. See Turkey, on Turkey see, Selahattin Turan, "John Dewey's Report of 1924 and His Recommendations on the Turkish Educational System," *History of Education*, 29, no. 6 (2000): 543–555; Ernest Wolf-Gazo, "John Dewey in Turkey: An Educational Mission," *Journal of American Studies of Turkey*, no. 3 (1996).
4. Studies of Dewey in Brazil have identified the importance of the nexus of race and nation in the formation of a social foundation for education. See Marcus Vinicius Da Cunha, "John Dewey, The Other Face of the Brazilian New School," *Studies in Philosophy and Education*, 24 (2005); Jerry Dávila, *Diploma of Whiteness: Race and Social Policy in Brazil, 1917–1945* (Durham, NC: Duke University Press, 2003), especially chapter 5; Paulo Ghiraldelli Jr. and Cody Carr, "What is Pragmatism in Brazil today?" *Studies in Philosophy and Education*, 24, 2005; Ana Waleska P.C. Mendoça, Libania Nacif Xavier, Vera Lucia Alves Breglia, Miriam Waidenfeld Chaves, Maria Teresa Cavalcanti De Oliveria, Cecilia Neves Lima and Pable S.M. Bispo Dos Santo, "Pragmatism and Developmentalism in Brazilian Educational Thought in the 1950s/1960s," *Studies in Philosophy and Education*, 24 (2005). See also Jaime Nubiola, "The Reception of John Dewey in the Hispanic World," *Studies in Philosophy and Education* (November 1, 2005); Gregory Fernando Pappas and Jim Garrison, "Pragmatism as a Philosophy of Education in the Hispanic World: A Response," *Studies in Philosophy and Education*, 24 (2005).
5. Few scholars have discussed the appropriation of Dewey in Mexico in any detail. Among scholars of Mexican history we find Alexander S. Dawson, *Indian and Nation in Revolutionary Mexico* (Tucson: University of Arizona Press, 2004); Alan Knight, *The Mexican Revolution, Vol.2: Counter-Revolution and Reconstruction* (Lincoln: University of Nebraska Press, 1990); Stephen E. Lewis, *The Ambivalent Revolution: Forging State and Nation in Chiapas, 1910–1945* (Albuquerque: University of New Mexico Press, 2005); Mary Kay Vaughan, *Cultural Politics in Revolution: Teachers, Peasants, and Schools in Mexico, 1930–1940* (Tucson: University of Arizona Press, 1997); Mary Kay Vaughan, *The Eagle and the Virgin: Nation and Cultural Revolution in Mexico, 1920–1940* (Durham, NC: Duke University Press, 2006); Mary Kay Vaughan, *The State, Education, and Social Class in Mexico, 1880–1928* (DeKalb: Northern Illinois Press, 1982). Among scholars of American history and culture we have Jay Martin, *The Education of John Dewey: A Biography* (New York: Columbia University Press, 2003); Steven Rockefeller, *John Dewey: Religious Faith and Democratic Humanism* (New York: Columbia University Press, 1994); Alan Ryan, *John Dewey and the High Tide of American Liberalism* (New York: W.W. Norton and Company, Inc., 1997); Robert Westbrook, *John Dewey and American Democracy* (Ithaca, NY: Cornell University Press, 1993).
6. See Engerman, David C., "John Dewey and the Soviet Union: Pragmatism meets Revolution," *Modern Intellectual History*, 3, no. 1 (2006).
7. See Jessica Ching-Sze Wang, *John Dewey in China: To Teach and to Learn* (Albany: State University of New York Press, 2007).
8. See the essays contained in Thomas Popkewitz, ed., *Inventing the Modern Self and John Dewey: Modernities and the Traveling of Pragmatism in Education* (New York: Palgrave MacMillan, 2005).
9. Rosa N. Buenfil Burgos, "Discursive Inscriptions in the Fabrication of a Modern Self: Mexican Educational Appropriations of Dewey's Writings," *Inventing the*

Modern Self and John Dewey: Modernities and the Traveling of Pragmatism in Education, ed. Thomas S Popkewitz (New York: Palgrave Macmillan, 2005).
10. Rosa Bruno-Jofré and Carlos Martínez Valle, "Ruralizing Dewey: The American Friend, Internal Colonization, and the Action School in Post-Revolutionary Mexico (1921–1940)," *The Global Reception of John Dewey's Thought: Multiple Refractions through Time and Space*, ed. Rosa Bruno-Jofré and Jürgen Schriewer (New York: Routledge, 2012).
11. Robert B. Westbrook, *John Dewey and American Democracy*, 205.
12. It is the nature of modern states to set limits to the diversity of life-worlds in order to pursue a developmentalist agenda. See, for example, James C. Scott, *Seeing Like a State: How Certain Schemes to Improve the Human Condition Have Failed* (New Haven, CT: Yale University Press, 1999).
13. Resolving the "national problems," a phrase that refers to Mexico's historical failure to become modern, would lead to the incorporation of Mexico into the universal domain of modernity and thus to full development, both economically and in terms of social consciousness. Andrés Molina Enríquez, a Mexican social scientist, coined the phrase to identify issues of poverty, land redistribution, and race, which he argued had prevented Mexico from reaching the modern. Thus Mexican social science (and the nationalist discourses that would define the appropriation of Dewey in the 1920s) set limits to the nationalist imagination that previous radicals had not. See, Andrés Molina Enríquez, *Los grandes problemas nacionales* (México: Impresora de A. Carranza e Hijos, 1909). For a discussion of Molina Enríquez's legacy see, Agustín Basave Benítez, *México mestizo: Análisis del nacionalismo mexicano en torno a la mestizofilia de Andrés Molina Enríquez* (México: Fondo de Cultura Económica, 1992) and Claudio Lomnitz-Adler, *Exits from the Labyrinth: Culture and Ideology in the Mexican National Space* (Berkeley, CA: University of California Press, 1992). According Claudio Lomnitz, for Mexican social scientists, the "definition of the Great National Problems and of their resolution . . . involve[d] incorporation [of Mexico] to a 'civilization horizon' that transcend[ed] Mexico's borders. The universal character of the modern constituted that" civilizational horizon for Mexican intellectuals. See Claudio Lomnitz, *Exits from the Labyrinth*.
14. See Cornell West, *The American Evasion of Philosophy: A Genealogy of Pragmatism* (Madison: The University of Wisconsin Press, 1989), 5.

1 Introduction: Race, Modernity and Nation in the Reception of Dewey's Pedagogy in Mexico

Introduction

The analysis of the reception of Dewey's pedagogy overseas has been mostly informed by binaries such as those of original/deviation and local/foreign that either measure the fidelity of overseas Deweyan project to a Deweyan original or that link Dewey unproblematically to the uses of his ideas in various overseas projects. I seek in this book to move beyond these conventions by offering two paradigms to interpret the appropriation of Dewey's ideas in Mexico for the purposes of building a nation-state during the 1920s. I first look at the Deweyan project in Mexico as a supplement to Deweyan pragmatic thought in education whereby the interpretation and implementation of Dewey in Mexico both responded and added to absences in Dewey's thought. Second, I look at the Mexican project as a form of asynchronous substitution whereby an education that responded historically to industrial capitalism as a historical process already in motion became in its Mexican appropriation a causal factor to generate an indigenous industrial nation. These paradigms explain, among many other issues, why the Mexican interlocutors of John Dewey rethought the process of socialized inquiry, a hallmark of the Dewey experimental schools at Chicago and Columbia, as consisting of two separate set of tasks: a project of *socialización* (socialization) informed mostly by Mexican history to create a homogeneous national society and a project to promote modern (and thus universal) cognitive practical skills to generate modernity from within the nation.

In offering these interpretative paradigms, I seek to open up avenues to a critique of Dewey's progressive ideas on education through the analysis of the historical use of his ideas in the world by positing that crucial aspects of his philosophy and educational writings became visible in its transnational dissemination rather than in his national (American) one. I believe this avenue of investigation will make the manifold interpretations of Dewey in the world relevant to the study of Deweyan ideas themselves rather than constitute a separate, interesting, yet unrelated chapter in the study of Deweyan educational ideas. Furthermore, I intend to make Deweyan ideas theoretically relevant to an understanding of the modern world precisely through a case study of one of its most important yet least studied implementation: the Mexican project of the *escuelas activas*. As the Mexican case demonstrates, and most cases of Deweyan appropriation in the twentieth century corroborate, the narrative of the transition of modernity informed the meanings Deweyan pedagogy acquired in its circulation abroad. Thus both the successes and limitations of Deweyan pedagogy in the world speak directly to the problematic of the nation-state, the role that education has played in the consolidation of that modern political structure and ultimately the relationship between Dewey's ideas and modern nationalism.

Race and Nation: The Dewey Project as a Supplement

Aguirre Beltrán has argued that although Sáenz's project was congruent with Dewey's ideas on education and democracy, he needed to supplement it with a racial project to make it effective. For intellectuals such as Moisés Sáenz, race explained the different historical outcomes that separated Mexico from the modern embodied in the United States: Mexico never enjoyed the homogeneous social foundation that permitted the forms of inquiry of the practical man to develop unencumbered by the inefficiencies of a racially plural nation. As a supplement, the project to homogenize Mexico's social body through education obeyed the necessity to resolve Mexico's greatest national problem: the plurality of its social world and the perceived lack of coherence that had made modernity impossible. Aguirre Beltrán's use of the term "supplement" recalls for us Jacques Derrida's notion of the "supplement," which may assist us in ascertaining the nature of the relationship established between Dewey's ideas and Mexico's implementation of them. For Derrida, a supplement (to an assumed original) "has not only the power of *procuring* an absent presence through its image; procuring it for us through the proxy *[procuration]* of the sign, it holds it at a distance and masters it. For this presence is at the same time desired and feared."[1] If we apply the notion of the supplement as defined here to the Mexican case, we could argue that the intrusion of race in a Deweyan project invoked an absence present in Dewey's writings: those of the racial histories of America—including the destruction of its native worlds—which had provided that nation with the possibilities for power and growth through the violent displacement of cultures contradictory to the dominant European spirit that eventually defined its foundation of shared values. This explains why the critique of Dewey focused almost exclusively on issues of America's origins.

Sáenz both desired and feared Dewey's America. As an object of desire, the United States represented modernity. As an object of fear, it embodied a power, politically as well as economically, that could undermine the sovereignty of the Mexican state. His efforts to make Dewey's presence public at all times took the form of a containment of that power, serving to delimit the autochthonous from the foreign, the autochthonous being the solution of the national problems related the heterogeneity of the national body; the foreign being the Deweyan ways of practical thinking that would make Mexicans modern. Claudio Lomnitz's thesis provides a good model to understand Sáenz's choices. According to Lomnitz, in order to reach modernity, Mexican intellectuals first responded to the "Great National Problems," the kind of issues concerning the historical obstacles to national development addressed by social thinker Andrés Molina Enríquez in his seminal essay "Great National Problems" or *Grandes problemas nacionales*. At this level, social scientists addressed issues of development and national conscience in ways fully "encompassed by national history." Whereas the findings of Mexican social thought did not rise to the level of "paradigms of rationality" as they did in Western or American social science, their resolution, argues Lomnitz, would lead Mexico to modernity. "Universality," argues Lomnitz, "will come later."[2] The resolution of the national dilemma creates the conditions for the rise of the nation to the universal realm of a fully formed nation-state. One can see how for Sáenz a project that resolved the historical problem of the Mexican nation—its racial heterogeneity and multiplicity of social contexts—would establish the necessary foundation for the practical man of modernity. Thus conceiving the socializing function of Deweyan education as distinct from the formation of individual character—one working on creating a nation by suturing historical wounds and homogenizing material and spiritual domains (the autochthonous), the other fostering new cognitive capabilities (the future, the modern)—constitutes an effect of the supplementary character of the interpretation of Dewey in Mexico.

Modernity and Nation: The Dewey Project as Asynchronous Substitution

Just as the supplementary character of Sáenz's Deweyan project produced effects that scholars may object were not truly Deweyan, the peculiarities of its asynchronous implementation in Mexico brought forth a set of consequences that transformed the Deweyan original. If we look at one key feature of Sáenz's Deweyan schools, the insertion of agricultural processes in the schools as a version of Dewey's insertion of industrial production at Chicago and Columbia, we find a case of asynchronous translation where Dewey's context for a new education—industrial society—gets replaced by the agricultural community. As Leonard J. Waks argues, Dewey's purpose in embedding learning in production responded to the unique historical event whereby the "factory system" replaced "the home and neighborhood system of production, in which industrial processes had 'stood revealed' to all, and every member of the household, including young children, had defined tasks."[3] Thus industrial society created a "void" when production moved out of the household and with it went the learning processes that trained the child with respect to the "physical realities and social responsibilities of life . . . only the schools remained available as agencies to provide this basic grounding in real-world experience and social responsibility."[4] That of course was not the case in Mexico. As we have seen, the parents' complaints of children performing in school the same tasks they performed at home and in the fields prove the point. After all, wasn't education supposed to open avenues of mobility for students away from the poverty of the village?

As opposed to American Deweyan schools, in Mexico the *escuelas tipos*, instead came to perform a utopian function as signs of the future modernity of Mexico. Sáenz's thought was historicist and evolutionary, and in formulating his understanding of how the school should reflect the principles of social life, he understood México's agrarian present as representing America's past; on the other hand, the future practical man of America's industrial present signified México's future. Thus making the nation visible displaced making the processes of production visible. Yes, at times the schools did perform in ways similar to progressive schools in the United States, but I argue that the utopian function overtook other qualities of the progressive education that Sáenz and his precursors wished to introduce in Mexico. Thus we can explain the confusions about the new method among village teachers and the "chaos" that inspectors and observers found in the experimental schools. The schools did create grounds for creative work and fostered children's inventions—the reports from the schools do indicate that—but usually they did so because children employed their imagination when filling the void created by teachers that could not or did not fully understand the foundations of the new philosophy of education.

Thus asynchronous appropriations do produce their own particular effects. In the example above, inserting processes of production in the schools acquired a causal function vis-à-vis modernity. Whereas in Dewey's project, progressive education responded to industrial changes in home and education, in Mexico, Sáenz and his precursors intended to generate modernity with the adoption of progressive methods. One could also extend Gellner's analysis of industrialization and the condition of permanent cognitive growth that it fostered to the Mexican project's goal of promoting practical thought. In the Mexican case, modalities of rationality posed as necessary by industrialization in the West came to be adopted to generate that same modernity in the Mexican nation.[5] Thus the effects of a historical event became its cause in the translation. In the early twentieth century, this understanding of the cognitive qualities necessary for modernity did not surface only in Mexico. According to Aaron Moore writing on technology in wartime Japan, in Europe during the early twentieth century, "certain forms of creative thinking, acting or being" along with the "values of rationality, cooperation and efficiency" that characterize modernity according to Weber, came to define the meanings of technology in modernity.[6] In Mexico, we have a project with its own technological imaginary dating back to the Protestants of the turn of the century, whose desire consisted in adopting technologies of association and education that would affirm and develop their values and would assist them in creating their own forms of modernity.

And thus we return to the persistent theme of empire and colonialism whereby Dewey came to be associated by proponents and critics alike with empire. The objective to transform ways of thinking in the Deweyan project overlapped—and in many ways gained legitimacy—with centuries of imperial history in Mexico where civilizational discourses associated those of European descent or European-educated subjects as *gente de razón* (people of reason) and counterposed that category against Natives of the Americas imagined oftentimes as children in need of tutelage. Thus the subject of Deweyan education acquired in Mexico qualities similar to Giorgio Agamben's *homo sacer*: outside the boundaries of civilization yet part of it as a result of their racial categorization by the *gente de razón*, a categorization necessary to the identity of *gente de razón* themselves.[7] Yet, whereas in Europe and the United States the distinction between Europeans and the Native Other (and the African in the slave colonies) acquired definite and strictly differentiated contours, in Mexico the civilizational discourse ambiguously demarcated the location of peasants and Natives vis-à-vis that of what Saenz persistently referred to as "Mexican." Thus the narrative of the transition to modernity that structured the appropriation of Dewey did not fit entirely that of South Asian modernity, for example, where according to Dipesh Chakrabarti, European historicist thought had placed Indians in the "waiting room" of history, not yet ready for self-rule.[8] In Mexico, the racial binaries of colonialism oftentimes collapsed—witness Sáenz's persistent claim that the Indian was both inside and outside the nation—and produced the ambivalences and unresolved tensions that made the project seemed chaotic and ultimately impossible to institute.

Ultimately, Dewey, through Sáenz, entered the Mexican intellectual space through acts of displacement: the agricultural community displacing the industrial society, the Catholic imaginary replacing the mystified view of reality created by capitalism, the nation-to-be displacing the factory system. In doing so, Deweyan education acquired new goals even when to justify Deweyan pedagogy, Sáenz and his followers borrowed from the national past to give meaning to the new. As Chakrabarty argues in the case of the dissemination of Marxism in Asia where the peasant displaced the proletariat as the revolutionary subject, "newness enters the world through acts of displacement."[9] When Deweyan education attempted in Mexico to relate people to each other so they would form a nation rather than using education as an instrument to raise consciousness of interrelatedness, we have a displacement whereby newness entered the world. When Sáenz defined the new subject of modernity in terms of rational subject of European and American thought, he in fact disguised this newness in order to formulate a logical justification of his project. Where this newness would have taken Mexico and how it would have continued to comment on Dewey's (and the progressives') own assumptions concerning the nation had the project succeeded, we will never know.

6 *Introduction*

Notes

1. Jacques Derrida, *Of Grammatology*, translated by Gayatri Chakaravorti Spivak (Baltimore: John Hopkins University Press, 1988),155.
2. Claudio Lomnitz-Adler, *Exits from the Labyrinth: Culture and Ideology in the Mexican National Space* (Berkeley, CA: University of California Press, 1992), xvi–xviii.
3. Leonard J. Waks, "John Dewey and Progressive Education, 1900–2000: The School and Society Revisted," *John Dewey's Educational Philosophy in International Perspective: A New Democracy for the Twenty-First Century*, edited by Larry A. Hickman and Giuseppe Spadafora (Carbondale: Southern Illinois Press, 2009), 82.
4. Leonard J. Waks, "John Dewey and Progressive Education," 82.
5. Ernest Gellner, *Nations and Nationalism*, 2nd edition (Ithaca, NY: Cornell University Press, 2009), 19–38.
6. Aaron Stephen Moore, *Constructing East Asia: Technology, Ideology, and Empire in Japan's Wartime Era, 1931–1945* (Stanford: Stanford University Press, 2013), 6.
7. Giorgio Agamben, *Homo Sacer: Sovereign Power and Bare Life* (Stanford: Stanford University Press, 1998).
8. Dipesh Chakrabarty, *Provincializing Europe: Postcolonial Thought and Historical Difference* (Princeton, NJ: Princeton University Press, 2007).
9. Dipesh Chakrabarty, "The Names and Repetitions of Postcolonial History," *The Ambiguous Allure of the West: Traces of the Colonial in Thailand*, edited by Rachel V. Harrison and Peter A. Jackson (Hong Kong: Hong Kong University Press, 2010), Kindle edition (loc. 171).

2 Radical Dewey
Deweyan Pedagogy in Mexico, 1915–1923

> *When we intended to issue regulations for the children, they had already done so by themselves; when we intended to demand punctuality, the child cared more about being punctual than ourselves . . . when we intended to talk to them about equity in the distribution of lands and profits, it was realized that they never desire for any one child to gain more than the other, or more land than the other, because they always saw that as an injustice; when we intended to teach them about virtue, they themselves praised the working child and chose their leaders by their virtues and not by their defects.*
> (Eulalia Guzmán, "Características de la escuela nueva")

Introduction

This chapter focuses on the uses of Dewey's ideas in Mexico before his appropriation in 1923 by the Mexican revolutionary government. During the early twentieth century, anarchists, socialists and radical teacher advocates of progressive education in Mexico invoked the name of John Dewey as an important pillar for a vision of a future Mexican society. Deweyan ideas circulated among radical pedagogues, sprouting in urban centers such as Mérida in Yucatán province, or in poor *barrios* of México City, where pockets of urban radicalism emerged concurrently with each other without the necessity of concerted action. Subsequently, self-professed disciples of Dewey founded the journal *Educación*, identifying Dewey as a member of the journal's board of editors. Few if any historians have paid due attention to any of these uses of Deweyan education in Mexico during this time.[1] This neglect may be due in part to the fact that most Mexican experiments with foreign education during that time withered or were successfully coopted by the national state. With scattered sources to encourage research and a common assumption that Dewey was no more than a name uttered on behalf of idealistic, quixotic, and perhaps contradictory experiments, scholars have neglected the intellectual foundations of the experiments that preceded the state project of the *escuelas activas*, the name given to the Mexican revolutionary experiment with Deweyan schools in the mid-1920s. Given this silence, the established interpretation of the role of Deweyan thought in Mexico holds that the popularity of Dewey's ideas should be understood purely in terms of its utility to a nationalist state desirous to establish social control over its population in order to consolidate capitalist relations.[2]

The importance of these early projects and discourses on Dewey in Mexico resides in the various ways they illuminate how Deweyan thought became embedded within the progressive nationalist Mexican imagination.[3] They demonstrate that when Dewey's ideas first circulated in Mexico, they stirred the imagination of radical sectors of Mexico who desired to establish in that nation a more equal and just society. Thus as Dewey became popular in Mexico, social justice and democratic life first constituted the endpoints of revolutionary education. This analysis will dramatize how later Dewey's import for Mexican intellectuals shifted from experiments that aimed for social justice and democratic life to ones that prioritized Deweyan education as an avenue for making Mexicans modern individuals, that is, self-conscious, practical, entrepreneurial and secular. Yet, before Dewey became "Americanized"—that is, understood as a key to unlocking the productive potential of the American modern subject—his ideas gained salience for its radical vision of the modern.

I begin by focusing on the intellectual foundations of the *escuelas racionalistas* or rationalist schools, which were experiments in anarchist education established during the first decades of the twentieth century. I then proceed to analyze the thought and aspirations behind the *escuelas activas* movement, focusing on the writings (and projects) of Eulalia Guzmán, discourses and debates among Mexican teachers, and finally, the emergence of the journal *Educación*, where Dewey's ideas gained supremacy among key Mexican pedagogues. I conclude by identifying correspondences between American progressivism and Dewey's own ideas with those of his Mexican interpreters.

The Anarchists' *Escuelas Racionalistas* or Rationalist Schools

Anarchists implemented in Mérida, state of Yucatán, a very important educational projects led by José de la Luz Mena, a Spanish immigrant, who established the first anarchist schools in 1917 in Chuminópolis. They were inspired by the pedagogy of Francisco Ferrer i Guardia, a working-class radical executed by the Spanish government in 1909.[4] The schools were called rationalists or *racionalistas* because of their profession of faith in the rational nature of man and the universal applicability of science, whose truths were deemed universal and objective.[5] "Science," Ferrer exclaimed in his book, "is the sole mistress of our life."[6] Dewey's pedagogy had impacted anarchist education in Europe before they moved to the United States and Mexico in the late nineteenth century.[7] Shortly after Spanish exiles and Mexican anarchists formed the first anarchist organizations in the city of Mexico, the writings of Ferrer, collected in the volume *The Modern School* and Dewey's works such as *The School and Society* and *How To Think*, began to circulate among leftist intellectuals along with Peter Kropotkin *Mutual Aid: A Factor of Evolution* and *The Conquest of Bread*, Mikhail Bakunin's *God and the State*, and Pierre-Joseph Proudhon's *What is Property? Or an Inquiry into the Principle of Right and Government*.[8] Mexican labor unions joined public readings of these books as they celebrated in 1914 the fifth year anniversary of Ferrer's execution.[9]

The anarchist project in Mexico did not necessarily intend to be purely a conversation with its American socialist and anarchist counterparts but instead aspired to be part of a more universal project of human liberation. Mexicans never claimed that their schools were purely Deweyan either, yet they invoked Dewey as a model for a very important dimension of their educational mission: the power of the school to re-create within itself a model for the future community. The document that set the legal foundations of the school, for example, identified two Deweyan postulates as basis of anarchist pedagogy: that all schools had to reflect the "principles of life" and the school had to become a "society in miniature" with no "antagonism" to society.[10] Organizing learning around agricultural and industrial work, the production of crafts, and the sale of manufactured articles in the market inserted production at the center of learning in ways analogous to Deweyan schools at Chicago.[11]

For these anarchists, the vision of a school as a "society in miniature" constituted the most attractive Deweyan idea because its implementation promised to liberate the mind of the student from the "artificial" order created in Mexico by Catholicism and which prevented individuals from relating to life and understanding its real logic.[12] It was a form of alienation that the school could remedy by creating within it a "society in miniature" that would reflect the "principles of life"—in other words, that would reveal to the student in the classroom how the real world worked and how it was produced so the student could name that world as his own. Removing religious mysticism would establish in the child conceptual avenues to a world deemed transparent and available to human knowledge and transformation. In this sense, they found congruence between Dewey's thought and Ferrer's mission to create purely secular schools removed from the influence of the church. Rationalist schools promoted this new orientation to life by encouraging students to publish their own newspapers, to read publications from different parts of the world, and to engage in the exploration of the natural world that surrounded them. They introduced student savings banks, a Republic of Workers, American Boy Scouts clubs, cooperatives, and other institutions in an effort to create a production cycle within the school that would reflect how life works in reality.[13] Thus anarchists proposed to create within the school a social order they identified as "natural," by which they meant democratic, secular, egalitarian and objectively real.

Anarchists moved beyond Dewey by construing this natural world as one characterized by freedom from any mediating form of authority. All forms of association that replicated or reproduced hierarchical relations were to be abolished. de la Luz Mena advocated the importation of a great number of pedagogical ideas inspired by American progressive education for that purpose, such as student clubs, pupil participation in school administration and student associations in order to provide the perfect environment for a fully democratized form of social inquiry. In the state of Tabasco, anarchists called for all forms of student contests to be eliminated and any kind of activity "organized around competition among students with the purpose of emulation" was frowned upon.[14] For Tabascan Professor Ochoa, sympathy and cooperation would substitute for competition.[15] He maintained that emulation would lead or degenerate into rivalry and envy, the opposite sentiments to solidarity.[16] An aesthetic of freedom that included unbolted chairs, open-air classrooms, and the elimination of "rows of rigid tables" would further encourage the "free associations of students and the bonds of solidarity and cooperation that [are to] characterize [this] new order."[17]

de la Luz Mena's 1917 tract entitled *De las tablillas de lodo a las ecuaciones de primer grado*—"From the Clay Tables to the Equations of First Degree"—promoted an atmosphere of "complete liberty" where students produced their own school projects simply by playing with "clay tables" and then naturally proceeding to the learning of mathematics, seemingly without teacher supervision.[18] Professor Elena Torres, speaking at the First Socialist Congress held in Motul, Yucatán, from March 29 to 31 of 1918, explained the schools' goals as the acquisition of two kinds of knowledge: a "knowledge of immediate application" to be acquired "by sowing fields, in workshops, in the experimentation cabinets of the same school," and a more sophisticated knowledge of "social life to be acquired in the conduct of life in the school, giving way to practices of liberty."[19] Scientific principles would be "deduced from ordinary work."[20] Inquiry, rooted in human experience and free of dogmatism and authority, would usher in a new man free to pursue, innovate, and create: a child-scientist. Anarchist activists defended Deweyan child-centered education during the Pedagogic Congress of 1915 in Merida specifically for that purpose.[21] de la Luz Mena argued that anarchist schools "must let children live for themselves; the child is a sun around which all factors of education move, he is the center of reference for all organization according to John Dewey."[22]

The texts, proclamations and regulations of these anarchist schools suggest that there was in fact a duality to this project. Another dimension to this project consisted in an active project of exclusions necessary to make the democratic order of the school possible. On the one hand, the notion of freedom inscribed in anarchist writing implied the destruction of the "artificial" barriers of Catholicism, its dogmatic impositions and its opposition to free inquiry. In this way, the school, structured around the "principles of life," could accommodate itself to a society whose logic became transparent. The school community—its social world of clubs, organizations, newspapers and activities—would find in the world a congenial environment for its own reproduction only when that world was free of any dogma.

On the other hand, racial considerations became paramount in the pluralistic world of Yucatán province, a social reality very much the opposite to the racially homogeneous classrooms of Europe, where only class differences impinged on revolutionary projects such as Ferrer's.[23] In Mérida, racialized fractures in social consciousness between school, society and home prevailed. Thus socialization, as an educational objective, acquired a much broader significance in an urbanized and racially miscegenated society such as Mérida. Most anarchist texts affirmed a civilizational mission to the Natives of Mexico as a supplement to the larger task of creating a democratic community inspired by European and American models.[24] This mission implied an intimate and accurate knowledge of the conditions of students' homes and their parents' social practices. Their culture had to be available for transformation the same way as the natural world. By displacing Native autonomy, society would be consistent with the "principles of life": secular, available to continuous inquiry and homogeneous. Nothing could have been more important in a nation of innumerable particularities such as Mexico, where many communities coexisted uneasily, and at times violently, with each other.

In spite of these tensions, Dewey's notion of the associated life shared an important place in anarchist thought, which aimed to achieve a democratic life in a world of limitless possibilities for individuals sharing the same purpose. Anarchists opposed anything that promoted uniformity and conformity in the schools. They eliminated textbooks, examinations, awards and punishments and rejected any form of mediating authority, such as the church and state. They justified anti-intellectualism on the grounds that the only knowledge that was practical was necessary for democratic life.[25] Anarchists demonstrated that radical aspects of Dewey's pedagogy could find a congenial atmosphere in Mexico. They helped advance the notion that ideas were the product of man's labor and his engagement with the world and that democratic life could be conceived as the end point of social revolution. This aspect of education that conceived democracy as its ultimate end constituted the most Deweyan aspect of anarchist education in Mexico.

The *Escuelas Activas* Movement

Whereas the *racionalista* project shared the universal aspirations of the worldwide anarchist movement, most other projects of education in Mexico who invoked Dewey reflected a firm commitment to the creation of a Mexican nation. This meant that the purposes of education focused on the creation of a nationalist consciousness that would facilitate a modern and just industrial order possible in Mexico. These two dimensions of modernity—nationalist consciousness and economic development—complemented each other. Nationalist consciousness spoke to the desire to create that underlying unity of purpose that would make possible material progress and that would socialize what Eulalia Guzmán, a principal actor in the movement and writer of *La escuela nueva*, denominated the "isolated individual,"[26] a common moniker for the subject atomized by a racially (and geographically) diverse society such as Mexico. It would realize the Mexican liberal dream of reconciling order and progress. This aim animated the *escuelas activas* movement that promoted the principles of progressive activity-based education in Mexico during the early 1920s.

The *escuelas activas* movement in Mexico City moved Dewey and American progressive education more to the center of their nationalist vision. Pedagogues such as Guzmán imagined Mexico in a comparative framework where the progressive aspects of American society stood as an important model for a future Mexican society. America consisted in an ordered and progressive social order where the methods and organizational capabilities of Americans explained its amazing progress.[27] This was the America found in the classroom but also the America that made these classrooms possible. In that classroom, Mexican teachers found discipline and order without the need of coercion. This was a product, according Guillermo de la Rosa, of America's "admirable political and administrative organization,"[28] which, as Guzmán claimed, reconciled order and progress in a synthesis of "utility and culture."[29] She expressed admiringly that in the United States "anything that is not of utility outside the school nor possesses an educational value to justify its inclusion in the program . . . is thrown out of the primary school in order to substitute for the simple equation and the percentage."[30] Science had replaced dogma: "Anything that harks back to scholastic discussions . . . is thrown out," she exclaimed.[31] The managerial liberalism teachers praised spoke to the teaching and use of science as form of inquiry and thought, exemplified by the use of the inductive method.[32] Guzmán and the Mexican teachers read modern forms of discipline encountered in the United States not as the product of its industrial society but as its cause.

In Guzmán's visit to New York's Angelo Patri's Deweyan schools, the Bronx experiment founded by school principal Angelo Patri, Guzmán spoke admiringly of the American classroom as a laboratory for democracy. Patri had used Deweyan education in public schools as an alternative to the enforced Americanization projects favored by other progressives, which he thought were coercive if not outright hostile to the student's heritage and language.[33] Here Guzmán observed the Dewyan schooling practices directly, which she compared to those of Tolstoi in Russia and Tagore in India.[34] Her recollections indicate that Patri's schools exemplified for her Dewey's "education for life," devoid of the dogmatic tyranny of book memorization and the political control it implied. She observed admiringly how "[students'] associations, cooperatives, elections, [were] not written on a school notebook, they wanted them living in the schools."[35] Patri's schools suggested for her the model for Mexico's "future social order." "Why do they need notebooks, why summaries of civics if they have the living practices of civic life," she exclaimed. "When [I] wished to talk to them [the students] about respecting the right of the other, they were already respecting the labor of others, because they understood the value of such labor and did not desire unto others what they did not desire to be done unto them,"[36] she concluded.

In her book, Guzmán lionized Arturo Oropeza's "Francisco I. Madero" school, financed in part by Mexico's Directorate of the Campaign Against Illiteracy, and founded in 1921 in Mexico City partly as a Deweyan activity-based school, whose purpose consisted in translating this atomized subject into a producer citizen or *niño productor* (producer-child), fully socialized by the social world of the school. This world consisted of social organizations such as banks, technical councils, irrigation committees, a Cooperative of Consumption, a second Cooperative on Production, and a Commission for the Regulation of Prices, which students could manage as a fraternal and egalitarian enterprise.[37] Students also formed a *Junta de Trabajo* or Labor Board, a Board for the Protection of Children, a Board of Justice, a Board for Material Improvements, and other corporate bodies to prepare them for a life of activism outside the school,[38] and engage in the solution of Mexico's national problems such as poverty and land and labor issues and create in the school Mexico's "future social order."[39]

Guzmán's ideas reflected the intense desire of Mexican intellectuals, ravaged by war and spiritually burdened by the poverty of Mexico, to imagine a nation where virtues flowed organically from human interaction and not from external authority. She wrote *La escuela nueva o de la acción* in 1923 as a manifesto for a new movement imagined along Deweyan lines of the cultivation of the self, scientific practice, communal work and cooperation, fraternity and mutual support. Discipline in the classroom, based on "liberty in work and happiness," would displace "awards and punishments." Classrooms were to become "fields of observation and experimentation . . . factories and workshops" and provide the basis for a new kind of experimental self.[40] Like many other liberals, she imagined the school's community as "natural" and providing the necessary common purpose to permit experimentation and creativity. In her discussion of Oropeza's school, she praised the classrooms' *desorden armonioso*, a common phrase meaning "harmonious disorder."[41] Eulalia Guzmán called it a "disorder that follows the varieties of life, within a natural order."[42] She praised Oropeza's students because they exercised in class their "broad faculties to govern themselves in order to give foundation and see with clarity the problems of life, and not to vegetate in a school within an environment of artificiality, more artificiality, pure artificiality."[43] The political order of the school, free from the religious oppression of the mind, could be self-sustaining and thus deemed natural. Oropeza himself related how "cleaning brigades," one of the first spontaneous associations formed by children, cleaned the school and swept the streets of the barrio and the front of each child's home.

Guzmán argued that in Oropeza's school there was no planning at all as students set the pace of learning. As in other similar experiments, textbooks, blackboards and maps, considered "material created for the exploitation of the child rather than his benefit," were eliminated. Oropeza claimed to have eliminated schedules, timetables and any kind of preconceived planning to allow children to dictate the pace of learning through their own work. Arturo Oropeza called agricultural tools a replacement for books and chalk something "natural."[44] Guzmán relates how Oropeza's students learned about their nation from their experience in school:

> at first . . . because the extension of land [in the school] was large and because relatively few students wished to work the land (a few students wondered why they had to work in school since they had always been convinced that in school one does not work but merely reads) . . . [the agrarian problem] did not arise in their minds . . . [according to Oropeza] "as soon as they saw the pecuniary results and the satisfaction they felt in being producers, the demand for land grew and all ask their teachers for their share of it . . . we saw with pleasure . . . how this problem was easily resolved by the children themselves . . . since they came up first with the idea that any share of the land had to be possessed equally by all and that for this sharing to be ordered they must appoint a commission of their peers. Thus children practiced elections, understood the value of the individual in the collectivity, and, felt the weight of the national problem of socializing land."[45]

One may doubt that students spontaneously created all these organizations in the school, let alone had time to even read a book, but the idea that students' personal and national interest possessed a natural correlation constituted the key point in this narrative.

She continued:

> when we intended to issue regulations for the children, they had already done so by themselves; when we intended to demand punctuality, the child cared more about being punctual than ourselves . . . when we intended to talk to them about equity in the distribution of lands and profits, it was realized that they never desire for any one child to gain more than the other, or more land than the other, because they always saw that as an injustice; when we intended to teach them about virtue, they themselves praised the working child and chose their leaders by their virtues and not by their defects . . . as can be seen . . . the problem of discipline resolves itself automatically as a result of a life of work, of liberty, which the children are living.[46]

Teachers' Debates and the Journal "Educación"

The more nationalist the educational project, the likelier the United States (and Dewey) became the focus of discussion.[47] In congresses, conventions and public meetings with leaders of the Secretariat of Public Education (SEP), radical teachers defended Deweyan pedagogy when it demarcated the domain of teaching as separate from that of the state and prioritized democratic and egalitarian social relations as the ultimate end point of modernity. Many teachers supported American child-centered education because it affirmed the inviolable bond between student and teacher. The Second Commission of the Second National Teachers Congress, held in Mexico City on December of 1920, declared itself in favor of Dewey's *escuela activa* as a way to individualize instruction, declaring that: "[if] all children were to be absolutely equal, if one child were to be identical to the other . . . then the school would fulfill its noble goals by instructing teachers with old ideas . . . [yet] texts show us that there is no such psychology of the child, but the psychology of this one child, and that one child."[48] The Congress expressed its approval of the new pedagogy declaring that its "basic principle is to be liberty, both for the pupils as for the teachers, without any other sanction than the sentiment of one's responsibility."[49]

Although opposed by teachers who argued that Dewey's *escuela activa* would promote chaos by fostering the radical individuality of each person and by claiming that no authority could evaluate the relationship between student and teacher, sentiment in favor of activity-based education grew.[50] In the First Mexican Congress on the Child held in Mexico City in 1921, Lisandro Calderón, condemned any education whose "principal objective," he argued, "was mastering certain symbols as the only access to culture."[51] Teachers who followed Deweyan progressive education in the Congress argued that education could not be secured simply by teaching culture through the European classics, as the newly appointed secretary of public education, José Vasconcelos, claimed, but by democratizing social relations among students.[52] Calderón defended American education as a place where "these transformations [had] been implemented rapidly"; "the American child," he argued, "has in the school a true place for work and education."[53] Thus the United States stood firmly, now more than ever, at the center of teachers' debates on Dewey.

Yet, these sentiments in favor of an education free from state constraints conflicted with the desire to unify the nation, a response to the weakness of Mexico, devastated by civil war and American imperial incursions, which intensified the need to unify a politically and racially fragmented nation in order to defend the state. Lisandro Calderón defended the use of Deweyan education in the schools precisely because it favored "a society . . . [that] maintains itself together because it labors in a common direction, possesses a common spirit and has, as a reference [point], common aspirations."[54] Calderón stressed that in Mexico, "the fundamental reason why the school today cannot organize itself as natural and unify society is precisely because it lacks this element of a common and productive activity. In the field of play and in sports we don't see a spontaneous and unavoidable social organization . . . [today's] schools are lacking in the motivation and cement of social organization."[55] Calderón continued:

> If our natural resources remained unexploited or if only foreigners were to take advantage of them, I would understand this as the result of our

deficient theoretical education. But if we get children used to action, their mental state will change; it will take off in new directions and will generate acts in a more positive sense. And the Motherland, who expects so much from her good sons and the course of progress, will finally be able to count on an army of workers well armed for the struggle . . . this does not mean that scientific speculation will be seen with indifference . . . what is wished is to orient education towards action.[56]

The preoccupation on national unity moved fears of racial degeneration or as Calderón put it, the "racial apathy" of the Mexicans,[57] to center stage. Creating a "national character" rested on the belief that racial miscegenation had produced the Mexicans' apathetic and atomized individual, an idea that reflected a growing consensus that race and modernity intersected only in that historical space where racial homogeneity prevailed. Calderón's intervention bears reproducing in full given the salience of race, now firmly at the center of national discussions on education among teachers favoring Dewey. Calderón stated that,

> our national character is generally apathetic and not too much inclined towards action. We must recognize this . . . the majority of the Mexican people proceeds from the mixing of two races: the Spanish and the Indigenous. The first one was proud, heroic, and a dreamer; the other one was resigned and sad, without aspirations and at times estranged from the social conditions of the nation, in spite of the fact that in the past it demonstrated its potent energy. From this mixture comes the Mexican people who are dreamers, who are heroic but also sad and resigned.[58]

Progress and melancholia did not mix.

Calderón's arguments demonstrate that the appropriation of American education, and especially Dewey, was intended to save the Mexican nation, not to Americanize Mexico. If it is true, as Calderón affirmed, that the Mexican school was to be transformed "just like School 45 of Indianapolis where children build a doll's house first by drawing a plan, gathering material, building up, decorating and endowing the new house with its park and cultivated land,"[59] it was equally true that the school needed to be purely Mexican. Yet, at the same time, the concern with common purpose and the need to build an industrial and powerful nation strong enough to withstand the erosion of sovereignty brought about by American penetration of markets and politics meant that the comparative disadvantage between the United States and Mexico stood as the implicit point of reference for the importation of foreign ideas such as Dewey's.[60]

Calderón's intervention also demonstrates how, along with the issue of national unity, another idea powerfully took hold of the imagination of these teachers: that Mexicans needed to reach a new "mental state" who could move the nation in "new directions" and generate modernity from within the nation. This moved the debate away from discussions of structural issues such as land redistribution. Polemical texts by José Antonio Rodó, Edmond Desmolins, Victor Arreguine and Gustav Le Bon had begun circulating in Mexico since the turn of the century, providing a public forum for the proliferation of discourses of racial decline and the ascendancy of the "Anglo-Saxon" race in world history profoundly influencing the teachers of *Educación*.[61] "If one wishes to summarize in one word the fundamental psychological differences that separate Latin learning from Anglo-Saxon learning, Gustav Le Bon states the first one rests only on the study of books, while the second one exclusively on experience," argued Deweyan supporters Lima and Rentería.[62] The solution was to educate a new practical man of modernity oriented toward *vida* or life.

The primacy of John Dewey to the teachers' movement, so much tied to these discourses, was cemented by the publication of *Educación*, a journal of politics and pedagogy published in Mexico in the years of 1921 and 1922 and sponsored by the Columbia University. John Dewey figured as a listed member of its editorial board along with other faculty of Teachers' College, such as William H. Kilpatrick. In its pages, the rhetoric of education coalesced around the *principio de la acción*, a set of techniques and proposals that unified all kinds of projects to formulate modern Deweyan classroom practices around the concept of activity or *acción*. The journal's ideas became the foundation for the *Bases para la organización de la escuela primaria conforme al principio de la acción* (Bases for the Organization of Primary Schools according to the Principle of Action), the law that inscribed Deweyan ideas in Mexican education and was published in the journal. The *Bases* supported the adoption of Kilpatrick's project method as a way to create the much-desired "harmonious disorder." It also promoted *centros de acción* to produce unity in the classroom when one single task stood at the center of group activity.[63]

Thus the significance of *Educación* resided mostly with a slight but significant shift, when writing on Deweyan education (and American modernity in general), toward the creation of a new subject of modernity and away from the previous emphasis on social justice and democracy. This meant a search for ways of thinking that promoted creative growth in the individual. Mexican teachers such as Manuel Barranco, Lucio Tapia, Marcelino M. Lima, Marcelino Rentería and Moisés Sáenz, perhaps the most important advocates of the Deweyan schooling in *Educación*, seemed overwhelmed (as most Mexican intellectuals) by Mexico's disempowerment vis-à-vis the United States in the particular and between Latin American and English-speaking nations in general. A model for a new Mexican subject, declared Barranco, was "the inventor, the discoverer, the wise."[64] Lucio Tapia declared that México needed to transform its men into pragmatic individuals who could produce not ideas, but things. Marcelino M. Lima and Marcelino Rentería called this new man the "Struggler-for-lifer" (in English).[65]

This "struggler-for-lifer" was entrepreneurial, akin to the American man of business, a Mexican version of the self-made man. For them, Deweyan education promised the transformation of the Mexican self from a Latin *"hombre teórico"* or theoretical man to a practical and entrepreneurial men edified by labor."[66] "God Himself assists the Saxon, while we ourselves kill each other over dogma,"[67] declared José Vasconcelos. The *Bases* went on to declare that the new education would provide "the foundation for scientific investigation . . . to awaken the child to action . . . to favor the instinct of the child."[68]

The Mexican Native stood in opposition to the entrepreneurial man. Deemed an "obstacle to progress," national unity needed the transformation of the Native into a "factor of production." "What solution is there for this national problem," wrote Tapia in *Educación*, "if the Indian cannot advance and we cannot back down?"[69] For Tapia, the teacher to the Indians would be a "new Messiah . . . bringing the Gospel of civilization."[70] For teachers such as José Bonilla, the Indian's life had to be absolutely modified and transformed, his family life severed from village loyalties, and his physical being separated from the home. Bonilla even proposed his own version of the school as "a community in miniature,"[71] imagining the school as providing an artificial environment that could favor the transformation of the Indian.[72] The writers of *Educación* all agreed that modernity necessitated the complete transformation of the Indian, a project not subject, of course, to democratic deliberation, but to state imposition.

The pedagogues of *Educación* assumed that racial homogeneity constituted the most important reason for American success, and even opponents of the Deweyans agreed. Antonio Caso argued that, "the collective soul of the Mexican has not coalesced yet in definite and characteristic form; and it is very difficult that there exists a proper and adequate scientific study of anything if the object itself of research has not yet realized itself in its integrity and plenitude."[73] According to José Vasconcelos, at this time the head of education in Mexico, "they [the North Americans] do not bear in their blood the contradictory instincts of the mixture of dissimilar races."[74] Although Vasconcelos condemned American "destruction" of American Indians, he conceived modern education in Mexico as encompassing Native life in its totality: "the flowering of the native within the domain of the universal."[75] Jurist Emilio Rabasa put it more succinctly: "the Anglo-Saxon communities, were founded in the New World not by conquest but by the occupation of land, and, instead of forming unions with the Natives, they denied them all contact with their race . . . increasing their hereditary tendencies of individualism, autonomy, and thus able to experiment without interruption in the practices of ordered government for their mutual benefit."[76]

These discourses on race tempered the optimism prevalent in the previous projects that invoked Dewey, casting a melancholic shadow over the very meaning of progress. Lucio Tapia imagined progress now "not [as] an angel," but as a "satanic exterminator of the Apocalypse."[77] In the name of progress, he said, Indians, "these ancient and great people who owned this land that we have violently taken away from them . . . the authors of the civilization we have destroyed . . . the masters of yesterday," have been "enchained and conquered."[78] Yet, progress being inevitable, the new educational mission for Mexico could be imagined as a tragic yet necessary continuation of the centuries-old European project of conquest, another *conquista*. The *Bases*' dictum that "the school must reproduce the environment of the home"[79] prefigured the state's mission to know the intimate life of its citizens and transform it for nation building purposes. The *Bases* committed the schools to "penetrate the current of material and spiritual progress of the society wherein [the child] will live and struggle," faithful to Dewey's desire to create a continuum between school and society,[80] but also setting the basis for state intervention. Schools were to be given the task of transforming the intimate lives of Indians to make way for civilization. The civilizational mission became thus an essential component of state projects based on Deweyan education, a mission justified as necessary to create a nation with a common set of values and where racial difference would not stand as an obstacle for the efficiency of the entrepreneurial national body.

End of the Military Phase of the Mexican Revolution

Pedagogical discourses invoking Dewey could have multiplied and transformed themselves in multiple ways as they had been doing since the earlier anarchist projects. Yet, historical contingencies led to Dewey becoming the patron saint of the Mexican revolutionary education in 1923. The military occupation of the state of Yucatán in 1915 by General Salvador Alvarado, which precipitated the demise of the anarchist and socialist experiments in education that had been established there, paved the way for the appropriation of Deweyan education by the national state. The Deweyan features of anarchists' schools appealed to Alvarado, who had familiarized himself with American pedagogy, especially new ideas emanating from the University of Chicago. Alvarado expressed an appreciation for the qualities of American pragmatism and Anglo-Saxon Victorian virtues in general. He became an avid reader of the literature of personal uplift, where Anglo-Saxon cultural traits offered clues to Anglo-Saxon success and character. He read Samuel Smiles, the Victorian writer and novelist, and the literature of uplift and self-esteem produced in the United States.[81]

For a man who believed that Catholic education had created an artificial world embodied in the oppressive figure of the authoritarian teacher who interpreted life for the child "by the dogmatic imposition" of his beliefs and "the fateful principle of *magister dixit*,"[82] the practicality of the American character reigned triumphant because it expressed the ability of the student to orient himself to experience. Dewey's notion of the "school as miniature community" compelled Alvarado to suggest how schools could create a national consciousness by providing a vision of the nation as a real entity through experiential learning. Schooling could create within the space of the school a vision of society "as it really was." He invoked Dewey in this respect when he said: "Education must be a social process; a process whereby the individual participates in the social consciousness of the people or the race he belongs to. The school is a social institution and for its proper functioning, for it to socialize the child, it must present the form of a small community wherein social life is represented in miniature as it really is, as it is seen in the home, in the neighborhood and in the field of play."[83] In Alvarado's mind, that "real life" was the nation. The Deweyan principle of the "school as a miniature community" and the "assimilation of school to society" formed the foundation for Alvarado's project to acculturate Mexican natives to civilization and create self-consciousness through work-based education. Socialization would teach them "how to read, write, or count . . . it means work . . . intelligent work . . . to work in a conscious mode."[84] In 1918, Alvarado passed a law for primary schools with fields, orchards, and workshops designed to derive learning from activities.[85] Boy Scout groups were imported from the United States to promote solidarity and the practical principles of everyday life.[86]

Along with the appropriation of progressive education techniques came the absorption of these same intellectuals into the revolutionary process, leading to the rise of Moisés Sáenz, a self-professed disciple of Dewey and former student at Teachers' College, to the sub-secretary of education in 1923. These pedagogues, many of them Protestants, had placed an enormous emphasis on the American entrepreneur as their model for the common man: an everyday man with extraordinary abilities and a practical *orientación para la vida* or "orientation to life." As Jean-Pierre Bastian has noted, Sáenz "took from Anglo-Saxon liberal Protestantism this concept of the individual engaged in an effort for the common good . . . [where] . . . private and public interest must coincide in the defense of a nationalism open to foreign pedagogical models and to the economic model from North America."[87] Most, like Sáenz, had been educated according to the principles of progressive education in mission schools and became useful for a state desirous to displace the power of Catholicism in the Mexican government. These intellectuals led a new phase in the dissemination of Dewey's ideas in Mexico.

Conclusion

It is difficult to evaluate the fidelity of these projects to Dewey's own thought since the Mexican actors for the most part invoked Dewey as a prophet of national salvation rather than seeking to engage the philosopher's works in depth. Positing the existence of a "true" Dewey may also constitute a problem when it veers into dogma. Mexico's early uses of Dewey occurred in a quasi-mystical engagement with American modernity and with the messianic possibilities of Dewey's education in particular and American progressive education in general. The nature of the dissemination of his ideas occurred mostly in relation to "maxims" such as the "school as a miniature society" or "the schools must reflect the principles of life." These powerful ideas structured an important phase in Mexico's educational history and constituted a powerful conceptual tool to conceive the future nation with the same messianic zeal that characterized the spirits of American educators in the early twentieth century. As Richard Hofstadter reminded us, progressive education "was presented to the world not simply as an instrumentality but as a creed, which went beyond the hope of this or that strictly educational result to promise some kind of ultimate salvation for individuals or for the race."[88] It would usher, as Dewey himself proclaimed, "the true kingdom of God."[89]

It is clear that from the beginning how to create an underlying unity for the nation—assumed by most Mexicans to exist already in the Anglo-Saxon racial fabric of the United States—constituted the main problematic in the appropriation of Dewey's thought in Mexico. Mexican teachers believed that creating a shared set of values would not occur in conditions similar to those of the United States, which had been indeed violent. "We cannot annihilate [the Indian] as the English colonials did with the Redskins or the buffalo and then gather them pitifully," exclaimed Salvador Alvarado, "and populate reservations and parks with them."[90] Mexico, facing a majoritarian native and mixed raced population, had to pursue other means to convert the Native. Acts of exclusion did not seem incongruous with the American progressive spirit. Social efficiency would have seemed a product of selection (and thus exclusion). Mexican intellectuals had visited various experimental schools in the United States, including Dewey's laboratory schools, which for the most part functioned by selecting both teachers and students in order to provide that common fabric without which the experimental school would not achieve its effectiveness. In other words, unity of purpose could be conceived as an external imposition: as in the laboratory's conditions of possibility.

Thus when pragmatism met revolution, to paraphrase Engerman, it gave way to force as the way to attain peaceful ends. Dewey had argued that when "certain ends are desirable," it did not mean that, "those ends and nothing else will result from the use of force to attain them."[91] Yet it was not clear whether he intended to apply this idea to all societies. Oftentimes he referred to the United States as a nation possessing an exceptional foundation for democratic life; under other conditions, force could be employed to "permit the method of intelligent action." In fact, Dewey claimed that,

> to profess democracy as an ultimate ideal and the suppression of democracy as a means to the ideal may be possible in a country that has never known even rudimentary democracy, but when professed in a country that has anything of a genuine democratic spirit in its traditions, it signifies desire for possession and retention of power by a class, whether that

class be called Fascist or Proletarian . . . the one exception—and that apparent rather than real—to dependence upon organized intelligence as the method for directing social change is found when society through an authorized majority has entered upon the path of social experimentation leading to great social change, and a minority refuses by force to permit the method of intelligent action to go into effect. Then force may be intelligently employed to subdue and disarm the recalcitrant minority.[92]

The issue of unity in Mexico was an ambivalent concept. Imagined at times as absent, at other times it was something actually real but impossible in practice due to the artificial order imposed by the church on society, which nurtured divisions among the national body. The discourse on the "principles of life" and the accommodation of the school to those principles veered between the descriptive and the prescriptive. At times it referred to an already underlying unity, which the school would redeem for the nation, at other times to a future "social order," which the school would cultivate. The discourse on the "principles of life," relying on an opposition between "real life" and an "artificial order," also replicated the logic of American progressive education. "The notion of education advanced at the turn of the century," writes Hofstadter, "was romantic in the sense that [progressives] set up an antithesis between the development of the individual—his sensibility, the scope of his fancy, the urgency of his personal growth—and the imperatives of the social order, with its demand for specified bodies of knowledge, prescribed manners and morals, and a personal equipment suited to traditions and institutions. Theirs was a commitment to the natural child against artificial society."[93] In Mexico, the ambivalence between the artificial and the real complicated the reception of Dewey.

Finally, the shift toward ways of thinking exemplified by *Educación* led to the prioritizing of individual growth over the concerns with democracy and justice. Democratic ends, of course, were not forgotten, but the uses of Deweyan education turned toward the teaching of productive ways of thinking—in other words, to ushering some kind of cognitive revolution in the Mexican self. This corresponded to Dewey's thought. Dewey did not reduce human activity to just growth and productivity, but his philosophy of education did emphasize productive forms of inquiry. According to Larry Hickman, Dewey's notion of inquiry, as the defining feature of his philosophy and the foundation for social scientific thinking in general, did just that.[94] Hickman argues that, "progress in the sciences, as well as in common sense inquiries, requires that the results of prior inquiries be treated as raw materials for further inquiries, and not as determinate results, established one and for all."[95] Nothing could have been more attractive for Mexican pedagogues of the time, concerned especially with how the Catholic Church fostered exactly the opposite vision in Mexico, militating against free inquiry and promoting a purely "consummatory" orientation to life.

Radical Dewey 23

In many ways, the Catholic order in Mexico thrived on what Dewey called in *Experience and Nature* "magical exercise and superstitious legend." He explained in that book how in a political order infused with magic, the "primary interest lies in staging the show and enjoying the spectacle, in giving play to the ineradicable interest in stories which illustrate the contingencies of existence combined with happier endings for emergencies than surrounding conditions often permit. It was not conscience that kept men loyal to cults and rites, and faithful to tribal myths. So far as it was not routine, it was enjoyment of the drama of life without the latter's liabilities that kept piety from decay."[96] This phase of experience," he continued, "manifests objects, which are final. The attitude involved in their appreciation is esthetic."[97] Larry Hickman explicates that for Dewey, "primitive magic and religious practices fail[ed] to become inquiry precisely when and because their interest [were] focused on intrinsic meanings as final and not as productive of further significance: extrinsic meanings or instrumentalities are merely incidental to such practices. These societies therefore reverse[d] the pattern of effective technological inquiry."[98] "As direct appreciative enjoyment exhibits things in their consummatory phase," wrote Dewey, "labor manifests things in their connections of things with one another, in efficiency, productivity, furthering, hindering, generating, destroying." Most teachers in Mexico invoking Dewey in fact searched for ways of thinking where, as Hickman argues, "production [would take] precedence over and [become] a guide to practicality."[99] Dewey's ideas in this matter came to possess an import for Mexican pedagogues because they identified the possibilities for progress within specific modes of thought or ways of thinking that were productive rather than purely consummatory. Magic led to the reproduction of familiar worlds and not to the creation of new ones.

By 1923, this vision of Dewey came to define the state project that followed in its Deweyan form: creating the practical man of modernity. His leader: Moisés Sáenz a Presbyterian minister and respected member among Mexican Protestants. Thus before dwelling of the state project, it becomes necessary to analyze a second node in the dissemination of Deweyan and American progressive ideas: the liberal ideologies of Mexican Protestantism.

Notes

1. The scholarship on the Mexican revolution in the 1920s is too extensive. Among works on Mexico that relate to aspects of Deweyan education during that time see, Alexander S. Dawson, *Indian and Nation in Revolutionary Mexico* (Tucson: University of Arizona Press, 2004); Alan Knight, *The Mexican Revolution, Vol.2: Counter-Revolution and Reconstruction* (Lincoln: University of Nebraska Press, 1990); Stephen E. Lewis, *The Ambivalent Revolution: Forging State and Nation in Chiapas, 1910–1945* (Albuquerque: University of New Mexico Press, 2005); Mary Kay Vaughan, *Cultural Politics in Revolution: Teachers, Peasants, and Schools in Mexico, 1930–1940* (Tucson: University of Arizona Press, 1997); Mary Kay Vaughan, *The Eagle and the Virgin: Nation and Cultural Revolution in Mexico, 1920–1940* (Durham, NC: Duke University

Press, 2006); and Mary Kay Vaughan, *The State, Education, and Social Class in Mexico, 1880–1928* (DeKalb: Northern Illinois Press, 1982). Some Americanists have referred to this period in the dissemination of Dewey's ideas in Mexico albeit briefly. Among them see, Jay Martin, *The Education of John Dewey: A Biography* (New York: Columbia University Press, 2003); Steven Rockefeller, *John Dewey: Religious Faith and Democratic Humanism* (New York: Columbia University Press, 1994); Alan Ryan, *John Dewey and the High Tide of American Liberalism* (New York: W.W. Norton and Company, Inc., 1997); and Robert Westbrook, *John Dewey and American Democracy* (Ithaca, NY: Cornell University Press, 1993). On Yucatán during this era see, González Navarro, Moisés, *Raya y tierra: la Guerra de castas y el henequén* (México: Colegio de México, 1970); Francisco Paoli and Enrique Montalvo, *El socialismo olvidado de Yucatán* (México: Siglo Veintiuno, 1974); Mary Kay Vaughan, *The State, Education, and Social Class in Mexico, 1880–1928* (DeKalb: Northern Illinois University Press, 1982).
2. For Mary Kay Vaughan, for example, Deweyan education in Mexico focused on bourgeois concerns with individual character as the basis for modernizing the nation rather with revolutionary structural transformations. Mary Kay Vaughn, *The State, Education, and Social Class in Mexico, 1880–1928* (DeKalb: Northern Illinois University Press, 1982).
3. All interpretations of Dewey in Mexico take for granted the nature of the nationalist discourses that appropriated Dewey in Mexico. If nationalism enters the discussion, it remains tied to a methodology that addresses it purely as sociological phenomena, rather than as a discursive one. On the importance of understanding nationalism as a discursive phenomenon; see Partha Chatterjee, *Nationalist Thought and the Colonial World* (Minneapolis, MN: University of Minnesota Press, 1986). According to Chatterjee, "the sociological understanding of the phenomenon of nationalism" would lead "inevitably towards a teleology, i.e., a theory of political development." In our case, for example, Vaughan conceives Dewey's pedagogy as serving a particular purpose within the narrative of capitalist development, which is to impose discipline and homogeneity on the work force. This kind of analysis of nationalism, of course, Chatterjee would find limiting, especially because it trivializes the place of nationalism in the history of ideas. I argue that the dissemination of Dewey's ideas in the world is indeed a problem of intellectual history.
4. The state of Yucatán was situated in an advantageous geopolitical location at the intersection of a vast flows of ideas and cultural forms emanating from Europe and the United States, ranging from European anarchism to Deweyan pedagogy, and including American baseball, which had been imported from the United States by Cuban immigrants to Yucatán. The *escuelas racionalistas* or rationalist schools constituted the most radical of these pedagogical experiments, and they became a model for other socialist schooling projects in México. See Vaughn, *The State, Education, and Social Class in Mexico*.
5. Ferrer's universalism began with his proposition that "truth was universal." See Francisco Ferrer, *The Origins and Ideals of the Modern School*, translated by Joseph McCabe (New York: G.P. Putnam's Sons, 1913), 19.
6. Francisco Ferrer, *The Origins and Ideals of the Modern School*, 101.
7. On Spanish anarchism see Carolyn P. Boyd, "The Anarchists and Education in Spain, 1868–1909," *The Journal of Modern History*, 48, no. 4 (December 1976).
8. See, Carlos Martínez Assad, introduction to *Los Lunes Rojos: la educación racionalista en México*, 1st edition, Carlos Martínez Assad, ed. (México: Secretaría de Educación Pública. Ediciones El Caballito, 1986), 9–20; José de la Luz Mena, "Tres conferencias del profesor José de la Luz Mena," *Los Lunes Rojos*, 49. See also Carolyn P. Boyd, "The Anarchists and Education in Spain", 22.

9. The most immediate source on Ferrer is his own autobiographical work, *The Origins and Ideals of the Modern School*; see also Carolyn P. Boyd, "The Anarchists and Education in Spain," and Murray Bookchin, *The Spanish Anarchists: The Heroic Years, 1868–1936* (Oakland: AK Press, 1997). On Ferrer's impact on American education see Paul Avrich, *The Modern School Movement: Anarchism and Education in the United States* (Princeton, NJ: Princeton University Press, 1980), 69–110.
10. "Fundamentos de la Ley de Institución de las Escuelas Racionalistas," *Los Lunes Rojos*, 25, 44.
11. This was also the method to teach mathematics. See Francisco Ferrer, *The Origins and Ideals of the Modern School*, 90.
12. See for example, Ibid., 73.
13. "Prospecto Plan de la escuela racionalista," *Los Lunes Rojos* (Mexico: Secretaría de Educación Pública Ediciones El Caballito. 1986), 40.
14. José Ochoa Lobato, "No aceptamos los concursos escolares," *Los Lunes Rojos*, 147.
15. Ibid.
16. Ibid., 148.
17. "*La voz de la revolución* (Mérida: Yucatán), Thursday, August 9th 1917, 35.
18. José de la Luz Mena, *La escuela socialista, su desorientación y fracaso: El verdadero derrotero* (A. Sola: México, 1941), 401.
19. Elena Torres, "El Quinto tema del Primer Congreso Socialista celebrado en Motul, estado de Yucatán," *Los Lunes Rojos*, 29.
20. Ibid.
21. Jose de la Luz Mena, *La escuela socialista*, 18.
22. José de la Luz Mena, "Tres Conferencias del profesor José de la Luz Mena: Tercera Conferencia," *Los Lunes Rojos*, 62. See also his defense of activity-based education for this same purpose: José de la Luz Mena. "Tres Conferencias del profesor José de la Luz Mena," 21–22.
23. This is evident in Ferrer's account of the class dynamics of anarchists' schools in Spain. See Francisco Ferrer, *The Origins and Ideals of the Modern School*, 44.
24. I used "supplementarity" here in the sense given to it by Derrida, as suggesting something lacking in the original and thus completes it, and at the same time, something that adds to the original. As we see here, that supplementarity in Mexico most oftentimes relate to issues of race and homogeneity. See Jacques Derrida, *Of Grammatology*, translated by Gayatri Chakravorti Spivak (Baltimore: The John Hopkins University Press, 1988).
25. "¡Sólo la escuela racionalista educa! Declaración de principios: fundamentos científicos y consecuencias sociales de esta escuela," *Los Lunes Rojos*, 147.
26. Ibid., 39.
27. This promise is clearly set forth in the instructions given by the president of Mexico, Venustiano Carranza, in 1914 to a contingent of Mexican teachers about to tour American schools during the years of 1914 and 1915. Eulalia Guzmán participated in these tours along with over one hundred teachers in three separate presidential commissions, which traveled to Massachusetts, New York, Philadelphia, Boston and Washington. See Venustiano Carranza, "Instrucciones a la segunda comisión," *Boletín de la Secretaría de Educación Pública* I, no. 2 (México: Talleres Gráficos de la Nación, Publicaciones de la Secretaría de Educación, November 1915), 84–85; "Instrucciones a la tercera comisión," *Boletín de la Secretaría de Educación Pública*, I no. 2 (México: Talleres Gráficos de la Nación, Publicaciones de la Secretaría de Educación, November 1925), 85.
28. Guillermo de la Rosa, "Informe de Guillermo de la Rosa," *Boletín de la Secretaría de Educación Pública* I, no. 2 (México: Talleres Gráficos de la Nación, Publicaciones de la Secretaría de Educación, November 1915).

26 *Radical Dewey*

29. Eulalia Guzmán, "Informe de Eulalia Guzmán," *Boletín de la Secretaría de Educación Pública* I, no. 2 (México: Talleres Gráficos de la Nación, Publicaciones de la Secretaría de Educación, November 1915), 137.
30. Ibid., 138.
31. Ibid.
32. María Dolores Mendoza, "Informe de María Dolores Mendoza," *Boletín de la Secretaría de Educación Pública* I, no. 2 (México: Talleres Gráficos de la Nación, Publicaciones de la Secretaría de Educación, November of 1915), 134–136.
33. For Patri's schools, see James M. Wallace, *The Promise of Progressivism: Angelo Patri and Urban Education* (New York: Peter Lang Publishing, 2006).
34. Eulalia Guzmán, "Características de la escuela nueva," Eulalia Guzmán, *La escuela nueva o de la acción* (México, 1923), 31.
35. Ibid., 37.
36. Ibid.
37. Ibid., 39.
38. Ibid., 37–39.
39. Ibid.
40. Ibid.
41. Manuel Barranco, "La escuela primaria del futuro," *Educación* 1, no. 1 (September 1922), 9 (also published in *Mundo Cristiano* July 6 1919, 22).
42. Eulalia Guzmán, "Características de la escuela nueva," 37.
43. Ibid., 38.
44. Ibid., 33–35.
45. Ibid., 38–39.
46. Ibid., 36–37.
47. The ideas of Dewey found their most ardent supporters among unionized teachers in Mexico City during the early 1920s, when the military phase of the Mexican revolution came to an end and the Mexican state—and Mexican society in general—reorganized itself.
48. *Segundo congreso nacional de maestros: Reunido en la capital de la República en los días del 15 al 28 del mes de diciembre de 1920. Obra escrita por el Profesor Higinio Vásquez Santa Ana, Srio. del referido Congreso y delegado de los estados de Jalisco, Michoacán y Chiapas* (Querétaro: Oficina Tipográfica del gobierno, 1923), 73.
49. Ibid., 74.
50. See for example the dissent of teacher Lopez Ibarra in *Segundo congreso nacional de maestros*, 56–57.
51. Lisandro Calderón, "El hábito de la acción en la niñez para combatir nuestra apatía racial," *Memoria del primer congreso mexicano del niño patrocinado por "El Universal"* (México, 1921), 248–249.
52. José Vasconcelos professed admiration for the American progressive tradition and initially embraced Dewey's idea of education as an important dimension of the modern education project of the revolution. Dewey exemplified for him the ideals of the practical subject as model to reject the dogmatic subject, legacy of the Spanish Catholic tradition. Yet, after his dismissal from the government, he rejected Dewey as anti-Latin and denounced the state project of the Deweyan *escuelas activas*, which had just gotten under way in 1923. The critical body of work on Vasconcelos is too numerous to mention. Among notable monographs see, Itzhak Bar-Lewaw M., *La Revista "Timón" y José Vasconcelos* (México: Casa Edimex, 1971); Mario Aguirre Beltrán, *Revista El Maestro, 1921–1923: raíces y vuelos de la propuesta vasconcelista* (México: Universidad Pedagógica Nacional, 2002); Joaquín Cárdenas, *José Vasconcelos: Caudillo cultural* (Oaxaca: Universidad José Vasconcelos de Oaxaca, 2002); Regina Aída Crespo,

Itinerarios Intelectuales: Vasconcelos, Lobata y sus proyectos para la nación (México: Universidad Autónoma de México, 2005); Claude Fell, *José Vasconcelos. Los años del águila* (México: Universidad Nacional Autónoma de México, 1989); and Luis A. Marentes, *José Vasconcelos and the Writing of the Mexican Revolution* (New York: Twayne Publishers, 2000).
53. Calderón, "El hábito de la acción," 248–249.
54. Ibid., 248.
55. Ibid. Here Calderón for the first time seems to argue that the much-desired "natural" order will not come about just by removing obstacles to liberty, but by actively and externally establishing the necessary "common purpose": thus we have two, not one, projects now. And again, he does affirm Deweyan principles and, at the same time, moves away from them if, as I read him, he suggests that the "element of a common and productive activity" is external to the project.
56. Calderón, "El hábito de la acción," 247.
57. Ibid., 246.
58. Ibid.
59. Ibid., 249.
60. Scholars have identified the "transition to modernity" not so much as a sociological phenomenon, but as a discursive trope, comparative in nature, which organizes and narrates the history of the nation as moving toward self-consciousness and thus modernity. See, for example, Dipesh Chakrabarti, *Provincializing Europe: Postcolonial Thought and Historical Difference* (Princeton, NJ: Princeton University Press, 2000).
61. See Víctor Arreguine, *En que consiste la superioridad de los latinos sobre los anglosajones* (Publicación de la Enseñanza Argentina: Buenos Aires, 1900); Edmond Demolins, *A quoi tient la superiorité des anglo-saxons* (Paris: Firmin-Didot et cie, 1898); Edmond Desmolins, *A science sociale depuis F. Le Play, 1882–1905: Classification sociale resultant des observations faites d'après la methode de la science sociale par Edmond Desmolins* (Paris: Firmin-Didot et cie, 1905). See also, José Enrique Rodó, *Ariel*. 2nd edition. (Madrid: Cátedra, Letras Hispánicas, 2003). For a scholarly analysis of this issue see, Castro Belén, introduction to *Ariel*; Detlef Müller, Fritz Ringer and Brian Simon, ed., *The Rise of the Modern Educational System: Structural Change and Social Reproduction 1870–1920* (Cambridge: Cambridge University Press, 1990).
62. Salvador M. Lima and Marcelino Rentería, "La escuela nueva de la acción: los errores de la vieja escuela," *Educación* 4, vol. 2 (August 1923), 243.
63. "Bases para la organización de la escuela primaria conforme al principio de la acción," *Educación* 3, no. 1 (January 1924), 2–6.
64. Manuel Barranco, "La escuela primaria del futuro," 62.
65. Salvador M. Lima and Marcelino Rentería, "La escuela nueva de la acción," 242.
66. Lucio Tapia, "Orientaciones de la escuela popular," *Educación* 5–6, vol. 1 (January, Febuary 1922), 569.
67. José Vasconcelos, *La Raza Cósmica* (Baltimore: The John Hopkins University Press, 1979), 57.
68. Bases para la organización de la escuela primaria conforme al principio de la acción," 6.
69. Lucio Tapia, "Caracteres Sociológicos de la raza indígena de México e institutos docentes que son necesarios para lograr su redención," *Educación* 4, vol. 2 (August 1923), 273.
70. Ibid., 276.
71. Bases para la organización de la escuela primaria conforme al principio de la acción," 2.

28   Radical Dewey

72. José María Bonilla, "Nuevas orientaciones a la educación nacional," *Educación* 2, vol. 1 (Septiembre 1922).
73. Antonio Caso, "Problemas Nacionales," *Antología filosófica* (México: Ediciones de la Universidad Autónoma, 1957), 214.
74. José Vasconcelos, *La Raza Cósmica*, 57.
75. José Vasconcelos, "Discurso inaugural del edificio de la secretaría," *Obras Completas*, vol. II (México: Libreros Mexicanos Unidos, 1957–1961), 800.
76. Emilio Rabasa, *El juicio constitucional: orígenes, teoría y extensión* (Paris: Ch. Bouret, 1919), 52. For an excellent discussion of Rabasa's contribution to Mexican intellectual life see, Charles A. Hale, "The Civil Law Tradition and Constitutionalism in Twentieth-Century Mexico: The Legacy of Emilio Rabasa," *Law and History Review* 2, vol. 18 (Summer 2000).
77. Lucio Tapia, "Caracteres Sociológicos de la raza indígena," 274.
78. Ibid., 273.
79. "Bases para la organización de la escuela primaria, 7.
80. Ibid., 2.
81. For Alvarado's early life see, Antonio Pompa y Pompa, prologue to *Antología Ideológica*, Antonio Pompa y Pompa, ed., 1st edition (México: Secretaría de Educación Pública, 1976).
82. Salvador Alvarado, "El Problema de la educación," *Antología Ideológica*, edited by Antonio Pompa y Pompa, ed., 1st edition (México: Secretaría de Educación Pública, 1976), 116.
83. Ibid.
84. Ibid., 103.
85. *Ley de educación primaria* (Mérida: Departamento de Educación Pública de Yucatán, 1918), 3. See also, *El Primer Congreso Feminista de Yucatán, convocado por el C. gobernador y comandante militar del estado, Gral. Don Salvador Alvarado* (Mérida: Talleres Tipográficos del "Ateneo Peninsular," 1916), 89–97.
86. Salvador Alvarado, "Carta al pueblo de Yucatán publicada en la Voz de la Revolución, 5 de mayo de 1916, aniversario de Gloria para la patria mexicana," *La cuestión de la tierra, 1915–1917: Colección de folletos para la historia de la Revolución Mexicana, dirigida por Jesús Silva Herzog*, Jesús Silva Herzog, edition (México: Instituto Mexicana de Investigaciones Económicas, 1962), 189–190.
87. Jean-Pierre Bastian, *Protestantismo y sociedad en México* (México: CUPSA (Casa Unidad de Publicaciones, 1983), 166.
88. Richard Hofstadter, *Anti-Intellectualism in American Life* (New York: Vintage Books, 1962, 1963), 367.
89. *The Collected Works of John Dewey*, 1882–1953, edited by Jo Ann Boydston (Carbondale and Edwardsville: Southern Illinois University Press, 1967–1991), EW5: 96.
90. Salvador Alvarado, "El Problema de la educación," 102–103.
91. *The Collected Works of John Dewey*, 1882–1953 294.
92. Ibid., 62.
93. Richard Hofstadter, *Anti-Intellectualism in American Life*, 368.
94. Larry Hickman, *John Dewey's Pragmatic Technology* (Bloomington: Indiana University Press, 1990), 11.
95. Larry Hickman, "Dewey's Theory of Inquiry," *Reading Dewey: Interpretations for a Postmodern Generation* (Bloomington: Indiana University Press), 1998, 179.
96. *The Collected Works of John Dewey*, 1882–1953, 71.
97. Ibid.
98. Larry Hickman, *John Dewey's Pragmatic Technology*, 41.
99. Ibid., 15.

3 Practical Dewey
Mexican Protestants and the Promise of America

> *The richness of life is seen upon reflection to depend, in large measure at least, upon the tendency of what one does to suggest and prepare for succeeding activities. Any activity—beyond the barest physical wants—which does not thus 'lead on' becomes in time stale and flat . . . not to elaborate the argument, we may assert that the richness of life depends exactly on its tendency to lead one on to other like fruitful activity . . . and that we may therefore take as the criterion of the value of any activity—whether intentionally educative or not its tendency directly or indirectly to lead the individual and others whom he touches on to other like fruitful activity.*
> (William H. Kilpatrick's *The Project Method*, 1918)

Introduction

The radical movements in Mexico that integrated Dewey in their pedagogy of social change shared two assumptions: one, that the communities they sought to mobilize through education in order to change social conditions had been produced by historical forces; in other words, they were already existing entities. Second, that the formation of these communities had preceded the rise of social consciousness of their identities and interrelatedness in the world. Thus the schools served the crucial purpose of creating that social consciousness among the members of the community—an awareness of the values they shared—and to teach the individuals in the community how they integrated into the wider world wherein the community resided. Education closed the gap between group formation and group consciousness and in the process prepared the community to transform an unjust social world. Thus we should understand their accommodation to society in this way: social justice constituted the end of social change. By social justice, they meant the redistribution of incomes and the advocacy of equality at all levels of society in order to reverse the historical inheritance of Spanish colonialism that had produced Mexican societies.

In the following two chapters, I focus first on the emergence of a different Dewey arising mainly out of Protestant communities in Mexico that had established religious schools in accordance with American progressive education. More specifically I focus on the vision of Moisés Sáenz, a

Presbyterian minister and major actor in the revolutionary government of the 1920s. Sáenz upended important assumptions that had informed Deweyan reception in Mexico by thinking not the community but the nation-state. The rhetoric of education of Protestant communities that he inherited prepared the way for a national project of education where Dewey figured as the prophet of modern ways of thinking and of a new orientation to life and one whose pedagogy would serve the purpose of creating a nation-state out of the infinite particularities of Mexico's many regional and local cultures. The creation of a "unified soul" were to spawn the practical man of modernity whose ways of thinking would generate industrial modernity within the nation. Sáenz's interpretation of Dewey displaced the original Protestant community's means-ends philosophy whereby democratic life served as the ultimate end of inquiry by transforming a major assumption of Dewey's philosophy: that unity served as the foundation of plurality. Instead, the project collaborated in a wider state effort to eradicate the innumerable pluralities of Mexico in order to create a national body whose eventual integration would serve as the foundation for forms of inquiry productive of modernity and for an autochthonous industrial and modern society.

The nationalist discourses that produced Dewey as a national project under Sáenz were not entirely imitative of American models, as its critics have alleged, but certainly were not wholly autonomous of them either. Sáenz both invoked and contained Dewey simultaneously. He nationalized Dewey through a simultaneous process of appropriation and distancing: selectively appropriating his pedagogy as a cognitive technology while demarcating its distance from Dewey in the mission to create a unified nation by means of a national state-building project. Thus a duality characterized Sáenz's project: on the one hand, he sought to create a new modern man where Dewey provided the main inspiration; on the other hand, Deweyan schools, integrated within the larger Mexican government's nation-building project, would also help create national community that could serve as the social foundation for the practical man. As a nationalist, the goal of creating a "national soul" was Mexican, not Deweyan, but very much compatible with the unity he believed Dewey's America enjoyed. This last point defines the limits of Deweyan influence in Sáenz. Without this important limitation, as Partha Chatterjee explains of Indian nationalism, Saenz's project "would not [have been] nationalist" (41). In this sense, and as a defensive appropriation of modernity, the project became a way to produce a nation-state, strengthen power, and protect national sovereignty from American capitalist expansion.

In this chapter, I will first take a look at the roots of Moisés Sáenz's progressive vision of education in the Protestant communities of northern Mexico. I want to emphasize here that the Protestant desire to socialize within an American organization imported by missionaries had as its purpose to provide material expression to already existing groups with definable religious values. In adopting American forms, Protestants not only affirmed their local identities but also created socialized worlds that buttressed forms of inquiry they valued as productive. In other words, it allowed for the cultivation of a new *orientación para la vida* or orientation to life. I will then turn to Sáenz's personal vision of America and how within this vision he prioritized inquiry or the ways of seeing of the practical man as embodied in the myth of an entrepreneurial corporate America. I will then shift to an examination of how Sáenz's integration into Mexico's national politics after he returned from studies at Columbia Teachers' College in New York began a process that nationalized his vision of progressive education, laying the foundations for the importation of Dewey as a national savior of Mexico. As a result of his experiences in New York, Sáenz introduced William Kilpatrick's project method in Mexican schools with the purpose of creating a new subject of modernity. Through the project method, Deweyan education was tasked with creating a new citizen and aid in the creation of a "unified" Mexican soul.

Whereas other projects in Mexico had already been implemented to homogenize identities and socialize plural worlds into one national uniformity, I argue that the crucial aspect that made Dewey a prophet for Mexican modernity relates to his philosophy of inquiry. As we will see in the next chapter, Sáenz conflated most if not all of these goals under the rubric of *socialización*, which meant the effort to homogenize identities and integrate communities into a nation-state, but also the cultivation of a new *orientación para la vida*—an orientation to life—to create an entrepreneurial subject, the practical man of modernity. I draw deep analogies between the political and educational vision of Dewey and Sáenz to demonstrate this point. I conclude that in transiting between "thinking the community" to "thinking the nation," the relationship between community and inquiry were fundamentally transformed from those originally crafted in the Protestant community. In thinking the community, Protestants adopted American organizations to structure communities with firm values; in thinking the nation, Sáenz adopted American education to cause a community into being: a Mexican nation-state.

Thinking the Community: Education and Inquiry in Mexican Protestant Communities

Moisés Sáenz was born in the northern state of Nuevo León in 1888. As a young man, he attended the Presbyterian Seminary and the *Colegio* in Coyoacán, Mexico, where he graduated from secondary school. In 1907 he was ordained as a Protestant minister. After obtaining his teacher's certificate at the *Normal de Jalapa*—a very important national Teachers' School— he traveled in 1912 to the United States to work for a master's degree at Washington and Jefferson College in Washington, Pennsylvania, a university founded by American Presbyterians. As was the case for many middle-class Mexicans, his family looked to an American education as an important asset, a purpose intensified by the Protestant orientation of the family. Upon his return to Mexico from Washington and Jefferson College, Sáenz entered public service and worked as director of education in Guanajuato, Mexico, and later as director of the *Preparatoria*—Mexico's Preparatory Secondary School—in 1919. In 1920, after working at the Secretariat of Education, Sáenz left for Columbia University and entered Teachers' College to work for a doctoral degree in comparative education. More specifically, he intended to study the organization and management of American secondary schools in order to translate that knowledge into a dissertation on the concept of the "high school" that would establish paradigms to reform Mexican education.[1] In 1922, he traveled to France to complete research for his dissertation—which he never finished—and then in 1923 returned to Mexico and reentered public life, convinced that Dewey's pedagogy could save Mexico.

Sáenz's biography testifies to the intense desire for American cultural forms by Mexican Protestant communities and to the ways these communities integrated their values into a narrative of progress that valued democratic life and American capitalism. Sáenz's family was part of a congregation whose converts came mostly from middling sectors of society, much like their counterparts in Central Mexico. American missionaries had placed their hopes for conversion on these middling levels, eschewing the traditional classes that supported the political order (the aristocratic upper class) as well as the mostly peasant Indian classes. Fearing association with the often corrupt, unpopular or dissipated American community in that region of Mexico, American missionaries similarly closed off interaction with local American resident communities, placing their monies and faith in the conversion of a nascent middle class.[2] Given the enormous commercial presence of American corporations in the north of Mexico, these Protestant groups felt confident in affirming the positive role of commerce in human relations without implying acceptance of the immoral practices of America's ranching, railroad, and mineral interests, especially in the North. They affirmed the liberal political tradition of Benito Juárez, who as president of Mexico had favored the immigration of Protestants as a civilizing force for Mexico because of their educational achievements. Historically, they supported the *Leyes de la Reforma* or Laws of Reform, a set of liberal anti-Catholic laws passed by President Juárez to subordinate the Catholic Church to the state and which redefined religion as a private concern.

Conversion to an American religion never meant acceptance of values foreign to the converts; they benefited them through the adoption of technologies of association and community formation that could provide a material and spiritual scaffolding for their movement and their values. Mexican Protestantism had its foundations in radical egalitarian movements that preceded the arrival of American missionaries in the nineteenth century (1872), and that came to life as a consequence of an industrialization process partly financed by American corporations in Mexico at the turn-of-the-century. The expansion of the railroads and the establishment of new textile factories, along with other dislocations associated with an incipient industrial society displaced these groups from their traditional social niche.[3] Some were groups of artisanal workers coming from rural areas, whereas others came from rural communities heavily affected by the expansion of haciendas[4] where the divestment of church property led to an expanding ranching economy and the exportation of coffee.[5] As "social sectors in transition,"[6] they found in American Protestant missionary organizations a source of economic support for their associations, a conduit to channel their political activities, and a way to fulfill their desire for modern schools.[7] American religious organizations allowed them to structure their social world upon the horizontal bonds of equality that became the basis for their communities.[8] As Jean-Pierre Bastian argues, these Protestant communities did not constitute a "unitary movement," but were "a series of congregations without organization but among which predominated an associative model that was . . . horizontal and in rupture with the vertical, clerical, and Catholic model."[9] These fraternal associations were similar to those of masons, spiritualists and occultist associations,[10] which also sought to express their desire for a democratic life though the quality of the bonds established among themselves.[11] They firmly adopted American forms to protect that orientation and the ideas that stood behind them: to modern ways of thinking corresponded modern forms of association and relations among individuals.[12] As Bastian argues, "while the organization model [of the Americans] won, the content was Latin American."[13]

Mexican Protestants did not feel that their nationalism or their principles had been compromised.[14] They looked to America, not as a teacher of new values necessarily, but as a teacher of good values whose technologies of association would support their own set of beliefs, which they understood to be aligned with those of the United States. Their relationship to American congregations was contractual, with missionaries providing resources to build temples and schools, while Mexican subjects provided converts and ideological commitments.[15] The conversion impetus toward adopting Protestant forms was informed as much by the promises of American culture as by specific community goals. The shared values forged during this process formed the unity that buttressed a diversity of theological commitments and religious expressions. For Protestant congregations in northern Mexico, the origins of their communities and the role that education played in them would have been seen congruent with the assumptions inherent in the vision of most American progressives. For progressives—and this would include Dewey—social formations preceded social consciousness of the community's connectedness to themselves and the wider society. For Mexican Protestants, then, the transition to a community of self-conscious members could only be achieved through the education of its members thus laying out the process whereby they would integrate themselves into the wider society.

The biography of these communities speaks to the crucial role ways inquiry stood in relation to socialized communities that facilitated a practical orientation toward life. Conversion to Protestantism had not created new social worlds but had transformed already existing local groups into communities through the creation of interrelated churches, schools and hospitals: the Protestant complex. This complex—church, school, hospital—expressed the various ways American organizational techniques structured communities and exemplified how these Protestant groups understood the reciprocal relationship between community and inquiry. The Protestant complex established a socialized field of action where the hospital, the school and the church worked together in a continuum, manifesting spatially the interconnectedness of democratic and practical social relations.[16] The complex, as socialized space, facilitated a radical pedagogy of democratic life based on a continuum between the school, the hospital and the church. "Protestantism," declared an article in the journal *El Abogado Cristiano*, "has always and in every place supported without conditions popular education, and for that reason next to every temple a school is raised."[17] Protestants made schools into the "main axis for the diffusion of religious ideas and the North American protestant politico-social thought."[18] The socialized community space enabled social bonds that were horizontal, immediate and transparent.

The empirical reality of this democratic space and its practical connection to society defined Protestant communities in contradistinction to Catholic social relations, which Protestants understood as artificial just as radical intellectuals had accused the Catholic Church of having established an artificial social order in Mexico. It was not uncommon to charge the politics of the Catholic order with un-naturalness. The accusation indicated that relations among citizens in a Catholic polity were not natural and transparent but mediated by the church and its signs. Protestants maintained that only unmediated interaction could be the sign of democratic relations among citizens, insisting that only citizen-to-citizen interaction could be considered natural. The political import of this notion was clear. Catholicism preached that the objective of education was to accommodate the pupil to the natural order of God. The Catholic curriculum rejected the social contract philosophy of Hobbes and Rousseau, which informed liberal politics as false. Authority emanated from God and could not reside in the body politic. For Protestants, the individual was not to be incorporated into a natural order, for such order did not exist.[19] Natural were the potentialities of each individual rather than given social orders.

Protestants accepted progressive education for its potential to liberate the inner abilities of the student. In their schools, Protestants advocated for a social field where the natural inclinations of the individual were given free rein, thus the child-centered orientation of the school where children cultivated their individual personalities living a "natural" life of investigation.[20] The continuum between church, school, and hospital facilitated social efficiency because it homogenized space and at the same time made the interactions within that space transparent. Protestant teacher Manuel Barranco described it as a "world where all will be related, intertwined, forming an organic unity" and where the child will "live in 'active' and 'concrete' relationship with the world" so that the child's "studies will be unified."[21] As a vision of a future sphere of political contestation, religion was strictly private. Within the classroom and school, then, faith could conceivably be a religious value as well as a secular value. As a religious value, faith preceded secular knowledge. Sáenz maintained, for example, that "to believe precedes to know . . . the facts of Christian life are first, the explanation of those facts, if they were to come, are a secondary thing."[22] As a secular value, it was a factor of trust in a social world where individuals would respect and practice *tolerancia práctica* or a pragmatic form of ethics toward each other because preserving the social order was in the best interest of all.[23]

Protestant pedagogy set itself apart from middle-class Catholic reform groups, which promoted a middle-class work ethic and a pedagogy of personal responsibility through campaigns against moral degeneracy, gambling, alcohol and other projects in public schools throughout northern states such as Sonora and Chihuahua, which were explicitly intended to educate the peasantry for an industrial society and designed to create the conditions for a disciplined working class.[24] Protestants instead made self-discipline an instrument toward a democratic society. As a social world, the Protestant complex attempted in practice to close the gap between the democratic promise of Mexico's liberal constitution and the social realities of Mexican political life. As communities they sought to embody the democratic meanings of *pueblo* or "the people" that the Constitution and the Laws assumed existed. They defended social democratic bonds as a priority and made education an even more important precondition that industrialization to an effective citizenship in contrast to the prevailing ethos of the elite liberal political ideology that justified industrialization and capitalism as a prerequisite for progress.[25] The Protestant communitarian vision reveals that American technologies of association provided a foundation for local communitarian bonds wherein a socialized world facilitated social efficiency and a practical education oriented toward the world.

Thinking America: Moisés Sáenz's Vision of the Modern Subject

I want to turn now to the specificities in Moisés Sáenz's thought, especially the ways he prioritized the productive dimensions of inquiry and the role the American corporate order played when he thought the community. In his Protestant writings, Sáenz stressed the productive dimensions of a new man of modernity defending the necessity of practical schooling not only for its democratic potential, but also for the way it promoted the ways of seeing of the practical man. Progressive education paved the way: the object of education was to eschew the accumulation of knowledge and instead teach how to think in order to create an empirical subject that could transform the world through his or her enterprise. In life, wrote Sáenz, "we make an effort to achieve all of that which economizes time and effort and we look attentively to results more than to the processes of how to obtain those results. Would it not be then . . . legitimate . . . to make an effort to economize time and effort . . . and do certain things, not so much for the 'mental discipline' provided, but for the results that accrue as a result?"[26] In ways similar to the American businessman, the school had to provide not so much "the opportunity to acquire information and accumulate knowledge," but also "the manner of acquiring such things."[27] Ways of thinking, strategic orientations toward the world, the productive dimensions of thought, all found a place at the core of Sáenz's emerging worldview.

The Protestant complex had served as the foundation for that practical subject: an individual oriented toward life and experience. For Sáenz, the American entrepreneur constituted the model for the common man that Protestants should wish to create: an everyday man with extraordinary abilities to transform the world. The entrepreneurial life based on an orientation toward life or *vida* was a constant message in the pages of Protestant journals such as *El Faro* (The Lighthouse), *El Abogado Cristiano* (The Christian Advocate), or *Mundo Cristiano* (Christian World). For Sáenz, the ways of learning of the American entrepreneur explained the power of American capitalism. The American businessman epitomized American practicality. Sáenz insisted that "the man of business does not proceed out into the world taking his business data," but obtains information from his insertion in the market, and, when evaluating this information, makes decisions that make sense and become valid.[28] He was a doer, a practical man with a social ethos whose actions reconciled personal and social interest. For Mexican Protestants, the development of a pragmatic spirit—the American "orientación para la vida"—explained American material progress. An anonymous writing of 1915 in the religious journal *El Abogado Cristiano*—"The Christian Advocate"—argued that the Puritan colonies had triumphed because Anglo-Saxons had followed

> "the logical steps of utilitarian ethics . . . infused in the blood and intellect of the Saxon, educating themselves . . . for life, [and] growing and multiplying," then repeating again "and growing and multiplying in such a way that in 136 years it [has] forged thirty three states, built powerful cities, constructed marvelous railroads, invented the dollar, king of business, applied steam to navigation, formed philanthropic millionaires, perforated the Isthmus of Panama and spreads its overflowing civilization now all over the world that perhaps will not see its dawn."[29]

This figure of the practical man conforms with Enrst Gellner's notion of the "eternal inquirer." According to Gellner, during the rise of industrialism in Europe, the bureaucrat (embodying the principle of coherence), the businessman (the principle of efficiency), and the teacher (the citizen) personified the nationalist vision of modern capitalist societies.[30] In modern industrial societies, the figure of the eternal inquirer found its economic counterpart in the entrepreneur and his or her "untrammeled selection of whatever means, in the light of evidence and of nothing else, serves some clear aim such as the maximization of profit."[31] Sáenz constructed the American entrepreneur as his version of the "eternal inquirer." The language of productivity and entrepreneurship, the conflation of things practical with business, production and industrial growth, and most importantly the vision of an open-ended realm of experience as a social fact, indicated the particular role that the American corporate order performed for Sáenz as the referent for understanding American modernity.

Whereas his political rival in the national scene, José Vasconcelos, had at one time imagined the American yeoman as an appropriate model for Mexico's future,[32] Sáenz summoned a corporate urban America where the American businessman and his practical ways of inquiry were the model. The American entrepreneur exemplified methods, ways of seeing the world, an orientation toward life or *orientación para la vida*. Sáenz even attributed the triumph of the Allies in WWI to American public intellectuals and educators who "searched with persistence for a formula more in accord with life [*la vida*]."[33] Glen Porter argues that Americans' conception of their nation and economic system figured as a "material paradise on earth" where "the work of the beneficent new corporate order became the core of [their] conceptions of themselves and their nation, and the core of how those from abroad saw the United States."[34] Sáenz adopted or subsumed that version of the American corporate order as he sought to define a modern future for his country.

If the organizational world of the corporation was an implicit model, so were other cultural organizational markers of American culture. For example, the American campus figured as an ordered and depoliticized space in the American high school.[35] While traveling in New York, Sáenz expressed admiration at the campus life of Columbia University where American sports and social clubs were not only an expression of the cooperative character of American democracy, but of Americans' reliance on experience as a basis for learning and forming character. American sports were among the preferred metaphors for defining pedagogy and establishing America as a model. "The great university of Columbia," Sáenz argued, "refuses to concede a diploma in any of its departments to one who has not learned to swim. Sports are essential to the education of the student."[36] College social clubs, sports teams and the organizational life of the American campus possessed powerful signification as referents for a modern democratic way of life. As editor of the Protestant weekly *Mundo Cristiano*—"The Christian World"—Sáenz emphasized the importance of this kind of socialization for Protestant youth in Mexico where church schools imported sports clubs with the intention of creating within the school a practical field for the application and creation of knowledge. "The field of play,"[37] declared Sáenz, "is saving the modern school from the bankruptcy of a pedagogical science focused on books."[38] American school activities such as sports clubs and competitions,[39] Boy Scouts,[40] literary and scientific clubs,[41] and all kinds of civic school organizations possessed not only the power to develop the social character of the individual, but also demonstrated the nature of American progress: the drive of the American associated individual to thrive in fraternal association with others and the creative spirit that social world made possible.[42] It made Americans entrepreneurial and productive.

Sáenz was an ordained minister and teacher, and Protestants had extended that entrepreneurial ideal to the figure of the preacher and the school teacher. *Pastores* or preachers were figures whose efficacy relied on the ability to transit through the secular and religious, and whose public speaking and leadership qualities reflected a politics oriented toward the life of the congregation. Such were the conditions for the practical man. The teacher-*pastor* was foremost a man of action, oriented towards experience, catering to and producing a democratic public within the congregation. For the most part, he supported the values of individualism and the work ethic associated with American capitalism. He was judged for his enterprising abilities in gaining converts and enlarging his congregations. The Christology of Sáenz's Protestantism accorded a similar quality to the figure of Christ, who was considered the explicit model for the Protestant subject, whether he was a minister or a schoolteacher. As Bastian argues, "Christ, understood as the Divine Teacher who teaches His disciples the rules of the active life—*vida activa*—[was] the foundation of the school teacher's activities, whose actions [were] similar."[43] Preachers radicalized their theology by articulating a strong democratic ethos that advocated an intelligent and well-educated populace as the only basis for a democratic community.[44]

Sáenz imagined his subject's world to be self-regulating, with no need for state coercion to create order. As an expression of the Protestant's practice of "ethical pragmatism,"[45] which imagined values as instruments for a better life and not as ends in themselves, good values were desired for the way they promoted social order and made the community cohesive. The violation of these values was severe and automatic. Sáenz's *Second Course of English*, a primer for the study of the English language, exemplifies this vision. Published in 1930 as an English as a second language course, it featured a storyline typical of many Protestant advice books. It involved a future businessman by the name of Gavin Pyce. Born in poverty, Gavin learned "to hate poverty," and carefully planned to rise in the world of business in any way he could. Yet life in corporate America was difficult and required hard work, which Gavin was not inclined to accept as his fate for the rest of his life. After nine years of working his way up in the bank, he decided to cheat the corporation where his father had found a job for him out of millions of dollars (the aptly named Aaron Burr National Bank of New York

City). Gavin's father had found this position for him after Gavin refused to become an attorney, according to his father's wishes.

Having successfully cheated the bank of millions, Gavin fled to Montevideo, Uruguay, in order to enjoy his money and avoid helping his girlfriend, whose mother was an invalid. He underwent a series of personal transformations in Latin America and Europe before returning to the United States when he thought he could not be recognized anymore. Yet, the case was still open, and the police managed to produce a "reel" or movie that was shown around the world. It showed Gavin as a left-handed writer recognizable to his friend Dick from the bank. As the world came to know Gavin, he felt terror at the thought that somebody would recognize his mannerisms. He surrendered peacefully, convinced that it would be a matter of time before this was so. In stories like this, Sáenz not only promoted what he called *sencillez* or simplicity, but also vividly portrayed a world that was self-regulated and where the work ethic constituted the most important value. Gavin was punished for having rejected his father's wishes to become an attorney and for having betrayed the corporation's trust, but he was found because in a world of similar individuals, any minor detail could give one away.[46]

Sáenz's social thought spoke to the fact that although practicality could be conceived as an American trait, it was a transmissible one, as long as social unity buttressed social practices oriented toward life: a technology of the socialized self.[47] This perspective reversed common assumptions held by most Americans and Mexicans of the times. He did not subscribe to the proposition that ideas possessed inherent value. Protestant social practices and Sáenz's writings instead reflected the fact that ideas were instruments for social action, which were effective when grounded in material structures that sustained democratic practices. For Protestants in a majoritarian Catholic nation, education, public service and loyalty to a liberal republic became essential to the reproduction of their communities. Sáenz's vision of community rested then on two assumptions: that the community shared common values and a vision of the future and that the members of this community were socialized individuals—*semejantes*—conditions that produced social order without coercion. Much later, as sub-secretary of education, in a radio address in Dallas in 1925, at the invitation of the teachers' association of the state of Texas—*Sociedad de Maestros del Estado de Texas*—Sáenz expressed his wish that (Americans and Mexicans) should become *semejantes* or fellow men to each other.[48]

Toward a Mexican Dewey

Sáenz's adoption of Deweyan pedagogy occurred after his sojourn at Columbia Teachers' College and his return to Mexico when, as sub-secretary of education, he made Deweyan education the pillar of the revolutionary government of the 1920s. The priority Sáenz gave to productive inquiry as the core of an education for the future model Mexican citizen went along with a project to make Mexico a nation state: practical ways of thinking were important as national traits and not just simply as a way of being in the community. In other words, once thinking the nation replaced thinking the community, the uses of education responded to the question of the transition to modernity: why had Mexico not become modern? How could Mexico become modern? The question would not anymore be how to live a good Christian life and become a democratic and productive member of a liberal Mexico but how education could produce subjects capable of generating modernity within the nation. A stronger emphasis on practical values as the mark and cause of modernity and the desire to create a unified nation as the social context wherein these values would be practiced, coupled with the conviction of the fundamental goodness of American industrial modernity, characterized this transition that eventually led to Dewey.

Protestants such as Sáenz were useful for a revolutionary Mexican government confronting the Catholic Church and determined to secularize education. The state had encouraged their participation, and Protestants participated significantly during the early decades of the revolution. Protestants were radicalized by this very insertion into the revolutionary political process.[49] Some held important posts in the revolutionary government, participating in various sectors of government service as police chiefs, governors, advisors to important figures of the revolution and educational experts for the Carranza administration.[50] Andrés Osuna, a Methodist minister, became superintendent of schools in the state of Coahuila and a major thinker in pedagogy and nationalism. He traveled several times to the United States, especially the American South, in order to observe and report on new educational trends.[51] Osuna preceded Sáenz as head of educational programs in 1915 and 1916, when he assisted the government of Carranza in establishing a new program of modern education for Mexico. He also served as governor of Tamaulipas and director of education for the state of Nuevo León. In fact, the years from 1914 to 1916 and 1921 to 1924 were fertile for the insertion of Protestants in the high echelons of government.[52] Although a very tiny minority, they were a highly organized group of intellectuals with strong loyalties to the liberal factions of the Mexican intelligentsia.

The possibility that John Dewey's ideas could be used for thinking the Mexican nation were facilitated when the liberal faction of the Revolution, led mostly by men from the northern frontier state of Sonora, won the military conflict that engulfed the nation from 1910 to 1920 and elected General Alvaro Obregón as president of the nation in 1920. With Obregón's victory, México's revolution stabilized, and the government began the reconstruction of the nation by casting a disapproving eye on revolutionary experiments that did not conform to the new politics of state-led development and unified nationhood. Among them were the political program of anarchists and socialists, and the progressive ideas that defined the *escuela activas* movement in urban areas. The central government not only crushed the anarchist and socialist governments of Yucatán and Tabasco but also coopted the progressive ideas at the heart of the pedagogy of revolution when General Salvador Alvarado invaded Yucatán in 1915 and along with his right-hand man, Gregorio Torres Quintero, ended the *escuela racionalista* movement.[53] For Alvarado, the internationalist character of anarchist ideology had to be replaced by the nation. If the anarchist believed in a universal history of man and a world beyond the nation-state, Alvarado proclaimed "the nation before itself."[54]

Sáenz's concern with the practical accommodated itself very well with the preferences of the Northern Mexicans that came to power in Mexico during the 1920s for whom the belief that the American practical spirit explained American progress prevailed among politicians that believed that northerners were more practical Mexicans than the rest. According to Michael J. González, the Sonorans "represented a frontier culture that valued entrepreneurship, public education, and limited democracy and resisted the centralizing tendencies of old Mexico as represented by Porfirian politics and the Catholic Church."[55] Obregón himself was a man who "depended less on ideology than on pragmatism." He prized a sense of practicality in the conduct of human affairs and possessed a keen sense for the value of experience, a pragmatic sense that he applied to his political decision-making.[56] The Sonorans who ruled the nation from 1920 to 1934 came from a region of México profoundly transformed by American investment and commercial might. Since the late nineteenth century, mining and commercial agricultural interests from the United States had penetrated the economy of Sonora and integrated the formerly isolated states into the national and international economy. Northern states that bordered the United States were among the regions in Mexico most affected by the expansion of American capital in Mexico. Mexicans there faced in American capitalism a force that was as productive as it was destructive, but one they could not control since they could not generate such wondrous wealth. The power of American commerce was felt not only in terms of technological superiority but also in terms of idiosyncrasies of business dealing and everyday inventiveness. Many Mexican businessmen had fallen into the role of mere intermediaries, losing the ability to create new enterprises themselves. American business interests not only had created their own company towns, but also had taken the initiative in hiring and managing the working classes, thus threatening to redraw the class and racial boundaries of the North.[57] This state of affairs was humiliating to Mexican businessmen and intellectuals, but to those in the North it was especially detrimental since American commercialism threatened to unravel the social fabric of their region.

Within the political space opened for him, Sáenz promoted a nationalist education whose rhetoric prioritized the nation as the locus of a future modern subject that would generate modernity but would also preserve the sovereign integrity of Mexico from the depredation of the very own system that was desired for the nation. In this process, he realigned his pedagogical priorities away from an emphasis on democratic life placing his faith in modern forms of inquiry as the solution to the dilemma of Mexican modernity. In that respect, the American missionary Cincinnati Plan had important implications for the ways Sáenz understood the role of Protestant Churches in Mexico, but more importantly for us, for the way it demonstrates that when thinking the nation, the nationalization of Dewey's ideas involved a preoccupation with the sovereignty of Mexico, a concern that reflects the fact that adopting Deweyan education did not intend to be an act of imitation but was in fact rooted in a defense of Mexican sovereignty: only by becoming modern could the nation acquire the power to defend its cultural integrity from a "new kind of conquest, the conquest by railroad and by bank."[58]

In what follows, I will outline the crucial moments in this evolution and identify powerful affinities between Dewey's philosophy and Sáenz's project to clarify the Deweyan foundations of the national project of education that Sáenz would lead in the 1920s. I will argue that in the evolution toward a Deweyan pedagogy, Sáenz redefined the relationship between the national and the local, the citizen and the state and the United States and Mexico.

Thinking the Nation: The Cincinnati Plan and the Pan-American Union

One important juncture in this trajectory was Sáenz's response to the American missionary Cincinnati Plan of 1916 where Sáenz upended the Protestant conviction that involvement in national politics meant affirming local (theological) beliefs. In 1916, major American Protestant denominations agreed in Cincinnati, Ohio to divide the Mexican territory to avoid competition among themselves for converts. They did this without the consent of Mexican ministers. Whereas most if not all major Mexican Protestant ministers decided to oppose the American decision and thus uphold their much cherished autonomy, Sáenz, writing as editor of *Mundo Cristiano*, defended the American strategy. Along with the Cincinnati Plan, he explicitly supported the American government's plan for a Pan-American union, a foreign policy initiative by the US government to strengthen its influence in Latin America and unite the continent along the commercial lifelines American corporations were creating. The American board of missions meeting in Cincinnati expected to use this foreign policy initiative as a vehicle for missionary activity. The primacy of national union was foremost in his mind in breaking with ministers' objections to the plan.

In doing so, Sáenz broke with a longstanding assumption of the supremacy of theology over politics. According to Deborah Baldwin, "the early missionaries (before 1905) [had] assumed an apolitical stance . . . in the early mission, politics was subordinate to theology . . . [an] emphasis [that] allowed a tenuous relationship to exist between the missionary and the Mexican minister as long as theology was considered separate from and superior to politics."[59] Sáenz instead subordinated theology to politics, ridiculing the position of those who considered it unethical to have to change denominations.[60] "'How is it possible that I must become a Methodist?' cries out the Presbyterian," said Sáenz. Sáenz defended the plan to his congregation as an efficient and cost-effective path to progress,[61] arguing that whereas "the sentiment of pride, tradition and loyalty are just and desirable to a great extent," they could stand the force of reason, "the human capacity for progress . . . [and] the spiritual advancement of the race."[62] The opportunities to create a national church overrode any concerns for the supremacy of local communities over national goals. The "construction of a [national] Church," he argued, was paramount and superseded the religious "particularism" of each congregation. The key goal was the creation of an Evangelical Church of Mexico to provide the global vision, the "world perspective," that was to complement national identities.[63] Sáenz explained that creating a unified Mexican nation was more important than defending theological differences between Presbyterians and Baptists.

Thinking the Nation: Sáenz at Columbia Teachers' College

Sáenz's letters written in New York while a student at Columbia University indicate how the nexus with American culture imagined by Sáenz evolved into a homogenous vision of American society as a corporate society whose social order was as beneficial as it was dangerous to Mexican sovereignty. They detail how in his two years at Columbia University, Sáenz cemented bonds with sympathetic American groups in both Protestant and business circles.[64] Sáenz spent a great deal of time lecturing on behalf of Mexico's revolutionary government, assuaging public fears that Mexico was under Bolshevik influence, and expressing his admiration for the educational and corporate institutions of the United States. In his lecture tours, he also addressed the Women's League for the Preservation of Peace headed by Jane Addams, Protestant congregations, and university groups.[65] Sáenz gave speeches to businessmen's organizations as well as to schools and community organizations praising the American business world.[66] In April of 1921, he met with religious leaders and other luminaries in New York City to explain Mexico's oil problem and to defend the Mexican government against the charge of Bolshevism. In that same month in New York, he continued his lecture circuit project, which he called "Pro-Mexico," and on April 11, 1921, he spoke on "Mexico in Reconstruction (*"Mexico en Reconstrucción"*) to a packed meeting of the Women's League for the Preservation of Peace led by Jane Addams. Diverse sectors of the American intelligentsia seemed to be homogenized, becoming indistinct actors in the larger canvas of American productivity.

He also spoke to the First Methodist Church in Yonkers and to a business club on Mexico's present problems (*"Algunos problemas de México en la actualidad"*) in Philadelphia, invited by Francis Taylor, a Quaker who had worked with Herbert Hoover in the reconstruction of Europe. He addressed the Executive Committee on Relief Work in Europe on the problem of petroleum and the oil business in Mexico. Presumably, he performed all of these public functions before countless other local audiences in New York City interested in Mexico.[67] By the end of the year, he had added more conferences, one of them with G. B. Winton, who worked for the *Comité Cooperación de la América Latina* [sic] or "Committee for Cooperation with Latin America," in order to lay the foundations for a project establishing a secular college in Mexico. Another conference with the Cosmopolitan Club of Columbia University at the invitation of Dr. Thomas Briggs, head of the Secondary Education Department at Columbia University, dealt with nationalist issues in Mexican-American relations. Sáenz was also invited by Dr. Babcock, a famous pedagogue and American Protestant, to address the International Convention of the Railroad YMCA. In his interventions, Sáenz expressed approval of American progress and efficiency, expressing his wish for a Mexican future that would equal the American present, but one that preserved Mexico's cultural distinctiveness and autonomy and most of all, its creative capacity.

Sáenz's purpose was to protect national sovereignty from the corrosive influence of American corporate power. He was not alone. His rival, José Vasconcelos, thought along the same lines in spite of their bitter differences over the Pan-American union. In a lecture in Buenos Aires, Vasconcelos echoed Argentinean intellectual José Ingenieros's argument (and Sáenz's) even as he opposed the Pan-American Union,

> the danger posed by the United States does not proceed from its inferiority but from its superiority: they are to be feared for they are great, wealthy and entrepreneurial. Our interest is to know if there are any possibilities to find an equilibrium to their power . . . and save . . . our sovereignty . . . the union of Latin America . . . our nationalities confront an iron-clad dilemma: whether to surrender themselves in submission and praise the Pan-American Union (America for the North Americans) or to prepare a common front to defend our independence thus setting the bases for a Latin American union.[68]

An irony lied at the core of Sáenz's position: the protection of Mexican sovereignty was problematically linked to an acceptance of the very system—industrial capitalism—he feared would erode the nation's independence. His responses to this question evidenced an innocent, yet certainly a firm conviction, in the ultimate goodness of industrial society. Whereas Vasconcelos invoked a united Latin American front to oppose American capitalist advance, Sáenz turned toward the entrepreneurial qualities of the modern self as the saving grace of Mexico.

Thinking the Nation: Sáenz and the Project Method

At Columbia University, Sáenz also came to the conclusion that out of the many progressive ideas tossed around in New York, William Kilpatrick's project method responded best to the project he deemed central for creating a progressive Mexican subject. Sáenz came into contact with these ideas through the international education department of Columbia University Teachers' College. Whereas there is no proof that Sáenz ever met John Dewey at Columbia University, Dewey emerged as prophet of Mexico's future modernity. Sáenz's acceptance of Columbia University's project method as the lynchpin of his educational plan for the nation is further evidence that for Sáenz the search for a productive subject constituted the major conceptual link to Dewey. If we are correct in arguing that Dewey's notion of inquiry constitutes the most important connection to Sáenz, then the centrality of the project method to Sáenz's project cannot be underestimated in an educational experiment that made the project method its core technique.

Sáenz became committed to an educational project with worldwide reverberations as Deweyan ideas came to have such a profound influence on the education systems of Leninist Russia, Republican Turkey, Republican China and Japan (before and after WWII). In nations such as Soviet Russia and Republican China, for example, the project method stood for Deweyan education in modern state-building projects initiated by Dewey's disciples. In China, the experimental schools of Tao Xingzhi, modeled after the Deweyan schools of Chicago and Columbia, were structured around the project method.[69] In Leninist Russia, the project method stood for American progressive education. Kilpatrick himself visited, as many American progressives did at the time, the Soviet Union as well as China, in order to learn about experiments in progressive pedagogy undertaken in nations that were close to the leftist imaginary of US progressives. The universalistic and humanistic language of Kilpatrick's methodology and language aided its dissemination around the world as a technique to create a modern self[70] in nations such as Japan, China, Turkey, Spain and Russia.[71] Many foreign intellectuals became acquainted with Dewey precisely through this set of techniques, which were given the immense mission of creating modern subjects in nations that understood their transition to modernity in terms of the rejection of traditional ways of learning and the redefinition of the relationship of the individual to the social world. Its association in America to the left-wing of the progressive movement and with the progressive critique of industrialization and Taylorism further aided its dissemination, for it promised to create a self that was modern, yet free.[72]

Upon his return to México, Sáenz insisted that the techniques of education produced at Columbia by William H. Kilpatrick as an avenue to a Deweyan education offered the remedy for México's historical condition of poverty and lack of development:[73] they would create entrepreneurial individuals, whereas the "society in miniature" created within the school would help socialize students into a unified national soul. As director of education for the state of Guanajuato, Sáenz began the introduction of these techniques learned from pedagogues at Columbia University and the laboratory schools in order to create new modern subjects. Kilpatrick's project method and Dewey's idea of the laboratory school converged on the notion that the school should function as a place for productive and entrepreneurial work.[74] Kilpatrick's emphasis on a productive and entrepreneurial self was reflected in how students generated their own knowledge by applying their own motivations or interests to the completion of projects in his classrooms. Only a productive life could keep the world open to new possibilities. Thus production stood at the foundation of social progress.

The project method figured as one of the most famous attempts in the United States to translate Dewey's philosophy of democracy into a classroom technique that could be implemented by the average teacher. Kilpatrick had been a former disciple of Dewey, having been first his doctoral student and then colleague at Teachers' College at Columbia University. In 1918, Kilpatrick published his seminal essay entitled "The Project Method," which proclaimed the cultivation of what came to be defined as a new "concept of the Self" for Americans. For Kilpatrick, free inquiry stood at the center of Dewey's social vision of a productive life oriented toward a social world understood as open-ended, contingent and human centered. Translating Dewey's philosophy of inquiry into classroom technique, Kilpatrick intended to "civilize Americans," instructing them to understand life as experimental, purposeful and productive. His philosophy was reflected in the statement that "the purposeful act is the typical unit of the worthy life," that man's "inner urge" was the driving force in classroom practice, as it was in the world, since it led to "action . . . guiding its process . . . and furnishing its drive."[75] "The Project Method" became a sensation in America and the main avenue for teachers to access the pedagogy of Dewey. It was a new American gospel.

One of the attractive features of the method relates to Kilpatrick's reconciliation of production and ethics. He argued that in the classroom, human purpose reconciled "practical efficiency" with "moral responsibility." This philosophy attracted those who wished to imagine a productive self distinct from the models provided by industrial America. According to Kilpatrick although not

> all purposes were good . . . the worthy life consists of purposive activity and not mere drifting. We scorn the man who passively accepts what fate or some other chance brings to him. We admire the man who is master of his fate, who, with deliberate regard for a total situation, forms clear and far-reaching purposes, who plans and executes with nice care the purposes so formed. A man who habitually so regulates his life with reference to worthy social aims meets at once the demands for practical efficiency and of moral responsibility . . . such a one presents the ideal of democratic citizenship."[76]

As his own words indicate, Kilpatrick's ideas were more than just about production, but also about authorship: the ability of the self to recognize himself in the world. In this regard, Kilpatrick contrasted the practical subject to the American slave. He argued that

> it is equally true that the purposeful act is not the unit of life for the serf or the slave. These poor unfortunates must in the interest of the overmastering system be habituated to act with a minimum of their own purposing and with a maximum of servile acceptance of others' purposes. In important matters they merely follow plans handed down to them from above and execute these according to prescribed directions. For them another carries responsibility and upon the results of their labor another passes judgment. No such plan as that here advocated would produce the kind of docility required for their hopeless fate. But it is a democracy, which we contemplate and with which we are here concerned.[77]

The American slave was indeed a producer, but he was not the author of his production because what he produced was not the end result of his purpose. The similarities to Sáenz's vision of peasants and Mexican Indians in a Catholic society were powerful.

The Political Vision of Dewey's Critique of Inquiry

There are powerful analogies between the political dimensions of Dewey's critique of inquiry, the philosophical underpinning of the project method and Sáenz's social vision and critique of Mexican underdevelopment. The fact that historians of Mexican education have ignored this aspect of Dewey's ideas has made the connections between Dewey and Sáenz impossible to identify, especially when the assumption has been that Dewey was simply a prophet for industrial capitalism and its need to produce passive workers. By understanding the political dimensions of Dewey's theory of inquiry, the parallels between Dewey and Sáenz's ideas (and not just Kilpatrick's) will sharpen, and a new dimension to the Mexican revolutionary project of mass education emerges. These parallels reveal connections between Dewey's vision of a non-free society with Sáenz's perception of the nature of Mexico's Catholic society.

Dewey's thought provided an explanation for how productive inquiry could become inhibited in individuals and thus respond to the question of how Mexico had failed to become modern. Although Dewey did not reduce all human activity to the technological and productive,[78] his epistemology and philosophy of education emphasized productive forms of inquiry as necessary for a free society. As we have seen, this emphasis provided the core for Kilpatrick's method and constituted the major appeal to Sáenz because it linked productive inquiry to progress. According to Larry Hickman, Dewey's technological vision of inquiry was not only the defining feature of his philosophy; it was also the foundation for social scientific thinking in general: "progress in the sciences, as well as in common sense inquiries, requires that the results of prior inquiries be treated as raw materials for further inquiries, and not as determinate results, established one and for all."[79] For Dewey, inquiry was an ongoing process that continually generated new meanings in an active and continual reconstruction of experience. Inquiry, as a reflective activity, was always instrumental for the production of further meanings. Thus things that were practical could not have final ends: they were part of a ceaseless chain of production and creation of new meanings. Intelligent social practices involved the constant production of new meanings so that "production takes precedence over and becomes a guide to practicality."[80] The notion of the practical that emerged from Dewey's writings on logic and method, which was consistent with pragmatists' assertion that all knowledge is grounded in experience, stressed the acquisition of knowledge as a permanent human condition, one with no final end. Social inquiry became "practical" then only when it led to the "enrichment of the immediate significance of subsequent experiences."[81] Dewey meant that an aesthetic experience might be productive only if the enjoyment of the beautiful was incomplete, leading to new, satisfying experiences. Although Dewey did not reject purely aesthetic pleasure, he did not prioritize it if it was not productive.

The historical framework wherein Dewey located productive inquiry was as important. Dewey's political vision of the productive self possessed a historical dimension that responded to the question of why some people were prevented from becoming productive selves. For Dewey, productive thought provided the quintessential engine of historical change. Whereas practical inquiry was productive, what he called primitive, magical or religious inquiry was not. Unproductive societies were dependent on "consummatory" thinking, which for Dewey meant purely aesthetic and thus not productive ways of thought.[82] According to Dewey, these consummatory experiences were essentially "non reflective" and not subject to "cognitional interest." He argued that for individuals or societies engaged in non-productive inquiry, "things are experienced but not in such a way that they are composed into an experience."[83] There is no active engagement with these experiences, and no "taking of some things as representative of other things."[84] They are purely familiar, unproblematic experiences. This characterized "closed worlds."

This aesthetic state characterized societies with little or no progress. Dewey argued that historically "it was not conscience that kept men loyal to cults and rites, and faithful to tribal myths. So far as it was not routine, it was enjoyment of the drama of life without the latter's liabilities that kept piety from decay . . . this phase of experience manifests objects, which are final. The attitude involved in their appreciation is esthetic."[85] Larry Hickman explicates that for Dewey, "primitive magic and religious practices fail[ed] to become inquiry precisely when and because their interest [were] focused on intrinsic meanings as final and not as productive of further significance: extrinsic meanings or instrumentalities are merely incidental to such practices. These societies therefore reverse[d] the pattern of effective technological inquiry."[86] They led to the reproduction of familiar worlds, and not to the creation of new ones. They were not progressive. In such worlds, non-productive thought is locked in a political relationship of subordination to productive inquiry. For Dewey, in a primitive society, those who were engaged in instrumental meanings or forms of inquiry that were productive remained separate from the rest of society for whom meanings become purely intrinsic. Progressive forms of inquiry constituted the preserve of the elite, which profited from the people's practice of consummatory experiences. The instrumental meanings of magic or of the elite remained hidden from the public because, as Hickman notes, the public "regard(s) the meanings of magic as purely intrinsic. In such cases, instrumental meanings are shared only within a limited group whose members do not participate for one reason or another, in a larger community."[87]

The analogies between Dewey's vision of societies where the powerful control those locked in unproductive ways of relating to the social world for the political benefit of an elite was totally congruent with the intellectual universe of Moisés Sáenz. Sáenz's vision of Catholic social order of traditional México was similar to Dewey's version of the "magic" state. For Sáenz, Mexico's Catholicism was "artificial," close-ended and largely dependent on the superstitious attachment of the peasant and Indian to the Catholic order.[88] This idea was prevalent among Mexico's pedagogues, such as the ones we discussed in the previous chapter and for whom "artificiality" figured as characteristic of everyday life in Catholic Mexico. If the Catholic priesthood was productive, the peasant was not. Productive forms of everyday social practices were impossible until productive inquiry could be extended to society in its entirety. It was not a question of what to learn but how to learn.

Thinking the Nation: Practicality as a National Trait

Yet Sáenz moved beyond Dewey when he thought of practicality as a national character trait and not just a quality of the individual and when he imagined the nation as the only possible social basis for inquiry of this kind. He did recognize that among Mexicans there were pragmatic practices called *saberes prácticos*, but they were ineffectual because of their purely local character. Social intelligence required a national canvas.[89] For liberals such as Sáenz, the nation was "incoherent" to itself[90] because it lacked unity; thus it was not legible to itself.[91] Individuals remained "atomized"[92] because no homogeneous social world existed to make their social practices practical—that is, intelligible and knowable to each other. The Code of Morality for the *escuelas activas* drafted by Sáenz admonished that the "isolated individual would not be able to construct a city or a railroad ... or a bridge."[93] México, as opposed to the United States, lacked coherence. For Sáenz, Mexicans lived in a fragmented world. Without a unified national context, Mexican men became "isolated" and resolved problems "empirically," that is, in an improvisatory manner.

There is no doubt that by the 1920s, the only context that mattered for Sáenz was the nation. The nation had replaced the community in his rhetoric of education and nation. His desire to create a nation as the social foundation for his modern subject poses important questions to the philosophy of progressive educational ideas. They speak to an important debate on the nature of Kilpatrick's project method: what social order would ensure the possibilities of productive inquiry? Kilpatrick's notion of the social context was weak, mostly evaluative, stressing the value judgment of one's peers. Dewey, on the other hand, remained more concerned with the group or collectivity acting in concert and shaping society.[94] Dewey's contention was inspired by his observations of workplace democracy derived from his experience with the labor movement during his life in Chicago. Robert Westbrook observes that Dewey's understanding of how workers established egalitarian associations on the factory floor informed his understanding of how school activities should work in a democratic classroom.[95] For Sáenz, inquiry would require a unified national context that only the state could ensure. Industrialism demanded the homogenizing of all social contexts as necessary for the reproduction and growth of the industrial system. According to Ernest Gellner, in order to socialize knowledge and create interchangeable individuals, society cannot tolerate heterogeneous spaces with conflicting epistemologies. Capitalism cannot survive without a homogeneous singular social space.

Thus, along with teaching modern inquiry, the socializing aspects of Deweyan schools or *socialización* would become a major aspect of the state-building project that Sáenz initiated in 1923. This also meant the end to racial or cultural particularisms. Once he entered the national stage, the social problem of the incorporation of the Indian into civilization reshaped Sáenz's national vision once more. The task of education, as Sáenz would say many times, was now consciously "dual." Creating a "national soul" meant a civilizing mission to the Indian, thus inscribing race fully in the Deweyan project. Deweyan education in Mexico would then intersect with the socialization concerns of Sáenz and the overall project of creating a nation by civilizing the peasant and the Indian. A second dimension of Deweyan education would be directed toward the creation of these "new active agents" that could take the nation into the modern and the universal. The implementation of these ideas will be addressed in the next chapter.

Notes

1. Moisés Sáenz to Miguel Alessio Robles, n.d., box 123, file #245-Si-8, Obregón Calles Collection, Archivos Generales de la Nación, México City, México.
2. See Deborah J. Baldwin, *Protestants and the Mexican Revolution: Missionaries, Ministers, and Social Change* (Urbana and Chicago: University of Illinois Press, 1990), 4–10.
3. Jean-Pierre Bastian, "Las sociedades protestantes y la oposición a Porfirio Díaz en México, 1877–1911" *Protestantes, liberales y francmasones: Sociedades de*

ideas y modernidad en América Latina, siglo XIX (México: Fondo de Cultura Económica, 1990), 135. See also, *La Antorcha Evangélica* 1 (July 7, 1876); José María Chávez, *Censura e impugnación del folleto del C. Juan Amador, titulado El Apocalipsis o revelación de un sans culotte* (Guadalajara: Tipografía de Rodríguez, 1856); cited in Jean-Pierre Bastian, "Las sociedades protestantes," 135.
4. Ibid.
5. See Prefecto del Distrito de Zitácuaro a secretario de Gobernación, Morelia, 20 de octubre de 1880, file 1, 1–2, Ramo Gobernación, Sección Libertad de Cultos 1880, Archivos Generales de la Nación; Daniel Rodríguez a Hutchinson, Tuxpan, 20 de agosto de 1880, Correspondence and Reports (1871–1911) 1886, vol. 53, 226, Archives of the Presbyterian Church of the United States, Presbyterian Historical Society, Philadelphia, Pennsylvania; *Actas de las conferencias anuales de la Iglesia Metodista Episcopal de México* (México: Imprenta Metodista, 1885–1911, 1889, 1902), 34, 38, 41; Jean-Pierre Bastian, "Las sociedades protestantes," 139–140.
6. Jean-Pierre Bastian, *Protestantismos y modernidad latinoamericana: Historia de unas minorías religiosas activas en América Latina* (México: Fondo de Cultura Económica, 1994), 117.
7. Ibid., 99.
8. The democratic politics practiced by the congregations aligns with the horizontal relationships typical of liberal models of political association consonant with Benedict Anderson's vision of nationalism. See Benedict Anderson, *Imagined Communities: Reflections on the Origins and Spread of Nationalism*, revised edition (London: Verso, 1991).
9. Jean-Pierre Bastian, "Las sociedades protestantes," 135.
10. Reynaldo Sordo y Cedeño, "Las sociedades de socorros mutuos, 1867–1880" *Historia Mexicana* 1, 129 (1983): 79 cited in Jean-Pierre Bastian, "Las sociedades protestantes," 135. See also *Roma y el evangelio: estudios filosófico-religiosos, teórico-prácticos hechos por el círculo cristiano espiritista de Lérida y reimpreso por el círculo espiritista "Buena Esperanza" de Monterrey* (Monterrey: A. Lagrange y Hermanos, 1876) also cited in Jean-Pierre Bastian, "Las sociedades protestantes," 135.
11. Francisco Bulnes, *Juárez y las revoluciones de Ayutla y de Reforma* (México: Antigua Imprenta de Murguía, 1905), 373; Regis Planchet, *La Cuestión religiosa en México o sea la vida de Benito Juárez* (Roma: Librería Pontificia, 1906), 153; cited in Jean-Pierre Bastian, "Las sociedades protestantes," 135.
12. Jean-Pierre Bastian, *Protestantismos y modernidad latinoamericana*, 93.
13. Ibid., 104.
14. ibid., 105.
15. Jean-Pierre Bastian, "Las sociedades protestantes," 136–137.
16. Jean-Pierre Bastian, *Protestantismos y modernidad latinoamericana*, 157.
17. "Las escuelas protestantes no educan en su seno a los traidores," *El Abogado Cristiano* (June 25, 1914), 383.
18. Jean-Pierre Bastian, *Protestantismos y modernidad latinoamericana*, 144.
19. See *Programa de filosofía, Colegio de San Juan Nepomuceno, Saltillo, Coahuila* (México, Saltillo: Tipografía La Perla Fronteriza), 8–9; "El Patriotismo como deber educacional," *El Testigo* (Guadalajara, January 15, 1904), 22; *El abogado cristiano ilustrado* (México, January 6, 1910), 12; cited in Jean-Pierre Bastian, "Las sociedades protestantes," 144.
20. Moisés Sáenz, "¿Quién es el verdadero agente de la educación?" *Mundo Cristiano*, December 25 1919. See also "¿Es la escuela una preparación para la vida?" *Mundo Cristiano*, December 18, 1919.
21. Manuel Barranco, "La Escuela Primaria del Futuro, *Mundo Cristiano*, July 6, 1919.

52   *Practical Dewey*

22. Moisés Sáenz, "Editorial del 6 de Julio de 1919," *Mundo Cristiano*, July 6, 1919, 2.
23. According to Protestant teacher Flores Valderrama, the Protestant school had to "teach what the official schools had not and will not be able to teach, that is, a practical tolerance to all religious ideas and the mutual respect owed to all civilized men." Flores Valderrama, "Educación y no solo instrucción," *El abogado cristiano ilustrado* (México, November 13, 1902), 13.
24. See William E. French, *A Peaceful and Working People: Manners, Morals, and Class Formation in Northern Mexico* (Albuquerque: University Unive of New Mexico Press, 1996).
25. Deborah J. Baldwin, *Protestants and the Mexican Revolution*, 165–171; Jean-Pierre Bastian, *Protestantismos y modernidad latinoamericana*, 129, 147.
26. Moisés Sáenz, "Lo esencial en la educación del estudiante," *Mundo Cristiano*, December 11, 1919, 559. One must notice how in this piece, "in life" is formulated in the comparative, American life being the implicit model. Obviously given the artificial nature of Catholic education, this concept of acting in life was not possible.
27. Ibid.
28. Ibid.
29. Moisés Sáenz, "El cuatro de Julio," *El Abogado Cristiano*, July 8, 1915, 209.
30. See Ernest Gellner, *Nations and Nationalism*.
31. Ibid., 24.
32. José Vasconcelos, "Conferencia dictada en el "Continental Memorial Hall." De Washington, la noche del 9 de diciembre de 1922, a invitación de la "Chataucua International Lecture Association," por el licenciado José Vasconcelos, Secretario de Educación Pública," *Educación* 1, vol. 2, May 1923, 1.
33. Moisés Sáenz, "Lo esencial en la educación del estudiante," 559.
34. Glenn Porter, *The Rise of Big Business, 1860–1920* (Wheeling, Illinois: Harlan Davidson, Inc., 1973, 1992, 2006), 117.
35. Part of the drive to import the American high school into Mexico was to destroy the power of political parties. In Mexico, as is still the case today, political parties were organized in the university, and university students then organized secondary school students to mobilize them at will. No sphere of secondary school life was left untouched by politicization. To the Mexican system, Sáenz opposed the American high school, where students were dedicated to study, and political life was mirrored in sports, debate and other kinds of American-style clubs. Today, Sáenz is remembered as the creator of the Mexican secondary system. His goal of depoliticizing the campus tragically failed. Today, in neo-liberal times, many of these secondary school groups, without a political compass, have degenerated into groups called *porros*, which vandalize and terrorize students and even control the spaces of the high school that are the preserve of the principal. For Sáenz's ideas about reforming the high school and his response to criticism of his school reform plans see, Moisés Sáenz, *La escuela preparatoria. Estudios realizados por acuerdo del consejo de Educación Pública y llevados a cabo por los señores profesores Andrés Osuna, Moisés Sáenz, Galación Gómez, José Arturo Pichardo, Emilio Bustamante, y José Romano Muñoz* (México: Departamento Editorial de la Dirección General de Educación Pública, 1917) in *Folletos sobre educación en México 1917* (México, 1917–1938).
36. Moisés Sáenz, "¿Es la escuela una preparación para la vida?," *Mundo Cristiano* (December 18, 1919), 583.
37. "Field of play" here means *campo de juego*—that is, sports.
38. Moisés Sáenz, "¿Es la escuela una preparación para la vida?," 583.

39. Ibid. These forms of organization would also become a crucial aspect of Sáenz's rural school projects. See Rafael Ramírez, *La enseñanza por la acción dentro de la escuela rural* (Mexico: Ediciones de la Secretaría de Educación Pública, Mexico 1925, 1942), 23, 35.
40. Boy Scouts were also introduced later in Sáenz's rural school project albeit rethought to integrate Mexican historical and folkloric traditions. See Moisés Sáenz, *Reseña de la educación pública en México en 1927* (México: Publicaciones de la Secretaría de Educación Pública, 1927), 33.
41. Moisés Sáenz, "¿Es la escuela una preparación para la vida?," 583.
42. Ibid.
43. Jean-Pierre Bastian, *Protestantismos y modernidad latinoamericana*, 160.
44. Deborah J. Baldwin, *Protestants and the Mexican Revolution*, 132–139, 171.
45. See "Reglas Generales de la Iglesia Metodista Episcopal del sur en México," *El Evangelista Mexicano*, August 1879, 29; see also Jean-Pierre Bastian, *Protestantismos y modernidad latinoamericana*, 107.
46. See Moisés Sáenz and Cristoph F. Steinke, *Segundo curso de inglés* (México: Herrero, 1930).
47. Edmundo O'Gorman has argued that in the course of Mexican history, conservative thinkers, and to a great extent liberal intellectuals, vigorously opposed the transmission of American values into Mexican society because history was understood as an emanation of essential spiritual values. Thus cultural traits were impossible to transmit. Not only were they essential to the genius or *geist* of nations, but also the histories of nations constituted the material expression of the historical development of these values. Mexicans who looked at American history as the unfolding of essential Anglo-Saxon values thought that the importation of American forms was fallacious, if not outright treasonous or sacrilegious. O'Gorman called this historical divide between Anglo-Saxons and Latins *la gran dicotomía* or The Great Dichotomy, an unbridgeable separation between Mexico and the United States buttressed by the notion that each nation represented the unfolding of an essential and morally opposite trait or spirit. See Edmundo O'Gorman, *México: El trauma de su historia*, 1stedition (México: Ciudad Universitaria: Universidad Nacional Autónoma de México, 1977).
48. The world *semejante* is, of course, the signifier for "fellow man" (or woman) in English, but it also indicates similarity in Spanish, or a certain kind of likeness. Thus two things that are *semejantes* are similar. According to the English language dictionary, a fellow is somebody in a similar position to oneself: thus the project of translating fellow into *semejante* had, at some point, to deal with the issue of race and the body; in other words: what are we going to mean by being located in the same position. It is important to recall that for many intellectuals, America's *geist* or spirit was essentially racially homogenous, that is, Anglo-Saxon.
49. See Deborah J. Baldwin, *Protestants and the Mexican Revolution*, 132–142; Jean-Pierre Bastian, "Las sociedades protestantes, 158–162.
50. See Deborah J. Baldwin, *Protestants and the Mexican Revolution*, 132–142.
51. See Andrés Osuna, *Elementos de Psicología Pedagógica* (México y París: Librería de la Vda. De Ch. Bouret, 4a. Edición, 1917). See also Deborah J. Baldwin, *Protestants and the Mexican Revolution*, 136.
52. See Ibid., 137–139.
53. I discussed this issue in chapter 2, *Radical Dewey*.
54. Efrén Núñez Mata, "Salvador Alvarado y la educación nacional," *Historia Mexicana*, 11 (1962): 430.
55. Michael J. Gónzalez, *The Mexican Revolution, 1910–1940* (Albuquerque: University of New Mexico Press, 2002), 119.

56. Ibid., 182.
57. See William E. French, *A Peaceful and Working People*. See also, Héctor Aguilar Camín, *La Frontera Nómada: Sonora y la Revolución Mexicana* (México City: Secretaría de Educación Pública, 1985).
58. Moisés Sáenz, *Some Mexican Problems: Lectures on the Harris Foundation* (Chicago: The University of Chicago Press, 1926), 17.
59. Baldwin, *Protestants and the Mexican Revolution*, 37.
60. Since the Cincinnati Plan divided the Mexican territory for Protestant missionary activity, it was possible for Baptists in one area of Mexico to now work for Congregationalist missions if those areas came under the purview of the Congregationalist Church.
61. Moisés Sáenz, "El Plan de Cincinati," *Mundo Cristiano* (July 10, 1919), 26–27.
62. Ibid., 27.
63. Moisés Sáenz, "Editorial del 6 de Julio de 1919," 2.
64. Moisés Sáenz to Miguel Alessio Robles, November 2, 1921, box 123, file #245-Si-?, Private Secretary of the Presidency of the Republic, Obregón Calles Collection, Archivos Generales de la Nación, México City, México.
65. "Nota del secretario Alessio Robles," n.d., box 123, file 245-S1-8, Obregón Calles Collection, Archivos Generales de la Nación, México City, México; "Carta del Palacio Nacional a Moisés Sáenz del 17 de noviembre de 1920," box 123, file #245-S1-8, Obregón Calles Collection, Archivos Generales de la Nación, México City, México.
66. "Memorándum de la Presidencia de la República del 27 de abril de 1921," box 123, file 245-S1-8, Obregón Calles Collection, Archivos Generales de la Nación, México City, México; "Carta de Moisés Sáenz al C. Presidente Álvaro Obregón del 27 de abril de 1921," box 123, file #245-S1-8, Obregón Calles Collection, Archivos Generales de la Nación, México City, México.
67. See for example, "Carta de Moisés Sáenz a la Presidencia de la República", April 27, 1921, box 123, file 245-S1-S (8)?, Obregón Calles Collection, Archivos Generales de la Nación, México City, México; "Carta de Moisés Sáenz al President Obregón," April 27, 1921, box 123, file folio 245-S1-S (8)?, Obregón Calles Collection, Archivos Generales de la Nación, México City, México; "Note of Moisés Sáenz to Secretary Alessio Robles, April 27, 1921, box 123, file 245-S1-S (8)?, Obregón Calles Collection, Archivos Generales de la Nación, México City, México.
68. José Vasconcelos, "Por la unión Latino Americana. Discurso del 11 de octubre de 1922, ofreciendo el Banquete de los escritores Argentinos Imprenta Rafael Reyes, San Salvador, 1992," 1922, box 25, file 104-B-21, Obregón Calles Collection, Archivos Generales de la Nación, México.
69. See for example, Su Zhixin, "Teaching, Learning and Reflective Acting: A Dewey Experiment in Chinese Teacher Education," *Teachers College Record* 1, vol. 98 (Fall 1996): 126–152.
70. See for example the essays contained in Thomas S. Popkewitz, *Inventing the Modern Self*, ed. Thomas S Popkewitz (New York: Palgrave Macmillan, 2005), especially Thomas S. Popkewitz, "Inventing the Modern Self and John Dewey: Modernities and the Traveling of Pragmatism in Education—An Introduction," 3–36.
71. Sáenz asserted that once the *escuelas activas* project got underway in 1923, "out of a clear sky, a bulletin came forth from the Department of Education ordering all teachers in federal public schools to adopt the project method . . . and to become modern." See Moisés Sáenz, *Some Mexican Problems*, 79.
72. See David B. Tyack, *The One Best System: A History of American Urban Education* (Cambridge, MA: Harvard University Press, 1974), especially part V, chapter 1, Success Story: The Administrative Progressives."

73. See for example, Moisés Sáenz, "Algunos aspectos sintéticos de la educación en México" *Boletín de la Secretaría de Educación Pública* 3, vol. V (México: Talleres Gráficos de la Nación, Publicaciones de la Secretaría de Educación 8, vol. VIII (México, 1926), 37.
74. Waks notes that it is not in Dewey, but only in Kilpatrick's narrower notion of the "social context" that the product becomes the sine qua non of social life, the way an individual becomes social: everything has to eventuate into a product; there is no room for consumption. See Leonard J. Waks, "The project method in postindustrial education," *Journal of Curriculum Studies* 4, vol. 29 (1997): 397. Yet we know that Dewey had room in his philosophy of social life for "consummatory" experiences, some of which he valued more than the merely productive. It is only when "consummatory" experiences are the end-in-itself of whole publics that they are dangerous. In this sense, then, it may be argued that Dewey's prioritizing of production and Kilpatrick's project method as a technique for creating modern selves and model citizens do converge one way or another in the idea of production, of the product.
75. William Heard Kilpatrick, "Danger and Difficulties of the Project Method and How to Overcome Them. Introductory Statement, Definition of Terms," *Teachers College Record* 4, vol. 22 (1921): 297–305.
76. William Heard Kilpatrick, "The Project Method: Child Centeredness in Progressive Education," *History Matters*, http://historymatters.gmu.edu/d/4954/
77. Ibid.
78. Larry Hickman, *John Dewey's Pragmatic Technology* (Bloomington: Indiana University Press, 1990), 11.
79. Larry Hickman, "Dewey's Theory of Inquiry" *Reading Dewey: Interpretations for a Postmodern Generation* (Bloomington: Indiana University Press, 1998), 179.
80. Larry Hickman, *John Dewey's Pragmatic Technology*, 15.
81. John Dewey, *Experience and Nature* in The Collected Works of John Dewey, 1882–1953, edited by Jo Ann Boydston (Carbondale and Edwardsville: Southern Illinois University Press, 1967–1991), MW 10: 330.
82. For example, John Dewey, introduction to *Essays in Experimental Logic* (Chicago: The University of Chicago Press, 1916), 322; also John Dewey, *Art as Experience* (New York: Minton, Balch and Co., 1934), 42.
83. Ibid., 35.
84. John Dewey, introduction to *Essays in Experimental Logic*, 4.
85. John Dewey, *Experience and Nature* (La Salle: Open Court Publishing, 1965), 70.
86. Larry Hickman, *John Dewey's Pragmatic Technology*, 41.
87. Ibid., 42.
88. See for example, "Código de Moralidad de los niños que concurren a las escuelas primarias," *Boletín de la Secretaría de Educación Pública* 7, vol. IV (México: Talleres Gráficos de la Nación, Publicaciones de la Secretaría de Educación Pública no. illegible, vol. VI, October 1925), 107; see also Eulalia Guzmán, *La escuela nueva o de la acción*, 38.
89. Some scholars maintain that Sáenz may have believed at some point that Indians did not possess this kind of modern practicality at all, but for the most part he wanted to democratize inquiry in the conviction that Indians were capable of civilizing and thinking the modern. For the idea of *saberes prácticos* see, Gabriel Zaid, *El Progreso Improductivo* (México: Siglo Veintiuno Editores, 1979).
90. Sometimes referred to as "a nation of excessive heterogeneity." See for example, Moisés Sáenz, *La educación rural en México* (México: Talleres Gráficos de la Nación, 1928), 8.
91. See for example, Carlos Basauri's essay, "La etnología de México," Carlos Basauri, "La etnología de México," *Boletín de la Secretaría de Educación*

Pública 7, vol. IV (México: Talleres Gráficos de la Nación, Publicaciones de la Secretaría de Educación Pública, October 1925); Lucio Mendieta y Núñez, "Importancia Científica y práctica de los estudios etnológicos y etnográficos," *Boletín de la Secretaría de Educación Pública* 1, vol. IV (México: Talleres Gráficos de la Nación, Publicaciones de la Secretaría de Educación Pública, 1925), especially page 196; Moisés Sáenz, *Some Mexican Problems*, 53; Eulalia Guzmán, *La escuela nueva o de la* acción, 39.

92. The idea was almost identical to that of Salvador Alvarado, who decried the atomization of the individual in Mexico as one sign of the nation's inability to become modern. See, for example, Salvador Alvarado, "Carta al Pueblo," 202–203; Salvador Alvarado, "El Problema de la educación," *Antología Ideológica*, 108–110.
93. "Código de Moralidad de los niños que concurren a las escuelas primarias," 107.
94. See Leonard J. Waks, "The Project Method in Postindustrial Education," 391–405. Waks also argues that Kilpatrick's notion of the social context "suggest something much narrower than Dewey's concern with community life in the school as a precursor to participation in the cooperative redirection of industrial society. Kilpatrick's social condition emphasized value judgment through the consideration by peers; a 'social context' is a context for evaluation. The girl making a dress is working in a social context because' other girls at least are to see the dress. The social situation is necessary for the comparative evaluations of . . . projects . . . for Dewey . . . the social idea was based on a systematic analogy with a group of dedicated problem-solving scientists united by shared interests and the willingness to communicate their findings and evaluate them by shared criteria to achieve their shared goal—the expansion . . . of knowledge. Individuals as masters of their individual fate were of no particular moral significance for Dewey unless they were also operating in a specific context—one where their common fate was collectively mastered." Leonard J. Waks, "The Project Method in Postindustrial Education," 396–397.
95. See Robert Westbrook, "Schools for Industrial Democrats: The Social Origins of John Dewey's Philosophy of Education," *American Journal of Education* 4, vol. 100 (1992).

4 Moisés Saénz and the Revolutionary Project of the *Escuelas Activas*

The preeminence of closure over openness . . . manifests itself as love of the Form. It contained and encloses intimacy . . . the double influence of the indigenous and the Spanish engenders our predilection for ceremony, formulas, and order. The Mexican . . . aspires to create an ordered world in conformity with clear principles . . . nobody, to express himself, needs to resort to the continuing invention that a free society demands"
(Octavio Paz's The Labyrinth of Solitude, 1950)

Introduction

According to Moisés Sáenz, in 1923 the Mexican state instructed "all . . . schools to become 'schools of action'" and a "certain advice and an absolute command was given to teachers to conform to the new ideas." According to Sáenz, this "was an order to become modern overnight . . . the 'project method' was duly expanded; John Dewey became a gospel . . . learning by doing was the watchword."[1] Education in México would be known as *"aprender haciendo"*[2] or learning by doing after Dewey's own pedagogy. Sáenz enthusiastically affirmed that,

> Dewey, with his philosophy of socialization, with his emphasis on reality, on self-activity and self-expression, became a watchword. Dewey [has] performed two great services for [Mexico]. He has confirmed our philosophy of education and has liberated us from the servitude of formal school equipment. Inasmuch as the school is a place where free activity is to have play, where growth, and self-expression making for growth, is the only rule, we can have schools without costly standardized desks, without a standard building, under the eaves of the thatched roof of the old farmhouse, under the trees . . . he has gone beyond pedagogies into the realm of mere common sense.[3]

The Dewey project would bring about "confirmation" and "liberation." It would confirm Mexico's own approach to education—to create a "national soul"—and it would liberate the nation from the stigma of poverty by establishing the grounds for modernity. The crucial aspect, the ultimate purpose, of Deweyan pedagogy for Sáenz was to foster new ways of thinking and entrepreneurial activity demystified by religious or political ideologies in order to create a new practical man who could engender the modern within the nation and thus incorporate Mexico into what Claudio Lomnitz denominates "a 'civilizational horizon' transcending Mexico's borders": the realm of the modern.[4]

This bifurcated vision of historical change where the modern lies at the end point of historical change explains two intertwined goals of Sáenz's project: one the one hand, the project of *socialización* or the socialization of the school through the homogenization of social contexts both material and human; and on the other, the promotion of Deweyan inquiry in the schools through the adoption of new methods of teaching imported from Columbia University's progressive schools. Socialization in general responded to the solution of these "Great National Problems" in the schools in the sense that in seeking to integrate social contexts by accommodating the school to society, it would homogenize racial and cultural worldviews and establish the basis for social efficiency thus creating a "national soul." Whereas it also promoted industrial work in the school to incorporate students into the capitalist process of economic development, the purpose was not to promote industrial education but to embed production in the process of learning. The social reconstruction promoted by *socialización* would then buttress Sáenz's promotion of a new orientation to life—*orientación para la vida*—to produce enterprising subjects with an open-ended view of the world and cognitive capabilities inherently creative and productive. Sáenz's philosophy of education assumed that a sense of practicality imagined as a cognitive dimension of socialized individuals constituted the condition of possibility for permanent industrial growth,[5] rather than industrial society having posited these ways of knowing as advantageous to its own reproduction.[6]

Whereas aspects of the project spoke to the concerns of Dewey's *How to Think*, it was *The School and Society* that resonated with Sáenz. "*School and Society* is a book we know and love," Sáenz told an audience at the University of Chicago.[7] "Motivation, respect for personality, self-expression, vitalization of school work, project method, learning by doing, democracy in education—all of Dewey is there."[8] By "there," he meant the state rural schools, which became the locus of Sáenz's Deweyan experiment after the demise of José Vasconcelos' cultural missions project during the Obregón administration. Moisés Sáenz took over the educational project of the Mexican Revolution under the administration of President Calles. Sáenz called his project the *escuelas activas*. The Deweyan experiment's most prominent and public phase ran from 1923 to 1929 until it was officially replaced in 1934 by President Cárdenas' socialist education. It was in the rural schools that Sáenz began to implement the new methodology of the *escuelas activas* with the major purpose of creating new habits of thought and new ways of conceptualizing the social world. As we have seen, Sáenz admired the United States and as a student at Columbia University had become fascinated with the social efficiency he saw embodied in the American college campus and in its corporate order. There the magical values of the American modern flourished: discipline, initiative, and productivity without the need for coercion and central planning. Its pedagogical vehicle: the laboratory schools of John Dewey; its major tool: the project method.

One precursor of this practical man could be found in the appropriation of anarchist pedagogy by General Salvador Alvarado (discussed in chapter 2), whose pedagogy rested on the belief in the power of American practicality and who established schools within which a miniature society, standing for the nation, would provide indigenous people with a referent for a national consciousness. A second precursor for this modern subject had been José Vasconcelos' *el técnico*, the technocrat modern subject, who could synthesize in his person the practical values of the Anglo-Saxon and the spiritual values of the Latin subject (I discuss this issue at length in chapter 5). When Vasconcelos lost his political battle with the modernizing forces represented by the teachers' associations within the SEP, Moisés Sáenz's coterie of followers replaced him in the Secretariat of Education and *el técnico* never developed beyond a simple vision of Mexicans as pragmatic and of Mexico as a nebulous version of Jefferson's yeoman republic.

In what follows, I will explicate how Sáenz's objectives were translated into a set of model experimental schools called *escuelas tipos* where the new methods were tested and exported to the rest of the nation. These schools provide the best evidence of how Sáenz implemented Dewey's pedagogy during the 1920s and constitute the proper foundation for an analysis of Dewey's influence during the Mexican revolution. It was in these schools where Moisés Sáenz set the basis for the creation of subjects that could produce the modern. I will also identify the limits of the project and what those limits say about Sáenz and Dewey's pedagogy in times of revolutionary change by providing a brief survey of selected case studies of school practices that may be gleaned from the archival evidence.

The Legal Framework: The "Bases" of the *Escuela Activa* for Mexico's Rural Schools

Although several conflicting agendas gave birth to the national law known as the *Bases para la organización de la escuela primaria conforme al principio de la acción*—"Basis for the organization of primary schools according to the principle of action"—officially published in 1926 by the SEP and which established the *escuelas activas* and Deweyan education as the pedagogy of the revolution, Deweyan qualities predominated in it. At its literal level, the *Bases* intended to create a modern labor force and a racially homogeneous nation loyal to the nation-state. For that purpose, its major instruments included the fostering rural schools with Spanish language instruction (rather than in indigenous languages), education programs intended to create a new working class, and a conciliatory politics of culture celebratory of Native Mexican culture. At this level of the law we find the location of nationalist politics as the resolution of the great national problems: the necessity of creating a nation-state and a homogeneous population with a shared set of values at its foundation. Here labor (*trabajo*) would become the center of school activity and the "primordial element of socialization" giving life to the "principle of action," that is, labor as the basis of the "life of the child."[9] The law explicitly rejected vocational schooling as its goal and instead defended its objective to create citizens through work. For example, work in school would not be about learning how to make bread, but that the production of bread would become a "center of interest" out of which all kinds of possibilities for learning and instruction would arise, as for example the study of chemistry or the history of the evolution of an industry.[10]

At a higher level, the law aspired to create a practical man of modernity in the figure of the associated child, an "active element that observes, investigates, compares and gives real and concrete form to the purposes of school work."[11] The law described how socialization and inquiry worked together:

> If the primary school is a small community and if in every community manual, motor and constructive activities constitute the dominant functions of life, it is natural that it [the school] will initiate the child in these activities, getting him in contact with the active life that surrounds him so that he may understand them, appreciate them and feel them according to his possibilities. In that way the student through his muscles in action and his mental activity will penetrate into the currents of material and spiritual progress of the society where he will live and struggle . . . the active work of the student will be the medium through which, in the short period of school life, the child will acquire the indispensable elements for a life in a civilized society.[12]

The new education, according to the law, would produce a child with an orientation to the world unmediated by religious or political ideology, but guided by scientific curiosity. An orientation to the world meant relating to the material world as "a reflection of social life," for example knowing how things were made, where they originated and how they circulated. "The child," said the law, "when laboring to make a product will have to know all the science involved in its preparation so that he will not become an empirical operator," that is, an isolated individual improvising on chance observation.[13] Explicitly invoking the name of Dewey, the law affirmed the school's objective to fuse science and art, the theoretical and the practical, so that a methodic investigation to the world involved a physical engagement with it.[14]

For this associated child, the schools would create the "social base" necessary for his creative and productive activity. The "social base," a utopian vision of Mexico's future as a nation-state, would reconcile creativity and order, authority and democratic life, creating a shared sense of purpose to form the basis of a new national community where, according to the law, a "harmonious disorder" would prevail.[15] The organic community at the heart of this "harmonious disorder" would produce its own order out of socialized labor conditions: a "division of labor adjusted to the particular activities of the children . . . [where] leaders will arise to organize labor . . . the strong, the skilled and the able will earn the esteem, respect and applause of their peers . . . [and] the strong will assist the weak and the able the handicapped."[16] It may have been a future utopian society, but it would be built upon materially existing human activity and natural resources. The production of a self-sustaining social order figured as one of the most salient features of the new society. According to the *Bases*,

> a natural environment that is a reflection of social life [would] provide to the student incentives to engage in work that requires the cooperation of his peer . . . and when this labor become a center of interest that demands cooperation, the sum of the efforts of a group of children (such as the construction of a common fund, of a bank, the raising of animals) . . . will spring forth the desire to assist one's comrade, the necessity to search for a benefit for the family . . . and the consciousness of the social benefit that is the result of a practical task. Through this procedure, the child socializes his conduct because he is working in the same direction as his peers with whom he finds himself closely connected through a common purpose.[17]

The "social base"—the homogeneous foundation of the social world— would make the rise of the practical subject feasible. The Mexican subject, conceived as an isolated subject, would become an associated individual because he would know the nation. Mexico, as professor Matías López, federal director of the state of Hidalgo asserted, would move away "from a stage of ferocious individualism" to one "where the spiritual unity of Mexico would become true."[18]

Moisés Sáenz's Deweyan Project and the *Escuelas Tipos* (Model Schools)

In 1924, with the presidency in the hands of Sonoran General Calles, Moisés Sáenz, recently arrived from Columbia University and appointed as subsecretary of education, established a series of schools called *escuelas tipos* or model schools to serve as laboratories for the new method and meant to become, as he called it, the "vanguard of the new educational movement."[19] There he began prioritizing those aspects related to inquiry, which, according to his personal understanding of Dewey's pedagogy, would foster new cognitive capabilities in Mexican subjects. Although Sáenz's ambitions had led him to believe that he could establish these schools over the entire territory of Mexico, by 1925 only nineteen schools of this kind had been established due to the state's lack of resources. Yet they contained Sáenz's vision of Deweyan education for Mexico. These new model schools were established in Tuxtla Gutiérrez, Saltillo, Guanajuato, Pachuca, Puebla, Querétaro, San Luis Potosí, Tlaxcala, Aguascalientes, Chihuahua, Colima, Guadalajara, Monterrey, Oaxaca, Culiacán, Nogales, Ciudad Victoria, Morelia and Zacatecas. They reached, at their peak, an attendance of 2,323 males and 792 female students, 300 male adults, and 138 female adults. The *escuelas tipos* served as the model for the creation of a new federal network of primary schools and secondary schools as well as a laboratory for social workers and teachers to be trained in the new system.[20]

The centerpiece of the system was the rural school with its dual mission: on the one hand, the creation of a racially homogenized citizenry through the socialization (and thus civilization) of the Mexican Indian (and Indianized peasants) and the erasure of autarkic Indian communities. This would be achieved by the teaching of Spanish as the national language, the spread of mass literacy education, the improvement of the sanitary and hygienic life of rural areas, the establishment of petty industries and rural cooperatives, and the general education of peasants and Indians. On the other hand, the creation of a practical man of modernity through an education promoting Deweyan open-ended inquiry similar to the Mexican Protestants' *orientación para la vida* to create an enterprising pragmatic subject: Sáenz's major objective in framing the entire project of *escuelas activas* as a Deweyan experiment. All supporters of Deweyan education, identifying Catholic education and culture in general as fanatic, sought to displace the church with the state school as the center of civic life, branding Catholic education as medieval or feudal. For all of them, accommodating the school to society meant accommodating the school to the nation. As it had been for Alvarado, the only "real life" was the nation. Thus the concept of the "nation-state" displaced the "community."

Both goals—socialization and practical inquiry—were intertwined as they originally were in the *Bases*. For Sáenz, revolutionary education needed to create a shared set of values, the homogeneous context that inquiry necessitated to be effective, and become a national character trait. This shared context would provide a foundation for entrepreneurial selves, fostering modern "disciplinary values" so that "just and correct notions of discipline" would become habit in "socialized" individuals. Second, it would cultivate the "utilitarian or practical value" that produced entrepreneurial forms of inquiry. These objectives would provide an identity to the future modern nation: entrepreneurial selves, modern systems of discipline that eschewed physical coercion and a homogeneous consciousness achieved through the state's use of culture as instrument of rule.[21] The first domain—socialization—constituted the precondition for the second domain and has understandably become the only focus of scholars assessing the influence of Dewey in Mexico at the time; the second domain identified the conceptual space wherein Deweyan pedagogy made its mark in Mexican history. Dewey's pedagogy thus became implicated in an extremely complex and vast universe of political agendas and versions of the modern, some of which supported state violence to accomplish national integration.

The Geography of the Rural School as an Organic Community

The spatial structure of Sáenz's schools in Mexico resembled in many ways that of Dewey's Chicago schools. Ida B. DePencier has illustrated how Dewey's Chicago experimental schools worked and how they highlight Dewey's concern with production and inquiry. According to Pencier, Dewey's classrooms worked on a continuum between home and school, which provided "no break between the child's home activities and his first contact with the school." This feature socialized both the home and the school, thereby providing one single context for the child's learning. Second, production served as the foundation for social life in the school and the basis for learning and productivity. Through the completion of tasks, students engendered the curriculum as "reading, writing, arithmetic, and spelling would [grow] out of [the child's] need to get information and communicate." Third, the school, as a "community in miniature," provided the basis for bonds of solidarity among children rather than individual competitiveness. Fourth, the school's mission was to create productive and creative selves prioritizing the child's "curiosity" as the foundation of the principle of discovery, scientific work and investigation. Fifth, projects and problems stimulated investigation, creating discipline and social cohesion without the need for authority. According to Pencier "no prizes, no false incentives, no standards imposed by adults would be used—or needed." The subject—the child—was placed at the center of the social world of the school, which, in its spatiality represented the "totality of the world of production." It was crucial for the child to understand the material world wherein he lived, for this "would arouse his curiosity, stimulate him to investigate, and challenge him to look at the world about him." Thus Dewey's schools structured the social world of the school in such a way that the productive spirit of the individual stood at the center. The key was to socialize the child's world, to unify social contexts—home, public world—and to ground all learning in the material world through labor, communicative practices and investigation.[22] For Dewey, unifying social contexts did not mean creating new relationships between individuals and their social world. As a pedagogical technique, it assumed the actual interrelatedness that the industrial revolution had produced but that the individuals could not perceive by themselves anymore because the home and the school had been separated from the world of production by capitalism.

For Sáenz, though, its value consisted in its causative powers: that it could lead the individual to visualize the world differently and integrate it through his work. Faithful to Dewey's idea that the school had to reflect social life, Sáenz planned rural schools to contain all aspects of rural society within its premises. The geography of the schools had been decreed by the *Bases* themselves and ratified by the executive office of government. According to a presidential decree, all *escuelas activas* or active-learning schools were to contain "cultivated plots, facilities for the raising and care of domestic animals, the manufacturing of petty industries . . . preparation of meals, the construction of furniture and toys, *curtiduría* and painting of leather . . . arts and crafts production."[23] General Salvador Alvarado, who first attempted in Yucatán to adapt Dewey's ideas into education, had asserted that the school was to be *una comunidad en miniatura* (a community in miniature),[24] or as Dewey put it, "a miniature community or embryonic society."[25] Others referred to it as a *comunidad en pequeño*, or a small community.[26] Sáenz accomplished this goal by dividing the geography of all rural schools in three specific sectors: a classroom, an annex where animals were raised and a cultivation plot or orchard (*huerto*) with a flower garden outside the school building. The core of the annex was the *huerto*. In this orchard, students cultivated an agricultural life typical of their environment or locality.[27] It represented agriculture as practiced outside the classroom. The space of the school provided students with an "orchard garden" signifying the agricultural world; a "flower garden" to cater to the "aesthetic inclinations of the Indians"; a "workshop" signifying industry; and other "work" areas where students would engage in projects and learn through them. Students, along with fellow villagers, also worked to construct a plot of land outside the premises of the school reserved for agricultural work.[28] The fabric of rural life was its productive life: its industries, the agricultural work of the community, the raising of animals for consumption, the small industries that characterized rural life and its school.

Since the industrial social life that structured Dewey's laboratory schools was not congruent with México's agrarian society, students were to solve problems through the fabric of rural life. In their classroom activities, students engaged the totality of their social world established in the school in order to engage in productive learning. This world of production gave meaning to Sáenz's goal to establish an *educación para la vida* or education for life. Life in this case was defined by the product of man's engagement with his environment, which in Mexico's case signified rural life. The major purpose of this scheme consisted in creating a new kind of Mexican self where the individual could "see" his world as outside himself and thus act on it through entrepreneurial projects designed to produce artifacts, agricultural products or any activity or commodity that conformed to the economic needs of the community. Linking the school to the community meant not social conformity, but the very opposite. Sáenz hoped to create new modern selves that could visualize new possibilities for transforming their rural worlds and thus create a new modern nation.

In spite of its progressive thrust, Sáenz's Deweyan project assumed that the practical cognitive qualities that he so valued were absent in the "traditional" Catholic mind-set of the native Indians and peasants, if not the overall Mexican population. This idea conformed to Dewey's principle that, historically, progress could only be possible when the traditional structures ("givens") of "primitive societies" (as in Catholic Europe in medieval times) gave way to societies in which inquiry was democratic—that is, extended to all members of society and open-ended and thus not dogmatic. Productive inquiry, in turn, depended on the ability of the individual to problematize his world, which is exactly what Sáenz believed conformist, "racially apathetic" and "passive" Mexican Indians and peasants could not do. The explicit goal of transforming Native societies by eradicating their autonomy, displacing their languages, substituting their religious beliefs with a national ideology and homogenizing their everyday life conformed to the necessity of creating an underlying unity, the "shared set of values" that made the laboratory schools and America, in Sáenz's mind, so socially efficient.

The instrumental purpose given by Sáenz to each space conformed to Dewey's insistence that intelligence consisted in the manipulation of "meanings" to solve problems and produce new events and new possibilities. Socialized intelligence formed a crucial aspect of Dewey's critique of inquiry. In seeking to replicate in the schools the conditions for life as experimental, Dewey wished students to see the various components of their social world, including ideas, as residing outside themselves. Decontextualizing the familiar—the orchard, the house, the school and the animals—in the Mexican classroom was precisely intended to facilitate that kind of experimentalism and produce subjects able to transform everyday objects into meaningful units. Sáenz's school moved away from the vocational education ideal because it was imperative for the modern subject to understand spaces, ideas and things as tools for inquiry,[29] and the best tools for this purpose were those derived from everyday life.[30]

Understanding social artifacts this way demonstrates how Sáenz intended to translate Dewey's technological view of inquiry into a pedagogy for Mexican schools. Students had to see, and visualize, all social aspects contained in the space of the school—ideas, objects, previous solutions to other problems, other projects, spaces—as tools for experimentation. Sáenz intended pupils to imagine everyday formations such as the classroom, the plots of land for agricultural work, the garden, arts and crafts workshops and spaces for raising animals (such as chickens, pigs, rabbits and cows)[31] as things "teeming with meaning." Thus students and teachers drew plans to construct plots, build fences, divide parcels and construct drainage. In the orchard, agricultural work had to be complemented with other sections of the annex such as animal husbandry, the care of pet animals and petty industry workshops, for example.[32]

The Project Method in the Rural Schools

The project method became the main avenue to transform the relationship of students to the world and foster new cognitive skills based on a secular understanding of reality distinct from the dogma of the Catholic Church. Sáenz proclaimed that schools would become "projectories" or "places where projects were hatched."[33] A project, to be successful, had to lead "like a series of satellites" to small problems whose theoretical development . . . allows us to be placed in communication with far away situations."[34] Not only must a project be productive, but its findings should eventually be used in any other context. Abstract ideas were to arise only from experience. "The little school," he said, "is taken as a center of a project" by students, teachers and community members. All instruction implied a project conceived as "investigation, information and scientific coordination."[35] The interrelationship of all projects made the school a productive enterprise leading to the practical man.

This objective was furthered by the problem-solving techniques of the method Sáenz had previously introduced in Mexico, which were wedded to the notion that knowledge was productive only when leading to the creation of more knowledge or when it engendered the ability to problematize the world.[36] Kilpatrick wanted "activity leading to further activity."[37] Thus no project could have that kind of "consummatory" quality that Dewey described as not leading to further inquiry and growth—that is, human experiences he considered as possessing a purely or "honorific" "aesthetic quality." As a scholar of the times observed, the responsibility of Deweyan education was, "to cultivate . . . reflective thought [originating] in a doubtful, problematic situation . . . [this was] the method of experimental inquiry and discovery which has won dominion in the world of knowledge."[38] Kilpatrick had asserted that in the project method purposeful activity must "lead on," that is, it must possess the "tendency to lead one on to other like fruitful activity." "We may therefore take as the criterion of the value of any activity—whether intentionally educative or not its tendency directly or indirectly to lead the individual and others whom he touches on to other like fruitful activity, he argued."[39] He tied this possibility to a means-end philosophy where skills, situations and ideas "acquired as an end can be applied as means to new purposes. Skills or ideas arising first in connection with certain ends may be singled out for special consideration and so form new ends. This constitutes one of the most fruitful sources for new interests,"[40] a key idea in the production of a social life based on the idea of unlimited growth.

Thus Sáenz insisted that, "another error that must be avoided is to consider the project method as an end in itself (*una finalidad en sí misma*) and not as the learning procedure it is."[41] A project could not be confused with its results. This method of evaluation explains why students were puzzled when realizing that completing projects given to them in school was not the basis for evaluation. It also explains why Sáenz expressed discontent when he chided parents for praising their children's projects for its purely aesthetic qualities. "It is not rare," expressed Sáenz, "to listen to expressions such as these: How beautiful are the projects exhibited at such and such school!

Have you seen the project on cotton of school N., or the project on history of zone Z.? One would believe that these were real plans, projects to be realized, when in reality these were diverse works performed on a specific theme, that are assumed to have been executed as a result of the development of the project, but that could have been the product of it or not."[42] One could take issue with Saénz's attitudes toward parents who were simply praising their children for completing their projects and for upholding them as models for others, yet his comments show the zeal of his conviction that the mentality of Mexicans had to change, especially in these small matters: projects gained value as plans for further production; they were not ends-in-themselves. The parents' aesthetic vision of the project was incorrect. Projects, like any enterprise, did not have certain and final ends. They were the product of uncertainty. To say that a project was "beautiful" would lead simply to the imitation of the project and not to the creation of a new one.

Gregorio Torres Quintero, among the earliest of Dewey supporters and former secretary of education in Yucatán, explained how the project method worked in Mexican classrooms:

> the teacher and his disciples must inaugurate a new topic or project in each meeting. The children then begin to ponder, comment and ask questions. This is the time to discuss and conference, rather than to learn a lesson. The topic is taken as if it were from real life. Then right away [children] begin looking for information. It may be found in the library, in field trips, in mutual consultation or with the neighbors of the community. At irregular times, not precisely every day, the pupils come together to conference on the same topic. Each child contributes with the best information he can. Each has conducted his own research, not as an assigned lesson, but in conformity with his inclinations and interests. In this conference all opinions and all data will be compared. Everybody will learn more or less according to their preparation or their individual interests.[43]

This was the essence of the "*escuela por la acción*," he averred,[44] which was to create what Quintero denominated as the "thinker-idea" and the "thinker-action," a practical man. The use of discussion groups, a novelty at the time, promoted this vision of a future society organized around communication and the exchange of meanings and information. Projects were like enterprises. They articulated continuous inquiry as the essence of growth and made continuous inquiry dependent on what seems like an abstruse philosophical point: that in any human activity, the results of that activity cannot be seen as the necessary endpoint of its original purpose. They were to be seized as an opportunity for further inquiry.

Another necessary component of the worldview promoted by the project method in Mexico spoke to the idea that it was necessary for students to understand how things in the world interrelate to each other and how they acquire value in terms of their interdependence. For this purpose, Sáenz imported another technique from Columbia University called correlations, translated to Spanish as *centros de correlación* or *trabajos de correlación*.[45] Among the techniques introduced at Columbia, this technique more than any other spoke to the industrial conditions prevalent at the time in the United States and exemplified the human-centered/secular purpose of the method. As a consciousness-raising device it intended to convey to the American student the interrelatedness of industrial processes, whose connections were not visible since production had been torn asunder from the home by the industrial revolution. This technique responded to Dewey's major concern to locate the student at the center of the world (and not that the student was the center of the world, which was another progressive interpretation of Dewey different from Kilpatrick's). In American classrooms, students were asked, for example, to identify how chains of commodities—such as copper, rice and money—circulated, changed and transformed the world. Each example led to questions that produced the curriculum: from geography to mathematics, from art to science.

In Mexico, it specifically furthered the notion that to understand ourselves we need to understand the material world through processes of investigation: it is a world we have created and therefore we own. Correlation techniques conveyed the idea that the world we produce is connected to ourselves by our own purpose and that the things we produce can be connected among themselves in an infinite number of ways. Things possessed no inherent values, unless given value by human purpose and labor.

Rafael Ramírez, former head of Mexico's *misiones culturales* (cultural missions) and right-hand man to Sáenz during this era, explained how the system of correlations worked in the care of the *huerto* (orchard):

> the cultivation of a school *huerto* should not be employed only to teach vocational agricultural education. Teaching of general subjects may be motivated also by the activities of such labor . . . [the students] have the precious opportunity of growing up 'by employing their hands as well as their heads,' to learn by timely and accurate observation . . . the school *huerto* places the child in intimate contact with the natural environment, motivating him to observe it and study it directly, being thus able to gather information first hand, which are the best and most useful; the practices that are executed in measuring and surveying the *huerto*, when planting and when sowing and selling their products, will generate enough motivation to acquire mathematical knowledge needed; many language exercises may be inspired by agricultural work . . . drawing, geography and history, just like civic studies, may also find motivation in the labor of the *huerto* in a natural way, and even concrete notions of commerce . . . if teachers were to suggest the formation of savings banks and school cooperatives or if they motivate students to deposit in banks their profits in order to draw checks.[46]

Deprived of inherent values, associations between ideas and material life could be produced in an almost infinite number of ways; only human purpose could place limits on these associations. As Ernest Gellner reminds us in his study of nationalism and industrial life, in modern societies the belief in the existence of one single coherent world permits the association of words and concepts traditionally believed to pertain to autonomous worlds: this is unique to the epistemology of the modern world.[47]

Along with the system of correlations, Sáenz and Ramírez also introduced a technique from Columbia University referred to as the center of interest translated into Spanish as *centro de interés*. In connection to the system of correlations, all projects had to possess a *centro de interés* or center of interest that gave it compass and that related projects to each other (also assisting in the creation of the curriculum of the school through the project). Students and teachers produced curricula in the school as part of *correlaciones* or relations of ideas given shape in common through a center of interest that tied all projects in the classroom together. Students were encouraged to suggest their own centers of interest, but teachers were trained to provide them when necessary.[48] For example, associations could be formed to paint the school for a festival; a committee could be formed to organize a *fiesta*; the community could organize itself to build chairs for the *fiesta*; or the association of the *fiesta* could organize other activities. Or for example, a teacher could choose a topic as a center of interest such as "rice" and develop the curriculum from just that one word. These activities would then engender more traditional subject matter such as history (Why do we organize *fiestas*? What are the festivities about? What is their historical origin?), biology or geography (Where does the wood for the chairs come from?) and other fields of inquiry. When students were asked to install showers for one school, lessons were derived for the study of iron.[49] The study of a commodity—as in the study of copper, for example—would allow students to identify how a commodity was transformed from a mineral into a product, generating lessons in geography, commerce, chemistry and physics. Lessons on the study of rice similarly would lead to further projects on commerce, history and biology. Correlations and centers of interest led students to understand how things were connected but also how to produce their own set of associations. Projects themselves, as part of a chain of projects, would unceasingly create new projects in response to new problems. Projects were not meant to be understood simply as tasks, but as units of meanings or "great units of learning with concrete meanings . . . problems whose solution is dependent on those of other simple and secondary ones and which compels [the student] to perform another great number of activities both in common and in isolation."[50]

According to Rafael Ramírez, the purpose of Dewey's pedagogy in Mexican schools was for students to understand everyday objects as "instruments of culture"[51] the same way as books were supposed to be. Ramírez's statement reflected the project's opposition to the cultural politics of the

Vasconcelos era, where school work combined "intelligent instruction and productive work"[52] by having students access the essence of Western civilization through the reading of a great books library. As secretary of education he had established a national project to publish and distribute in all rural areas of México the great works of the West, creating mobile libraries and distributing approximately twenty thousand classics of science and literature, which were published for this purpose. One hundred and ninety-eight small rural libraries were established all over the nation,[53] and four hundred and forty-five state and federal libraries, provided an additional 17,760 books.[54] For Vasconcelos, democratizing education meant providing peasants and Indians with access to these timeless works in order to liberate them from the oppression of clerical hegemony and the encroaching oppression of industrial life. Militating against this version of intellectualism, Saénz's method claimed that learning through books was "incidental" when compared to the acquisition of what he called "more fundamental things in life." According to Saénz, "other activities [were] as important, if not more important." "How far," he claimed, "are we now from the traditional schools that only taught to read, write and count!"[55] In his essay *La Educación Rural*, Saénz claimed that the object was not to teach how to read but how to live: "writing and reading will naturally figure in it [the curricula], but always in subordination to the broader objectives that are followed, because the ideal is to teach to live."[56]

Thus Saénz ordered rural teachers to eliminate textbooks, tests and examinations and evaluate projects solely in terms of their ability to produce more problematic situations for learning, yet he did not oppose the reading of books. The method introduced the notion that ideas were the product of man's activities and not vice versa (another of the "principle of social life" to be reproduced in the schools). Rather than eliminating entirely the reading of books,[57] Saénz promoted specialized libraries, especially those dealing with issues concerning rural life, to be used as tools for learning. For example, he created 580 public libraries during the 1926–1927 fiscal year and encouraged the continuation of libraries containing the great books of Western civilization as long as books were used as instruments for the completion of school projects. What books were to be read, if any, would be left entirely to local school projects and their leaders. Thus Saénz shifted the rural libraries program by redefining the meaning of a book. Ideas contained in books were to acquire meaning through their use.[58] In rural schools, Saénz proposed that most if not all books should be about rural life and should be used to solve problems through school projects. Knowledge was related to production, and the school was a place for production.[59] The aesthetics of the classroom followed the same logic: workshop tables replaced old two-student desks[60] for example. "We are adjusting to Dewey's indications on this matter," said Saénz, "since instead of furniture for the school we now have furniture for work."[61] Thus education had been transformed: "children . . . have to take care of their chickens . . . cultivate their little plots, sowing their flower plants and, besides, the girls have their activities of sewing . . . knitting . . . the school is, then a great field of activities."

The instrumental logic of Sáenz and Ramírez set itself to destroy the hegemony of the Catholic Church over peasants' minds. For state officials of the new school, there were no sacred books and thus no sacred truths. *Escuelas activas*' teacher and teachers' instructor José de la Vega admonished teachers in Matamoros, Tamaulipas, that "in a project, as in any human association, nothing possesses an absolute value."[62] Sáenz and Ramírez's methods were in many ways a form of promoting a new social consciousness for a future secular society that would rely not on refutations of the church's ideas and values, but on the creation of new circumstances leading to new ideas, and new conditions and subjects: the belief that reconstructing experience led to mutual understanding. It aimed to create a new form of "common sense" to resolve common situations that would lead to an individual with an "open spirit."[63]

To teach how to live, though, meant for the subjects of education to live as rural citizens of the nation, to perceive one's entrepreneurial future within the rural fabric of Mexico's society and thus work to make it modern.[64] Sáenz bitterly excoriated Vasconcelos' grand project of the great books for Mexico's peasants and Indians. "A practice both easy and quotidian is that of theorizers that prescribe for all . . . to learn how to write, to learn how to count, and in order to achieve this [they build] a school and [send] teachers to the farthest corners of the mountains," said Sáenz, adding that after educating the Natives, they are sent to "dark and sad" places where "nothing is written, where no accounting takes place, places where their illusions had been eclipsed long ago and where their hungry stomach and hardened muscles have almost erased any trace of a soul."[65] "Why learn how to read?" he cried out. Thus Deweyan education rested on a particular kind of faith: that reconstructing the imagination of Mexican subjects would lead them to prefer the reconstruction of rural life and not, as it often happened, as an avenue to move to the cities as the only place for the practice of modernity. The creation of a "rural spirit," as Sáenz and Ramirez often called it, constituted a sine qua non condition of education. It meant "that the children would love the countryside and not prefer the city, being initiated in an environment where they will make the land productive and where they will gain a critical attitude towards the life that surrounds them."[66]

But how could this goal be achieved if Deweyan education was to remain faithful to a means-ends philosophy where no objective could be produced without force? What would prevent educated Natives from choosing urban modernity now that they were modern? The answer to this question leads us to the second goal of Sáenz's Deweyan educational project: the integration of the nation—materially and spiritually—through the socializing power of the school. Here the racial aspects of the project came to prominence and eventually defined the history of the project.

Socialización

The goal of socialization or *socialización*, a semantically complex term, implied first the creation of a continuum between school and community, or as Sáenz called it, "bringing into the school the currents of life from the community and making the school radiate influences to affect the community."[67] Just as school activities were structured around a center of interest, the life of communities would be structured around the state school's projects. "Our little school," indicated Sáenz, "is the center of interest of the village."[68] Stressing the intimate relationship of the school, as "social center for the community," to the rural community, Sáenz indicated how "the village serves as laboratory to the teachers . . . [how] they organize the men and the women into one form of organization or other, they vaccinate every inhabitant, they hold evening meetings with them, they teach games to the young people." This work contrasted with the church—as an institution and as a place—which provided access to higher truths the same way a book in traditional education provided access to intrinsic meanings. The concept of the school as "social center of the community" needed to be different: it had to be understood as a social tool for investigation and communication, a "nexus" in a wider net of "connections and vital relations" to benefit the *aldea* or village. It constituted a place to exchange information, whether through the socialization of the community or the use of the library, which was "not only for the school but for the community," and which through meetings of young people, children, adults, it was to become a "laboratory" for all.[69] The objective of the "school as social center for the community" was thus to democratize information for all. Following Dewey's idea that the school had to transform society, Sáenz conceived the new school as adversarial to the Catholic order of the society outside its walls,[70] rather than complicit with it. Within the school's confines a new "spirit of democratic liberty in work" would ensue with "equality in effort and concreteness in interest," and "where the relationships between teacher and pupil [will be] as natural and easy as is their nature, where one contemplates a perfectly integrated group with a community of ideals and interests and in complete cooperation to realize them."[71]

Sáenz expected school activities to organize themselves "spontaneously," producing a social differentiation distinct from that of México's agricultural society.[72] He also introduced organizational activities from American high schools, such as sports clubs,[73] sports competitions,[74] Boy Scouts,[75] and democratic elections to socialize learning as well as create a continuum between all social contexts. A major project was a savings banks project whereby students not only created "banks" in schools, but also deposited their savings in a nationwide savings bank created for this purpose. Sáenz argued that this practice agreed with Dewey's idea that "there should be an organic connection between the school and business life," yet, he added, "it is not meant . . . to prepare the child for any particular business, but that there should be a natural connection of the everyday life of the child with the business environment that surrounds him, and that [for] the school to clarify and liberalize this connection, to bring it to consciousness ... the youth needs to become acquainted with the bank as a factor in modern life."[76] The savings bank was one of the major initiatives of the *escuelas activas* and perhaps one of the few projects that survived the Deweyan experiment.

A major contradiction plagued this aspect of Sáenz's translation of the Deweyan goal of accommodating the school to society. On the one hand, it intended to be a strategic engagement with the world and not a vehicle for the reproduction of existing social hierarchies considered to be oppressive to the Indian and peasant. On the other hand, it explicitly precluded the possibility of accepting Indian or local cultural ways into the state project; on the contrary, the state project intended to displace local and religious ideas and structures and in its place, establish those of the nation-state. Sáenz's goal that the school must become "a social center for the community"[77] sought to displace the church with the state school as the center of indigenous communities and established a social order transparent to the state and to the school. For example, Sáenz understood that historically Indians had bartered signs in order to provide continuity to their former religious life, worshiping the Christian God publicly, but hiding their own gods behind the Christian sign. Thus there was always the danger that the same mechanics could be at work in the new project: bartering the church for the state school, but keeping religious devotion alive. Sáenz deemed such a trade unacceptable. Similarly, traditional social formations such as *cofradías* or religious brotherhoods were not welcome even if peasants and Indians used them to accomplish school projects, because they reproduced hierarchies or served as expressions of identity and thus were not deemed to be productive. In doing so, Sáenz disconnected the school from society to make way for new kinds of school clubs modeled after American high school campus organizations, none of them indigenous to the nation. Traditional American-style student clubs were acceptable and exemplified the kind of democratic politics that Sáenz admired. For Sáenz, they were most of all demonstrations of true democracy: they admitted—because they were democratic—all kinds of ideas without destroying the social bonds that constituted the association.

Democratic politics within the school were not supposed to have any relationship to political formations outside the school such as those involving established political parties. Sáenz prohibited any interference from formal political parties in the state schools, as was customary in Mexican secondary schools. His purpose was to disassociate secondary school from the political domination of the university, where these political organizations were formed. Mexican schools were then as now extremely politicized; under the old system, university students tied to political parties organized clubs in secondary schools. Formal political organizations networked students for their own purposes. In order to terminate this nexus, Sáenz introduced the concept of the American "high school" to Mexican education. In fact,

Sáenz is today acknowledged as the creator in México of the modern high school. With the American system of the "high school," Mexican schools were severed from the domination of the university and formal political organizations. In order to introduce his idea of democracy in education, Sáenz sought to destroy this connection.

Socialización also implied the necessary racial homogenization of the nation, which the *escuelas activas* was to facilitate through socialization. The racial politics of socialization, creating "bonds of solidarity" between Indians and *mestizos* first and a racially homogeneous nation as its ultimate goal, became a most violent and anti-democratic one. IQ tests, personality tests, the employment of racial categorizations and the deployment of the national census not only furthered the interest of the state in understanding its population but also this process of homogenization. Education called upon the state, as teacher Alfredo Sánchez O. defined it, "to forge a national character upon ethnic and well channeled basis."[78] Social homogenization promised to incorporate Indians into the nation and "create social life." Creating a new social life could conceivably erase the memory of the conquest (and thus the origins of everyday oppression), which impeded social relationships of trust and equality. Intellectuals argued that they could not communicate with Indigenous communities without necessarily confronting either explicit resentment or a variety of social practices whereby Indians marked their territory in everyday exchange. In this regard, Sáenz insisted that the new school promised an education with "no tradition."[79] It would establish its social foundations on a historical break with the past.

Thus socialization meant a civilizing mission to the Native Mexican, yet one distinct from imperial models—Spanish, British, liberal republican— because it would bring progress "without sacrifice":[80] it would not neglect the civilization of the Indian—as the Spanish had done—or confine them— as the Americans had done—to reservations; progress would not come at their expense. The civilizing mission would incorporate the "isolated" Indian into civilization, correcting an excessive individualism (the "atomized individual") product of isolation, and making them part of society as a precondition to a future modern nation that education would make possible:[81] social efficiency for the nation. "The great diversity of race groups . . . the isolation of the people, isolation both material and spiritual . . . all these factors work for the creation of a strong individualism, for the atomizing of group consciousness, and are, in a word, forces that hinder the process of national integration."[82] Thus the socializing power of the school could correct the "excessive heterogeneity" of Mexico, a national problem Sáenz claimed,[83] by creating new experiences, which could produce "like-minded" people[84] and who could give the nation coherence. Sáenz and the authorities of the Secretariat of Public Education, in seeking to build a homogeneous foundation for the nation, explicitly rejected that the project implied the racial inferiority of Mexican Natives. "The truth is this," claimed Puig Casauranc, head of the Secretariat of Public Education, in agreement with

Sáenz, that "the Indians . . . are not inferior ethnical elements but social groups that have been abandoned and kept separated from the rest of the population and civilization . . . this abandonment that has been perpetual and absolute for the Indians and the large numbers of Mexicans living in the country is the real primordial cause of the so-called backwardness of Mexico. This systematic and criminal neglect of self governments stems from the time of the Conquest."[85] Although much of this defense of the Native rested on romantic grounds, it nonetheless reflected the conviction that the project sought to foster the productivity and self-expression of Mexican Indians by converting them into "factors of production."[86] The project, said Sáenz, would "give expression to the genius of the people" and end their artistic repression.[87]

In many ways, socialization linked with the project to create practical subjects in the sense that socialization established the common foundation, the shared set of values, that were needed to sustain the work of practical subjects and made their work good for the nation and not just for individuals or families. Sáenz explicitly rejected that religion could provide that unifying vision precisely because the church had not provided peasants and Indians with the right education to understand the world—even religion—in rational terms. "In the Indian," according to Sáenz, "there is . . . [no] clear conception of Christianity such as European peasants have. Due to this fact and to the fact that the political action of the Catholic Church in Mexico has brought upon it the antagonism of the government and liberal groups since 1850, religion in my country can mean no unifying influence, no binding together of purpose, no spiritual kinship. The religious situation in Mexico is working against social unification rather than for it."[88] He did not deny that Mexico was a country, but it certainly was not a unified civilization (as the United States or as European nations).[89] Sáenz's *socialización* as a homogenization project cannot be understood apart from the much larger goal to make Mexican communities into a nation-state—"we are thinking in national terms," said Sáenz[90]—as a way for a strong and modern Mexico to protect its sovereignty.

In his analysis of Deweyan education in Mexico, one of that nation's most notable historians of the twentieth century, Gonzalo Aguirre Beltrán, opined that although Sáenz's project was congruent with Dewey's ideas on education and democracy, it needed to supplement it with a racial project to make it effective. According to Aguirre Beltrán, Sáenz's

> thesis of incorporation[91] is similar in its conceptions although not in practice with the social participation advocated by the school of action. Dewey assigns to democracy an important role in education; he concedes primacy to learning through activities performed with the widest participation possible in experience by the greater possible number of persons. This demands not only an ample degree of freedom to participate in such experience, but also the demolition of ancient racial, class

or sectarian barriers, which block that freedom of transit. Once again, the idea of homogenization becomes the prerequisite for the construction of a social order; a democratic school, where *indios* and *mestizos* live together, will teach children to act in their communities with the greatest degree of participation.[92]

Aguirre Beltrán suggests to us that even if Dewey never explicitly advocated the forcible racial homogenization of any nation—and thus the unification of historical consciousness that it implied—this racial agenda had to be implemented to make the *escuela activa* possible. Beltrán's analysis suggests how the project to create a universal subject generative of modern forms "demanded"—in Beltrán's own words—the racial homogenization of the Mexican nation in order for (Dewey's) to work in the first place. In other words, it demanded socialization as the homogenization of social contexts, whether racial or material. Beltrán's argument thus implies that racial homogenization was the implicit basis for the communicative world that characterized Dewey's schools in the first place and that made possible the organic solidarity of students joined in common purpose and with self-awareness of their place in the world. Although this argument may be challenged on many fronts, Mexican intellectuals all assumed it to be true. The project filled the "emptiness" left by the absence of race in Dewey's works on education, but so visible when Mexican intellectuals visited America; on the other hand, it offered a supplement to Dewey's own vision of America because it imagined itself creating in Mexico the racial homogeneity—and thus the social efficiency—assumed to exist in America or at the very least in Dewey's schools. It must have seemed that way to Sáenz when visiting the schools at Columbia or to visitors to the Chicago schools, whose students had been selected from racially and class-homogeneous sectors of society precisely because they provided a good foundation for social efficiency.

A Modern Self for the Mexican Nation (State)

Sáenz's *escuelas activas* formed part of a great number of state projects in the early twentieth century connecting state politics to the promotion of a new kind of self. If the notion of the modern self implies, as Dipesh Chakrabarti argues, the idea of the "generalized, disembodied self,"[93] then the Dewey experiment in México as a state project approximated that task through its techniques of problematization and the project method. Ernest Gellner's argument that this self orients itself to a world "open to interminable exploration, [offering] endless possibilities of new combinations of means with no firm prior expectations and limits . . . nothing but evidence [should] decide how things [are], and how they could be combined to secure desired effects,"[94] applies to Sáenz's project whereby students would come to understand the world as lacking any inherent meaning that is not given by human purpose. The techniques for identifying the transformations of nature into commodities and those having the student locate himself within chains of production also performed that task. They were designed for students to make all kinds of connections between things, spaces and ideas in order to generate more ideas or projects and based on a secular foundation that the human universe is man-created and all things are linked to each other—meaningfully—by human purpose.

This was an experiment that sought to produce in the individual a new will to knowledge, one that Sáenz believed the Mexican subject lacked. Mexicanist scholar Claudio Lomnitz offers a useful line of investigation when discussing the philosophy of Mexican social science investigation. According to Lomnitz, the thrust of Western social science depends on a will to knowledge, which seeks to make the familiar strange. The will to knowledge of Western science is progressive, accumulative and modern in the sense that it must not see any conclusion as foreclosed to further contestation. Topics are not "re-usable," but in constant reconstruction. Dewey scholar Larry Hickman speaks to this kind of reasoning when he links Deweyan philosophy to the possibilities for social scientific thought. Hickman claims that progress in the sciences is only possible when the world is problematized and when any end point of research becomes simultaneously as "raw material" for further research and investigation.[95] Conversely, says Lomnitz, the Mexican social scientist seeks to remap the familiar rather than defamiliarize it, which would be the opposite to the logic of Western social science.[96] With these distinctions in mind, Sáenz's experiment encouraged ways of addressing the world contrary to the majoritarian tradition in Mexican thought and the intellectual thrust of Catholicism in that nation. Sáenz's radical philosophy of education clashed with that of other nationalist Mexican intellectuals. In the next chapter, I will investigate how the Dewey project prompted a visceral reaction among these intellectuals and how this led to a critique of Dewey as a national danger to Mexican culture.

Yet for Sáenz, this project was as Deweyan as it was Mexican: this was not a contradiction. Here I would like to go back to the previous discussion on the *grandes problemas nacionales*. The rhetoric of becoming modern in Mexico meant resolving the great national problems of poverty and underdevelopment so that Mexico could enter the universal realm of modernity. If the practical man was the modern man and thus a universal figure for Sáenz, the national dimension clearly related to the national problem of creating a "unified soul." Thus there was something beyond Dewey's "most excellent doctrine" where the rural school's mission was to create the "Nation," integrating its elements in to a "unified soul." "But here among ourselves," Sáenz confided to his Mexican interlocutors, "where the Nation is yet to be fulfilled, it [the rural school] surpasses any norm and, not obeying anymore any pedagogical doctrine, but as daughter of the Revolution and instrument of the times, it advances the cause of the Motherland by becoming a factor of integration . . . to four million silenced (*mudos*) Indians and by presenting to all our dispersed members the idea of a united Mexico."[97]

Thus the school would always "think the nation."[98] And Sáenz, thinking the nation—"our problem is personal and unique," he wrote[99]—believed that the Dewey project's school—"thinking the nation" (*pensando en la patria*)—would lead the way to Mexico in the world.[100] Thus Dewey would lead Mexico into that modernity that was universal, but the expression of that modernity would be uniquely Mexican.

Case Studies

The project method intended to promote a new way for the subject to orient himself or herself toward the world: to view it as separate from oneself, yet interrelated to oneself, open to change and permanently in flux, and thus amenable to endless transformations. Reconstituting Dewey's urban schools into rural spaces was consonant with Sáenz's idea that he needed to adapt Dewey's schools into Mexican reality.

The archives have legated us with descriptions of actual schools operating during the years of 1925–1929, 1929, the core years of the experiments. Whereas most were probably not entirely reflective of the reality of everyday teaching, they do reflect the mythology that surrounded the implementation of Deweyan schools in Mexico.

The San Francisco Culhuacán School in México City, México

The socialized school of San Francisco Culhuacán, an indigenous town located on the margins of the Xochimilco Canal south of Mexico City, offers one case of an *escuela activa*. Sáenz declared it fully socialized in 1925 and working according to the precepts of the Dewey school. San Francisco Culhuacán provided a good place to start the project because it was a fully indigenous town of Nahuátl speakers, the original language of the Aztecs. Education officials considered the school to be partially incorporated into civilization for two reasons: the Natives also spoke Spanish fluently—they were bilingual—and their economy, although working according to the logic of Nahuátl customs, was also incorporated into the larger economy of the Valley of Mexico. According to Sáenz, although commercially engaged with the city of México, natives in San Francisco "prefer to live their lives in this village without paved streets or *veredas*."[101] It was the perfect backdrop for an experimental school. It possessed enough distance from civilization—racially—yet not entirely out of it economically.

In this model school, spontaneity ruled. The school did not appoint a director to run the school. Instead, each teacher assigned to the school worked on his or her own "little school," most of them located in diverse houses spread throughout the entire town. There were five of these "little schools" or "units," with one teacher coordinating projects among them, but without any status hierarchies implied.[102] A *sociedad de alumnos* or a students' association (most of them younger than sixteen) organized and directed the activities of the school and was granted real juridical personality or *personalidad real*.[103] Students created the association and thus practically ran the school, coordinating school activities with the five teachers of the "little schools" through the construction of the *huerto escolar*, which was divided into individual plots for cultivation by a team of students, with sections for the raising of rabbits, chickens, and pigs, and other sectors for the ubiquitous basket weaving and the manufacturing of light industries. Students generated their own knowledge along with teachers, who suggested links and associations and provided the broader picture in the classroom. The enterprise seemed to work well; Sáenz exulted that he had never visited a "more united and integrated school" in the entire nation. The children also organized their own savings bank, which lent money for the purchase of seeds, tools and other supplies. School enterprises and the students' associations generated formal learning. Students, for example, produced the curriculum strictly from all those activities related to the care of the *huerto*. Thus according to Sáenz, the students drew "plans for the plots, performed the accounting, wrote up a register of activities . . . and drew instruments of credit."[104] Sáenz praised the students' entrepreneurship and observed that the "teachers worked according to the children's projects, which are motivated by themselves as an integral part of their daily life."[105] For Sáenz, the school demonstrated that any locality could produce a school through the coordinated effort of the community.

San Fernando provided an example of what a laboratory school actually meant to Sáenz. Sáenz encouraged visiting teachers to the school to observe experimentalism as a way of life and come up with ideas for their own projects. The school offered a breeding ground for ideas, not models to be replicated. Sáenz did not necessarily desire schools such as San Fernando to become showcases that would lead to literal imitation. Each locality in the nation had to understand its own limitations but also its opportunities. That was the essence of the entrepreneurial life. Each school was partially tied to the state but constituted an enterprise of its own. Nor did the school have to operate as a capitalist enterprise. Entrepreneurship was not conflated with capitalism here. Sáenz encouraged the formation of "cooperatives," more egalitarian forms of industrial agricultural associations that were to be promoted by the state during the Cárdenas presidency after 1932.[106] San Fernando demonstrated that Sáenz neither desired the state to reproduce itself in the schools nor for social hierarchies to be replicated in the associated life of the school. His choice of San Fernando in 1925 as a model school or *escuela tipo* proves that Sáenz concurred with Dewey's respect for local communities, yet he vested that faith on a community's ability to come up with its own associated solutions as long as they were fully integrated in a process of state-led industrialization. Entrepreneurship was thus defined fully in terms of the productive and creative life.

80 *Saénz and the* Escuelas Activas

The Matomoros School in Tamaulipas, México

In Matamoros, Tamaulipas, México, inspector José de la Vega established another *escuela tipo*, a model school created for teaching the new method. By 1928, the school was in operation under the new system. From his report on his visit of 1928, one can obtain a glimpse of how a rural school in México operated according to the philosophy of two men from New York, the pedagogy of John Dewey and the methods of William H. Kilpatrick. de la Vega disposed of the traditional curriculum of the school and proposed to derive all subject matter from the everyday problems of students' lives. Students had to meet regularly with their teachers and reveal their everyday problems. It did not matter whether they were private or considered trivial, but according to de la Vega, all inquiry within the fabric of everyday life was productive. de la Vega wrote down students' problems to transform them into learning matter. Some of them were very simple, such as, "When I go out on vacation I need a suitcase to carry my things," or, "Sometimes I wish I could go to the movies on Sunday but I don't have money."[107] de la Vega asked students to identify problems related to the school such as the "lack of furniture," the "lack of showers," the "absence of a chicken house," having "no kitchen utensils," etc. Furthermore, they were asked to discuss problems related to the broader political community with rubrics such as "There are no bridges to cross the river." Teachers would also identify their own problems under rubrics such as "creating a newspaper," "we need to go camping," "we need chairs," etc.[108] After two hours of student-teacher sharing, de la Vega proceeded to create projects linking all problems he deemed important.

"Projects" became units grouping a diversity of these problems organized around a motif or specific goal using the *centro de interés* or "center of interest" method, which replaced organized subject matter in the classroom and whose resolution defined the course of the school year. For example, de la Vega determined that one project would be defined around the production of things: "making a desk for the Director; to construct a suitcase; to install showers; to paint and install floors in the showers, etc." Another project would focus on the larger problematic of association; for example, the reorganization of the library, the reorganization of the *fiesta* or festival, or an association for the dissemination of hygienic literature.[109] de la Vega asked students to organize themselves for the solution of these diverse projects and to make notes on any observation of empirical interest, and through their own associations, carry out these projects. Thus projects replaced categories such as biology, geography and other disciplinary categories.[110] All projects were correlated to convey the idea of the interdependence of human activities, such as when de la Vega created a project linking students, teachers and community members: they were to form a cooperative, fix up the central plaza and organize a sports competition as part of a town *fiesta* to benefit the school, and the larger community. For de la Vega, the project method socialized all learning, whereas at the same time teaching self-reflected activities that demonstrated how human purpose links all things. Thus the method simultaneously furthered Sáenz's goals to create modern ways of relating to the world and at the same time, the state's desire to socialize society thus homogenizing social contexts.[111]

This interconnectedness of all things social achieved through human purpose and labor was intensified by certain applications of the technique of correlation as distinct sectors of a project were linked to traditional subject matter. During the installation of showers, de la Vega connected the "history of iron" to the installation of showers. Rather than have the teachers teach physics and geography in the traditional way, students learned about iron as a metal, as a commodity and as part of the natural world through the project to install showers in the school.[112] Students initiated a lecture on the "history of iron" by sharing their empirical "observations" with the rest of the class. de la Vega then asked students to acquire data and annotate all evidence as information in their notebooks, especially the dates in which the materials for the installation were used.[113] Thus any project could lead to an infinite number of associations, creating by itself the class curriculum. It was important for de la Vega that students' activities produce the school curricula.

de la Vega also gave students *registros agrícolas* where students had to record teachers' instructions concerning work in orchards, their own observations and the course of each planting experiment.[114] Every orchard possessed a history, which the students had to carefully register, and which then had to be related to the teacher and other students in open class discussion sessions. Partly a record of planting, it was also a record of everyday experience, which led to the conversion of life experiences into abstract data out of which the student had to become self-conscious.[115] de la Vega instructed teachers that observations had to go beyond merely teaching agricultural skills, but to the self-awareness of how ideas are created and how they could be used later for further inquiry. de la Vega had students form discussion groups to create further problems, associate projects with their homes and communities and share evidence gathered in the field. Students were encouraged to keep track of their projects in writing and to make their own evaluation of the projects.

These methods and techniques offered a new way in Mexican education for students to communicate and relate to each other. In traditional schools, students read from books orally and in groups and did not take written exams, for the written word was distrusted. Each student was examined orally, one by one, by the teacher or corps of teachers in the classroom. Although methods involved a lot of memorization and recitation, the transition to the new system was about more than simply replacing the traditional methods of rote memorization: learning was productive and consensual, not "individual."

El Centro Anáhuac: The School as a Corporation

Many supporters of the *escuelas activas* equated the enterprise of schooling with a capitalist corporatized world. Alfredo Sánchez O., one of Sáenz's fiercest supporters and a teacher himself, called for the creation of an "associated child," a sort of technocratic vision of the future citizen.[116] Sánchez had been critical of the early efforts—1923–1925—to establish guidelines for the *escuelas activas*, and he argued that specific models of association were needed to guide teachers in the new methods. He decried the "chaotic state that prevails [in the school of action] for the diversity of manners whereby the vague and nebulous ideas disseminated in books, brochures and newspapers . . . have given way to the disorganization of the New School . . . I found myself a victim of its disorientations and confusions."[117] Sánchez argued that new orientations had to provide for a specific "rational order" wherein the new school could work. This new "rational order" or social context was the associated life understood in terms of institutions such as the capitalist corporation. Sánchez did not just invoke America as a model, but also argued that Korea had provided a social context for its progressive education based on "ethnic" or "organic" bases.[118]

For Sánchez, a social and democratic education necessitated the future citizen's immersion in a world of associations such as clubs, banks, newspapers, cooperatives, commissions, and social unions: to understand society was to understand the "functioning" of a corporation or business so that the child would understand the benefits of an associated life "without mental effort," as a matter of habit.[119] In his school *Centro Anáhuac*, Sánchez redefined the roles of students and teachers to create an *escuela activa* based around the notion of the corporation as the model of an active education. For example, Sánchez transformed himself from a teacher into an *asesor* or "consultant," while students, to perform their school work, established work cooperatives, mercantile associations, banks and city councils, learning through the "documentation and management of funds and mercantile transactions."[120]

According to Sánchez, students formed themselves in cooperatives or associations, hired their own workers, and administrated the "business." Students occupied "posts"—one per child was mandated, as some children, Sánchez notes, were occupying two posts at the same time.[121] They constituted themselves in social classes in a natural way with the purpose of bringing the project to fruition. Not all these activities were done from the first grade; Sánchez notes that students learned in gradual form, progressing grade by grade. Sánchez's purpose was for students to extend entrepreneurial epistemologies into all aspects of everyday life. Sáenz called the associated child a utilitarian child. "The child is utilitarian," he argued.[122] "He likes to take advantage of the opportunities he encounters . . . let's channel the child's ingenuity . . . children reach a stage of development through exchanges and transactions that derive a profit."[123]

It should not be surprising that visitors were amazed when they visited successful schools such as Sánchez's and witnessed children working at various activities within school grounds, most of the time with no supervision and seemingly with no coordination. This was the much commented and desired *desorden armonioso* or harmonious disorder, a creative enterprise within order.[124] For example, a school in southwest México, calling itself the House of the People, or *Casa del Pueblo*, visited by Sáenz in 1926, conveyed this idea well. Sáenz found around seventy-six children working individually or in small groups, some reading, others painting, sewing, planting in the *huerto*, whereas others struggled with a malcontented pig, a scene that Sáenz himself called, "the most exotic spectacle one could imagine in a school," especially for those "not aware of the development of the new type of rural schools in México."[125] Students were allowed to go home when their tasks were done, but there were always students left in the classroom to greet visitors or family. Sáenz noted the success of the system when students organized themselves to greet him with a fiesta and parade. The ability to translate ideas into organizations and organizations into ideas was the hallmark of the system even for children like these, at that time no older than sixteen.

Thus, teachers often converted their schools into operations that performed like commercial enterprises, for commerce provided the closest association to the kind of schools that Sáenz had in mind. Still it is important to note that Sáenz and school inspectors did not intend to convert schools into a "factory floor . . . [or a] commercial house, agency shop."[126] According to Sáenz, it was an, "exaggeration of utilitarianism given to school activities which has contributed by giving the schools a mercantilist and pseudoindustrial character."[127] Even if the school could conceivably perform such a role, as a project it always had to possess some meaning beyond itself, a "transcendental" goal according to Sáenz. To imitate in society a model created in school meant to operate according to primitive logic: to reproduce the familiar. This was the antithesis of the project method.

The Federal Schools of San Luis Potosí: The Limits to the Dewey Project

Few schools exemplified the future Mexican society that Sáenz intended to create as his project for the federal schools of San Luis Potosí. In the Federal Schools of San Luis Potosí, he launched a program to create schools "without pedagogy" where "it didn't matter to teach and read as long as one is teaching how to live!" In these schools "only the light of the classroom" would shine, and on any given day "peasants of the community" and what he called the "poor nostalgic *rancheros*" would come to the Mexican school to learn about the world and themselves. Once inside, he said, "we would all talk among ourselves with simplicity (*sencillez*)," perhaps laughing a little and then "read them something, share with them the many stories and the many epics there are to be told . . . [this will be] a school without pedagogy but worthy of its men."[128] This was the great community he envisioned.

Yet, by 1927, the schools signaled a turning point in the Deweyan project. The imagination of a future community of equals turned nostalgic, and the apparent failures of the Deweyan project began to take possession of Saénz's imagination. When he toured the schools that year, he encountered teachers who openly resisted the new method and others who had no idea of what the state desired to accomplish. Rather than a full-scale rebellion, teachers in the provinces simply could not understand what the new method was about, whereas others openly mocked it. For example, one of the Deweyan principles, the notion of the "world of production," in which schools had to insert themselves in the productive life of the community and reflect within its walls "the world of production," had become a source of confusion if not derision. San Luis Potosí was a mining region characterized by the extreme exploitation of young men by mine concerns and where most young girls found employment as *empleadas* or *mucamas* (housekeepers). Yet no attempts were made to reflect these "principles of life" in the school.

Most schools simply imitated the state plan set up by the government for the *escuelas activas*. They built chicken houses and pigeon houses for the most part, whereas a few others managed to have their own orchard and cultivation plot. Flowers and fruit gardens, symbols of abundance and faraway lands, died pretty quickly or were abandoned by teachers. The region being a desert, some teachers spent most of their time protecting the chickens from predators, whereas others saw their orchards disappear under the desert sun. In some towns, the flower and fruit gardens were established upon the grounds of former *haciendas*, which meant that the lands were under violent disputation by the community and local and state political bosses. In *La Presilla*, the *ejidatarios* or the peasants who now owned shares in the former *hacienda* opted for giving the town the orchard when it became impossible to decide who would get this precious land. The end result was the "constant depredation" of the orchard by angry *ejidatarios*.[129]

Very few managed to start their own production in the schools by making soaps, doing carpentry work, or dressmaking, manufacturing accessories for furniture, or various arts and crafts. Many of them resorted to creating crafts that conferred prestige upon the user, using fine cloth for dresses or *ixtle* (istle) for crafts. Saénz chastised the schools and the community for not "reflecting the principles of life." The productive life of the schools had to reflect the local economy. Cultural competence or cultural prestige as was promoted in the old school was not a productive endeavor.[130] Donning dresses with tropical fabrics or producing arts and crafts with fancy cloth did not promote growth and progress; it was akin to Mexicans in the desert eating strawberries because it was "European." Staging works of theater such as "The Sorrows of Young Werther" (*El mal de Werther*) could not be seen as a sign of progress when staged by young Indians in the deserts of San Luis Potosí.

In that case, which were "principles of life" that should structure learning in the schools? What could be the "world of production" that would inform the school's mission to create new productive selves? Sáenz's identified the desert as the social and economic world the schools were to engage, because it was the desert that characterized the economy and ecology of San Luis Potosí. He praised, for example, those schools that managed to build wells in the desert and find water. In the town of *Lo de Acosta*, he commended the school for adjusting its productive life to the desert by managing to find water to drink and for agriculture and sustaining a cultivation plot with beans and maize, which even made a profit for that school, which it then used to set up a cooperative mutual fund for purchasing school materials. The school had become a successful productive enterprise in the middle of the desert. The teacher of this school became an ideal for others because of her efforts in leading the school to become a productive center, thus fulfilling the ideal of the accommodation of the school to society. It was here that Sáenz exclaimed to the shocking surprise of his enemies that reading books did not matter when students were learning how to live.[131]

The successful resolution of the method's problems in the town of *Lo de Acosta* also demonstrated one important and conscious limit that Sáenz imposed on the Deweyan schools that he desired to spread to the rest of the nation. In the midst of extreme religious and political violence, the school's inner world could never reflect that violence. As opposed to the earlier urban experiments in progressive education that preceded the state project, class and racial strife would not intrude the walls of the school; it was an exogenous factor affecting the conduct of the schools, as Sáenz acknowledged during his visit to San Luis Potosí when he commented on the violence against orchards in water-starved towns or when he condemned the fanatical behavior of Catholic *cristeros* attempting to disrupt the conduct of the schools.[132] It reflected the strongest connection of Sáenz to Dewey's renunciation of violence as the foundation of a nation-building education system even as it confounded those who understood idea of the "school as a community in miniature" in opposite ways. In his visits to regions such as San Luis Potosí and La Sierra de Puebla, for example, the violent campaign of the state against the Catholic Church was for the most part ignored in his school reports and letters. The "accommodation of the school to society" did not recognize coercion as a way to hold communities together.

Nor did Sáenz, at least not initially, recognize the violence implied in the logic of his method when it came to changing the minds of Mexican Natives. Their understanding of the social world contrasted with the state's cartographic mind, but in the method proposed by Sáenz there was no recognition of their social world as part of the society the school should accommodate to. Many if not most of the communities that Sáenz visited were indigenous towns. In *La Concepción*, for example, Sáenz examined classroom practices in order to see if they conformed to the method and if progress had been made in the schools. He found that Mexican Indians could neither identify the name of the state nor the name of the town where they lived. "They could not tell where San Luis Potosí or Laredo is. On the wall, there was a map of Mexico, but they did not know what it represented; they could not tell either where the North was."[133] Indians' concept of time, of history and of space had to be transformed, but the method did not recognize that transformation as such, but only as a form of collective ignorance.

School reports suggest that indigenous and other peasants actually imagined the space of the school as the site of social engagement. Thus, rather than the school accommodating itself to the social world imagined by Sáenz, as the Deweyan philosophy seemed to dictate, indigenous students conceptualized the school as a place or a site for the engagement of distinct social worlds. The method deployed Dewey's idea of history and technology to define the social world the school would engage, rather than the contested historically defined social spaces that Mexican citizens—Indians and non-Indians—recognized as Mexico. The application of the method did not recognize the ability of the Mexican Indian to synthesize the secular version of time of the state with the religious calendar of the Catholic religion. Such was the case when Sáenz deplored an Indian official in a small town who remarked on the felicitous convergence of the *fiesta* of the Virgin Mary and the opening of the school. In this case, if for Indians there could be two calendars—one religious and another state-imposed—for the state-directed mind of Sáenz, one had to displace the other.

It could be argued that progressive schools in America, which to a great extent intended to facilitate the socialization of diverse immigrant groups, implemented the method correctly because they lived in an already secularized industrial society. But in a nation like Mexico, where memory, especially Native memory, contested the legitimacy of the state, the historical narrative of the European conquest, and the class and racial system that sustained society, socialization had to be imagined upon different grounds than those of the United States. Thus the epistemology of the Indian imagination had to be transformed in ways different from those of European immigrants to the United States. Historical memories had to be homogenized but based on the erasure of "ancient claims." Only then could the notions of the "accommodation of school to society" and the "principles of life" become valid. For that reason, every aspect of this project sustained the idea that socialization—as the site for the resolution of the problems of the nation—was the precondition to the larger goal of making the Mexican mind practical and modern, even when both goals were implemented simultaneously.

Finally, as in other school projects, the schools of San Luis Potosí enlisted the population at large in the construction of school projects, in the building of schools and cultivation plots, and in sharing the learning activities of the school. The community also received students and teachers whose mission was to teach modern habits, who participated in the school *fiestas*, and explained how the community could serve as a market for the products of the schools. These activities established consent, and the exchanges that sustained them were intended to cement the role of the school as motor of change and as a place for the exchange of information.[134] The pragmatism of these exchanges consisted in the fact that the relationship of the peasant to the school, as opposed to his relationship to the church, was imagined as consensual. Acts of cooperation with the school constituted peasants as agents giving consent to new state-citizen relationships.

In spite of the achievements of some of the schools in the region, Sáenz's tours of the region produced the first major self-critique of the project by Sáenz. The tours of San Luis Potosí had placed Sáenz in intimate and sustained contact with indigenous peasants perhaps for the first time in his life and that of the other officers of the SEP who traveled with him. Thus in his recommendations to the state, Sáenz argued that "thinking the Indian" without understanding the nuances of their social organization undermined the project. The vision of the Indian communities promoted by the state and education officials as "harmonious" did not reflect itself in the everyday experience of teachers and missionaries who had to deal with complex local political formations. Thus it was not the civilizational fatalism of the Indian peasant that made impossible the accommodation of the school to society; it was the "fatalism" of the education officer, which undermined the "dynamism" of the locality.[135]

Another symptom of the fragility of the civilization narrative that sustained the project occurred as Sáenz's doubts increased on whether civilization—and thus the modernity he sought to create in Mexico—was indeed good for the Indian, if not for Mexico as a whole. The Secretariat of Education, where Sáenz functioned as sub-secretary, was fully wedded to the civilizational mission that the state promoted and that anthropologists working within the department produced in their ethnographies. Sáenz, in what was truly an exceptional vision among these officials, began a measured yet persistent criticism of civilization with his tours of San Luis Potosí and in that same year La sierra de Puebla. In Potosí, he remarks that "nevertheless, once confronted with the *hacienda*, the grand and silent house that overlooks the sugar plantation (*ingenio*) . . . one feels that eternal tearing of the Mexican heart and then doubts assault us with the thought that would not it be better for the peasant (*ejidatario*) that moves through the countryside like little ants, would it not be better to continue making old-fashioned *piloncillo* rather than having industrial capitalism continue to do it."[136]

These critiques to the philosophy of the project reflected the historical ambivalence that characterized the discourse of civilization, on the one hand producing a critique of its foundations, on the other not preventing Sáenz from criticizing the poor "entrepreneurial" mind-set of rural Mexico and the "lack of ideological adaptation" exhibited by teachers unable to figure out ways to make the project feasible in the desert.[137] "It is not agricultural labor that necessarily characterizes a rural school," he chastised them. Teachers must not pretend to establish an agricultural social world within the premises of the new rural schools of the revolution when in fact the region was a desert. He instructed them instead to create a "functional" world that "reflected" the world of the desert and admonished them to bring into the school the economy of the household, such as spinning with *ixtle* or tanning leather. The Dewey school, according to Sáenz, should seek "the reflection of the school environment"[138] within the school. "It must establish," he said, "a spiritual relation . . . to the community, give the teacher a community consciousness, and make the school the house of the people and the people the house of the school."[139] In other words, where was the great community?

The Carapan Project

In the year of 1932, Sáenz embarked on a new enterprise separate from the *escuelas activas* project, which by this time had for all purposes ended under a new presidential administration. This new project, the *Estación Experimental de Incorporación del Indio* (Experimental Station for the Incorporation of the Indian), funded by the Secretariat of Public Education and its Department of Rural Schools, functioned as an educational laboratory for the future "incorporation" of Native Mexicans into Mexican civilization, which for Sáenz meant the secular national culture of Spanish-speaking Mexico. Sáenz established this experimental station in the state of Michoacán in Los Once Pueblos at its seat in Carapan. The laboratory opened in June of 1932 and closed in January of 1933 when Sáenz left the SEP.[140] Carapan's 800 indigenous people and 236 school-age children offered Sáenz the opportunity to work in a community where he could study "the Indian right at the time when he becomes Mexican."[141] This project has been cited as the last of the Deweyan experiments in Mexico because of the quite flexible approach to the civilizational mission and the activity-based education employed for *socialización* purposes. Whereas this is correct, I argue that the project actually departed in important ways from the Deweyan principles that Sáenz had espoused, yet it offers a valuable way to understand Sáenz's self-critique and the insights it provides (in retrospect) on the meaning of his *escuelas activas* project.

The experimental station intended purely to find ways to integrate Indians into the nation, and thus it sought more efficient paths for socializing Native Mexicans. Working on a mostly adult population, the station's curricula employed activities such as singing, reading newspapers, watching films, listening to music, learning how to tell stories and lecturing on national political and economic issues in order to establish a discussion-based learning culture in the classroom.[142] The emphasis on "thinking the nation," which had characterized Sáenz's national project, dominated instruction, but the techniques and goals had been modified. Carapan implicitly stood as a criticism of the state project of the *escuelas activas* as it moved away from the objective of creating a new modern self with new cognitive abilities focusing exclusively on the racial integration of Mexico. Sáenz explicitly criticized the "futility of so many sporadic and puerile activities of our so-called *Escuela de la Acción* (school of action): small trials and simulacra so fledgling and false that they did not serve even as stimulants for further action let alone as exercises valuable in-themselves."[143] The pedagogy, the method, had become an end in itself and had not worked as instrument for change. "The new school focuses on the most fundamental and immediate needs of the people: this the new school gets right," cried out Sáenz.[144] Why did it fail, then? It did because it did not "abandon its exclusive reliance on pedagogy." It had failed to become "a more encompassing social organism," explained Sáenz, "an instrument of civilization . . . of material improvement, of work."[145] It had failed to create a practical man of modernity.

It had also failed to socialize Indians as Sáenz had wished. As he traveled through Los Once Pueblos, he observed how the techniques to create a society-in-miniature within the school had been abandoned or neglected.[146] There was no "thinking the nation": Indians could not understand the context for the national newspapers that he read to them; they did not recognize the names of national officials as he read them biographies of dignitaries, what he called "the civil directory of Mexico."[147] They did not engage projects thinking of national integration, but to satisfy local needs. It had failed because the pedagogy had engaged Indians as an abstract population instead of focusing on each individual native, each particular locale. "The better we [knew] the Indian," he opined, "the more Indian they [became] to us."[148] The state had not respected their religious life by closing churches. Although not a Catholic, Sáenz concluded that closing "temples" had been a failure. As a negative technique, it had only strengthen the enemies of the Dewey project in the villages[149] in spite of the fact that the church promoted submission, opposed democracy and rejected firmly the idea of a world open to human interpretation. He favored now "positive acts of substitution and re-orientation, rather than suppression and persecution."[150]

In Carapan, the school had not replaced the church. In fact, when Sáenz arrived in Carapan, his committee met with active resistance from groups seeking to reopen the village church, which happened frequently because the station's schools occupied former church buildings. Passive resistance struck Sáenz even more deeply because it demonstrated the diverse ways that Indians dealt with worlds foreign to them through "dissimulation."[151] "The Indian obeys, but does not collaborate," Sáenz wrote in his memoirs, ironically echoing a truly national sentiment dating to the era of Spanish colonialism of Mexicans who obey, but do not comply. Thus social behavior could have two meanings with one level of signification concealed to the outsider. Sáenz's insights of the futility of civilizing the Indian, which had begun firmly in his travels to San Luis Potosí, deepened during his Carapan experience. Yet, rather than blame failure simply on "apathy," he came to realize that *apatía* did not signify a cultural (or cognitive) failure, but stemmed simply from "isolation." "What happens in the *Cañada* does not happen because the *comarca* is Indian," he concluded, "but because it has been isolated."[152] Isolated, that is, from civilization, from the center of national life. Although buttressed by orientalist convictions, Sáenz firmly believed that an appreciation of the positive qualities of Native Mexicans informed this process of socialization.[153] Yet, a deepening appreciation of the complexities of Native life did not mean an abandonment of his belief that the future of Mexico meant integration. "Mexico is by definition not a country of Indians or whites, but of Mexicans," he claimed.[154]

Perhaps in rebellion against the open-ended and flexible quality of Deweyan instruction in the *escuelas tipos*, in Carapan Sáenz found solace in a newfound scientism, condemning the "practicism" of the national project. He mused about finding a "mexicanization index" with positive values against which to evaluate assimilation.[155] In Carapan, he placed his faith in the power of the census and social science to catalogue and know the Indian objectively even as he criticized the *escuelas activas* project for objectifying them in the first place.[156] He found that rewarding people with money mobilized their entrepreneurial skills more than when they were taught to think the nation.[157] Wasn't that the real incentive behind the American entrepreneur's magical efforts? He also came to embrace the aesthetic dimensions of everyday life by promoting music, dance and popular arts, not for the market value they could produce, but as "gratifications of aesthetic life."[158] Observing how artistic production expressed shared cultural values and motivated his students to participate in class, he supported them and integrated them into the curricula.

Ironies of Carapan as a Progressive Experiment

It seems from the archival records of the project and from his own memoirs that, as the Carapan laboratory experiment came to an end, Sáenz abandoned even this brief foray into scientific rigor and Western colonial imaginaries, reimagining Mexico's integration (a project he would never abandon) in ways Deweyan pedagogues would embrace but that Sáenz articulated as an all-encompassing critique of the *escuelas activas* and Deweyan pedagogy. For example, he critiqued those who conceived the civilizational mission as a one-way street, instead proposing that cultural change must always imply mutual transformation and responsibilities. Socialization implied, he claimed, "mutual participation of benefits and responsibilities."[159] "When socializing the Indian," he added, "we will perforce socialize ourselves and this means that being good Mexicans means learning to be better Indians."[160] This acceptance of the Indian—"I believe that the Indian dwells within ourselves"—led to the realization that the Deweyan project and the Carapan laboratory were inherently colonial enterprises. But surprisingly, Sáenz avoided the romanticism of those embracing Indian culture while rejecting all ties to Western society. He expressed his belief that the enterprise could be justified if it became an offering implying that its potential rejection by the Native would be an inherent component of such an offer.

Thus Sáenz reaffirmed his commitment to the civilizational mission. It did seem that now, participating in a pedagogical project as a teacher rather than simply as a government official, Sáenz had become himself a practical man, working, as he recognized, "on the basis of intelligent improvisation."[161] Yet this new practical man worked within the self-imposed cage of the *mission civilisatrice* because ultimately what could never be abandoned was the reconstruction of Mexican culture within the structure of a nation-state, which was, after all, the political form within which Deweyey imagined the United States and that they desired for themselves. "A Mexico loyal to its indigenous ancestry will be more powerful in the struggle against imperialism than one merely Europeanized," he claimed.[162] The imperative of nation-building to strengthen Mexican sovereignty could not be abandoned.

Conclusion: The End of the Dewey Project

In his conference essay *México Indio* of 1934, Sáenz restated the necessary character of any *mission civilisatrice* as an offer of "any part of the civilization that we posses," an offer that by necessity rejected "the idea of superiority" and a recognition that the Indian did possess its own and independent political organization.[163] Yet, by that time, Sáenz's project had ended and the *escuelas activas* had been fully replaced by the *escuela socialista* (socialist school) under the new presidential administration of General Cárdenas. In most communities, the Dewey project had collapsed long before. Mexican teachers never understood how the project method worked and returned to traditional techniques of memorization and oral examinations. Education supervisors reported widespread disorientation and preference for *peor es nada* education ("better than nothing" education).[164] As one inspector informed, only "inertia, pusillanimity, abandonment and incapacity" ruled.[165] In classrooms, students idled away in class, sacrificing reading to manual work, or in many cases "took over" the classroom. When students worked together in school, they did so without investigating the "industrial possibilities" of the products they made and without researching the market in the surrounding area: they could not transform products into commodities.[166] Peasants complained that children performed in schools the same tasks their parents asked them to do on the farms. Parent thus asked why they should send students to do at school what they would do in the fields if they had no education: school and society distanced themselves from each other, complained an inspector.[167] In cities such as Juárez, the meaning of community and society were constantly complicated as families crossed the border and took their children to schools in El Paso for they understood community to extend beyond the political boundaries of Mexican towns.[168] Nowhere was the practical man of modernity to be seen.

In many rural areas, teachers mocked the method, whereas parents complained that their children were being asked to become Protestant.[169] "Passive resistance" from devout Catholics, whom the supporters of the *escuelas activas* called "fanatics" doomed the project in many areas of the nation. Rafael Ramírez, Moisés Sáenz's right-hand man, told the story of a teacher who implored him to explain how to generate the school curriculum from student work in the "orchard." Apparently, students had work in the "orchard," and this activity would lead to the study of chemistry, physics and history. In another instance Ramírez faced a female teacher who similarly could not generate a school curriculum out of the agricultural activities of students in the school chicken house. Ramírez asked her to take two chicken eggs (*"dos huevos"*) and come up with a lesson plan for the next day. On the following day, Ramírez showed up and found the teacher unable to come up with anything. Ramírez scolded her and told her she could very well teach chemistry by looking at the interaction of the *dos huevos* or teach history by invoking the story of how Christopher Columbus convinced Europeans that the earth was round by playing with an egg on a table. With the entire class in laughter, Ramírez concluded that the educational situation in Mexico was quite serious when a female teacher could not come up with anything to do with Ramírez's *huevos*.[170] Misogynist? Yes. An apocryphal story? Absolutely not.[171]

The Dewey project in Mexico exposed a deep irony in the translation of Dewey's ideas. The Mexican revolution responded to the desire of local communities to preserve their autonomy versus an encroaching state and a domineering provincial government. These communities expressed their love of Mexico through a deeply felt patriotism most often centered on national religious symbols. Dewey's philosophy did not necessarily oppose patriotism and certainly not the local. In fact, Dewey had castigated the rise of authoritarian states in Europe and the mythologized national histories that displaced local patriotic sentiment in Japan. In spite of this similarity of spirit, the Dewey project was framed within the larger and violent imposition of the national state upon local communities, most of whom attempted to negotiated with the state in order to preserve autonomy yet accept the features of modernity that they deemed acceptable. Furthermore, the project was implemented by a Mexican Protestant whose own community had formed in the nineteenth century when displaced members of the body public sought to defend their autonomy and converted to Protestantism as a way to provide a structure for their beliefs and values. Yet, the implementation of the *escuelas activas* obeyed the larger logic of the transition to modernity and the necessity of constituting oneself as a nation-state as the only possible way to become modern and simultaneously strengthen the Mexican state versus American imperialism. The belief that America's present was Mexico's future constituted one of the great problems of the narrative of the transition to modernity, which dictated that capitalist development was inevitable, but it also explains why Mexicans knew more and cared more about the United States (and Dewey) than Americans (or Dewey) did about Mexico. The proximity of Mexico to the United States prevented the "idea of America" from ever becoming fully romanticized as Dewey noted had been the case in China and Turkey. The prism of the "transition to modernity" should also explain why modern ways of thinking (as those believed to characterize the students of the laboratory schools) generated by industrialization in the United States were thought in Mexico to cause modernity, thus reversing their historical role.

Notes

1. Moisés Sáenz, "Newer Aspects of Education in Mexico," *Bulletin of the Pan American Union 9*, vol. LXIII (September 1929): 862.
2. Moisés Sáenz, "El Papel de la escuela de la acción en la República" *Boletín de la Secretaría de Educación Pública 7*, vol. IV (México: Talleres Gráficos de la Nación, Publicaciones de la Secretaría de Educación, México 1925), 76.
3. Moisés Sáenz, "Newer Aspects of Education in Mexico," 863–864.
4. Claudio Lomnitz-Adler, *Exits from the Labyrinth*, xvi-xviii.
5. In this sense, Sáenz was a man of his times. José Vasconcelos, later his bitter rival, had subscribed to the notion that the Latin man was a theoretical man whereas the Anglo-Saxon was a practical man. The Anglo-Saxon man constructed his world out of his experience of the world, whereas the Latin man reduced his experience of the world to a priori ideas. See José Vasconcelos, *La Raza Cósmica*, translated by Didier T. Jaén (Baltimore: The John Hopkins University, 1979).
6. On this last point see Ernest Gellner, *Nations and Nationalism* and Dipesh Chakrabarti, *Provincializing Europe: Postcolonial Thought and Historical Difference* (Princeton, NJ: Princeton University Press, 2000).
7. Moisés Sáenz, *Some Mexican Problems*, 78.
8. Ibid.
9. "Bases para la organización de la escuela primaria conforme al principio de la acción" in *Publicaciones de la Secretaría de Educación Pública 8*, vol. X (México: Talleres Gráficos de la Nación, 1926), 3.
10. Ibid., 6.
11. Ibid., 3
12. Ibid.
13. Ibid., 7.
14. Ibid.
15. ibid., 11.
16. Ibid., 5.
17. Ibid., 4.
18. See Dr. J.M. Casauranc, "Plática que sobre asuntos educativos y en respuesta a preguntas concretas de algunos señores profesores, sustentó el ciudadano secretario de educación pública, Doctor J.M. Puig Casauranc, el día dos de abril del presente año en la primera session del Congreso de Directores Federales" *Boletín de la Secretaría de Educación Pública 1*, vol. 4 (Mexico, April 1925), 10–12.
19. See Sáenz's report in Dr. J.M. Casauranc, *El Esfuerzo educativo en México: la obra del gobierno federal en el ramo de educación pública durante la administración del Presidente Plutarco Elías Calles (1924–1928): Memoria analítico-crítica de la organización actual de la Secretaría de Educación Pública sus éxitos, sus fracasos, los derroteros que la experiencia señala. Presentada al H. Congreso de la Unión por el Dr. J.M. Puig Casauranc, Secretario del Ramo en obediencia al artículo 93 constitucional*, Tomo 1 (México: Publicaciones de la Secretaría de Educación Pública, 1928), 27.

20. Ibid., 15–26.
21. Ibid., 50–51.
22. See Ida B. DePencier, *The History of the Laboratory Schools: The University of Chicago, 1896–1965* (Chicago: Quadrangle Books, 1967), 13–28.
23. General Plutarco Elías Calles, "Speech at the opening of the ordinary sessions of Congress" (September 1st of 1927) *México a través de los informes presidenciales, Volume II, La Educación* Pública (México: Secretaría de Educación Pública, Secretaría de la Presidencia, 1976), 178–179.
24. Salvador Alvarado, "El Problema de la educación," 116.
25. John Dewey, *The School and Society and the Child and the Curriculum* (Chicago: The University of Chicago Press, 1991), 18.
26. Moisés Sáenz, *El papel de la escuela de la acción en la República*, 74.
27. See also General Álvaro Obregón, "Speech on September 1st of 1924 at the opening of the 3rd Congress on its first year of sessions" (September 1st 1924) in *México a través de los informes presidenciales*, 166.
28. "Circular del 15 de febrero de 1923" quoted in Rafael Ramírez, *La enseñanza por la acción dentro de la escuela rural*, 18, 22.
29. See for example the discussion on libraries in Moisés Sáenz, "Conferencia del Señor Moisés Sáenz, subsecretario de Educación Pública, dictada ante el Primer Congreso Nacional de Bibliotecarios, el día 18 de marzo de 192," *Boletín de la Secretaría de Educación Pública* 4, vol. VI (Mexico, 1927), 21–25.
30. Dr. J. M. Casauranc, *El Esfuerzo educativo en México*, 157.
31. These various annexes are described in various reports of the Secretariat of Public Education. The most complete is that of Sáenz in *El Esfuerzo educativo en México*, 21–28.
32. See for example, Rafael Ramírez, *La enseñanza por la acción dentro de la escuela rural*, 13–47.
33. Moisés Sáenz, "Newer Aspects of Education in Mexico," 862.
34. José de la Vega, "Informe de José de la Vega. El método de proyectos aplicado a las escuelas normales rurales" *Boletín de la Secretaría de Educación Pública* 5, vol. VII (Mexico: Secretaria de educacion publica, May 1928), 316.
35. Dr. J. M. Casauranc, *El Esfuerzo educativo en México*, 157.
36. In contemporary scholarship, Claudio Lomnitz has addressed this issue directly. The will to know of "First World" social scientists is that of making the strange familiar and the familiar strange. The will to know of the Mexican intellectual, the essayist or *pensador*, is to "reframe the familiar." Empirical research proceeds mostly from the former; the latter is mostly "discarded into a pool of reusable symbols," and as "artistic perceptions of social reality," do not lead to an accumulation of knowledge. See Claudio Lomnitz-Adler, *Exits from the Labyrinth*, 8–9.
37. William Heard Kilpatrick, *Foundations of Method: Informal Talks on Teaching* (New York: Macmillan, 1925), 141.
38. John L. Childs, "The Civilizational Functions of Philosophy and Education," *John Dewey and the World View*, edited by Douglas E. Lawson and Arthur E. Lean (Carbondale: Southern Illinois University Press, 1964), 6–8.
39. William Heard Kilpatrick, "The Project Method: Child Centeredness in Progressive Education," *History Matters*, http://historymatters.gmu.edu/d/4954/
40. Ibid.
41. See Sáenz's report in Dr. J. M. Casauranc, *El Esfuerzo educativo en México*, 195.
42. See Ibid.
43. Gregorio Torres Quintero, "Coordinación de los programas de las escuelas federales con los de los gobiernos locales" in *Memorias de los trabajos realizados en la junta de directores de educación federal, verificada en la ciudad de México,*

del 24 de mayo al 2 de junio de 1926 (México: Publicaciones de la Secretaría de Educación, 1926), 91.
44. Ibid.
45. See for example, Rafael Ramírez, *La enseñanza por la acción*, 29; Moisés Sáenz, "El Papel de la escuela de la acción en la República," 74. This technique was originally introduced in Europe by Decroly and taken by Dewey to Chicago.
46. Ibid., 16.
47. Ernest Gellner, *Nations and Nationalism*, 21–23.
48. Rafael Ramírez, *La enseñanza por la acción*, 29.
49. José de la Vega, "Informe de José de la Vega," 219–220.
50. See Sáenz's report in Dr. J.M. Casauranc, *El Esfuerzo educativo en México*, 193.
51. Rafael Ramírez, *La enseñanza por la acción*, 9.
52. General Álvaro Obregón, "Speech at the opening of the 30th Congress in its Second Year of Sessions" (September 1st 1923), *México a través de los informes presidenciales, Volume II, La Educación* Pública (Mexico: Secretaría de Educación Pública, Secretaría de la Presidencia, 1976), 159.
53. Ibid., 151.
54. ibid., 156.
55. Moisés Sáenz, "Algunos aspectos sintéticos de la educación en México," 34.
56. Moisés Sáenz, *La educación rural en México*, 25.
57. Moisés Sáenz, *La educación rural*, 33.
58. Rafael Ramírez, *La enseñanza por la acción*, 8.
59. See also Moisés Sáenz, "El Papel de la escuela de la acción en la República," 80.
60. "Informe del director de educación federal en el estado de Tamaulipas, con relación a las escuelas primarias, correspondientes a los meses de noviembre y diciembre de 1927" *Boletín de la Secretaría de Educación Pública* 3, vol. VII (México: Talleres Gráficos de la Nación, March 1928), 72.
61. "Informe del director de educación federal en el estado de Tamaulipas, 72.
62. José de la Vega, "Informe de José de la Vega, 217.
63. Moisés Sáenz, *La educación rural en México*, 21.
64. Moisés Sáenz, *Some Mexican Problems*, 74; Moisés Sáenz, "Algunos aspectos sintéticos de la educación en México," 36.
65. Moisés Sáenz, *La educación rural en México*, 10.
66. Moisés Sáenz, "Discurso pronunciado por radio en Dallas, Texas, E.U.A. (November 26, 1925) in *Boletín de la Secretaría de Educación Pública* 1, vol. V (México, January 1926), 29.
67. Moisés Sáenz, "Algunos aspectos sintéticos de la educación en México," 37.
68. Moisés Sáenz, *Some Mexican Problems*, 70.
69. Moisés Sáenz, "Algunos aspectos sintéticos de la educación en México," 33.
70. See Westbrook rightfully makes this point in his biography of Dewey. See Robert B. Westbrook, *John Dewey and American Democracy* (Ithaca, NY: Cornell University Press, 1991).
71. Moisés Sáenz, "Algunos aspectos sintéticos de la educación en México," 33.
72. See for example Moisés Sáenz, "El Papel de la escuela de la acción en la República," 77.
73. For example, Rafael Ramírez, *La enseñanza por la acción dentro de la escuela rural*, 23, 35–36.
74. See for example, Moisés Sáenz, *Reseña de la educación pública en México*, 18, 33.
75. Ibid.
76. John Dewey, *The School and Society and the Child and the Curriculum* (Chicago: The University of Chicago Press, 1900, 1991), 77–78.
77. Moisés Sáenz, "Algunos aspectos sintéticos de la educación en México," 33.

96   *Saénz and the* Escuelas Activas

78. Alfredo Sánchez O., "Rectificaciones y aclaraciones sobre la escuela nueva" *Boletín de la Secretaría de Educación Pública*, 24. Sánchez compared Mexico to Korea in this respect. It was quite common to make frame the dilemmas of Mexico's modernization in comparison to Japan or Korea, nations whose modernization would have been facilitated by their martial character and racial homogeneity. See also new school teacher José Juan Tablada on the martial qualities of the Japanese and their "intact" genius. José Juan Tablada, "El libro de un educador" *Boletín de la Secretaría de Educación Pública* 5, vol. V (México: May 1926), 22; also published in *La Prensa* (March 20, 1926).
79. See for example, Moisés Sáenz, "Algunos aspectos sintéticos de la educación en México,"36; also, Moisés Sáenz, *Some Mexican Problems*, 74.
80. Ibid., 72.
81. The nationalist discourses that addressed the incorporation of Native Mexicans into society at this time suffered from a great degree of ambiguity concerning the location of the Native in history with the Native at times referred to as truly Mexican and as a Mexican-to-be subject simultaneously. This is due in part to the very aporetic nature of nationalist language in nations such as Mexico where the foundational past or origins of the nation was located in the bodies and histories of people who had been conquered during the founding of the *patria* or fatherland by the colonial power. In this case, Sáenz made a distinction between Mexican and Indian wherein the Indians' civilization process corresponded to their transition into national society (racial homogeneity) as a precondition to modernization (thus making the Indian into a Mexican was both a modernizing and a modernizing-to-be transition). In fact, integration without sacrifice meant exactly that according to Sáenz: "through our little rural school we are trying to integrate Mexico and to create in our peasant classes a rural spirit. To integrate Mexico. To bring into the fold of the Mexican family the two million Indians; to make them think and feel in Spanish. To incorporate them into that type of civilization which constitutes the Mexican nationality. To bring them into that community of ideas and emotions which is Mexico." See Moisés Sáenz, *Some Mexican Problems*, 72.
82. Ibid., 57.
83. Moisés Sáenz, *La educación rural en México*, 9.
84. Moisés Sáenz, *Some Mexican Problems*, 60.
85. Dr. José Manuel Puig Casauranc, "Speech at Teachers' College, Columbia University, New York (23rd & 24th of March 1926) *Boletín de la Secretaría de Educación Pública* 4, vol. V (México, 1926), 5; also published separately and in English in *Addresses delivered by Dr. J. M. Puig Casauranc, Secretary of Public Education of Mexico, the 23rd and 24th of March, 1926, at Columbia University, New York* (México: Talleres Gráficos de la Nación, Secretaría de Educación, 1926).
86. Sáenz spoke oftentimes of the aesthetic virtues of the Mexican Indian or their "artistic temperament" or "soul." He also extolled their character as "wonderfully patient," "quiet," and physically strong. "Oh, the music and the dancing and the painting and the weaving of the Indian," he exclaimed, "his love of form and his instinct for color!" See Moisés Sáenz, *Some Mexican Problems*, 73. Casauranc went even further by claiming that the "artistic power" of the Native was of such "high order" that it conformed with the Indian's "physiological features of racial superiority" (size of the eye, teeth and the length of the intestinal tubes according to him) conformed to that power. See Dr. José Manuel Puig Casauranc, "Speech at Teachers' College," 4. Most of these attributions, though, feminized the Indian vis-à-vis the European superior rational powers. According to Claudio Lomnitz "the principal ideologists of Mexican nationalism [in post-revolutionary México] imagined the *mestizo* as the product of a

Spanish father and an indigenous mother . . . it made the Spanish Conquest the origin of the national race and culture . . . and even more important, the identification of the European with the male and the feminization of the Indian fit well with the formulation of a nationalism that was at once modernizing and protectionist." See Claudio Lomnitz, *Deep Mexico, Silent Mexico: An Anthropology of Nationalism* (Minneapolis, MN: University of Minnesota Press, 2001), 53.
87. Moisés Sáenz, "Newer Aspects of Education in Mexico," 877.
88. Moisés Sáenz, *Some Mexican Problems*, 57–58.
89. Ibid., 59–60.
90. Ibid., 60.
91. Aguirre called Sáenz's project the thesis of incorporation because at its core it aimed to create a nation by the racial homogenization of the Indian and mixed race—*mestizo*—population. His project thus attempted to incorporate the Indian into civilization as opposed to creating segregated areas for their uplift as was the case (in their minds) in the US reservation system.
92. Gonzalo Aguirre Beltrán, "Introducción: El hombre y su obra" Rafael Ramírez, *La escuela rural mexicana* (México: Fondo de Cultural Económica, SE/80, 1981), 27.
93. For a discussion of this notion of the modern self, see Dipesh Chakrabarti, *Provincializing Europe*, 117–148.
94. Ernest Gellner, *Nations and Nationalism*, 22.
95. Larry Hickman, "Dewey's Theory of Inquiry," 179.
96. This nationalist Mexican will to knowledge has not led to the production of empirical research in the way that European and American universities have, and has not resulted in the accumulation of knowledge that Western social science promotes. See Lomnitz-Adler, *Exits from the Labyrinth*, 8–9.
97. Moisés Sáenz, *La educación rural en México*, 25.
98. Ibid.
99. Moisés Sáenz, "Newer Aspects of Education in Mexico," 877.
100. Moisés Sáenz, *La educación rural en* México, 25.
101. Moisés Sáenz, "Una escuela socializada" *Boletín de la Secretaría de Educación Pública* 6, vol. IV (September 1925) (México: Talleres Gráficos de la Nación, Publicaciones de la Secretaría de Educación Pública, vol. V, no. 15, 1925), 246.
102. Ibid.
103. Ibid.
104. Ibid., 247.
105. Ibid.
106. Ibid., 246.
107. de la Vega, opus cit., 218–219.
108. José de la Vega, "Informe de José de la Vega," 218.
109. Ibid., 219.
110. According to Kilpatrick, "the purposeful act [was] the typical unit of the worthy life" and thus projects reify purposes. See William Heard Kilpatrick, "The Project Method," http://historymatters.gmu.edu/d/4954/
111. José de la Vega, "Informe de José de la Vega," 219.
112. Ibid.
113. Ibid. see also Ramírez's account on how to use the "huerto" school practice in Rafael Ramírez, *La escuela rural mexicana*, 17.
114. Rafael Ramírez, *La escuela rural mexicana*, 30.
115. Ibid., 29.
116. Alfredo Sánchez O., "Rectificaciones y aclaraciones sobre la escuela nueva," 28.
117. Ibid.

98 *Saénz and the* Escuelas Activas

118. Ibid., 24–25.
119. Ibid., 28.
120. Ibid., 29.
121. What he meant was that children were occupying more than one "post," as it became difficult to convince some students to play employees. For some students, it was good to have a "post," maybe even two. As we will see, the transgressions to the method tell us quite a bit about the way student-teacher interaction transformed the experiment in Deweyan education.
122. Alfredo Sánchez O., "Rectificaciones y aclaraciones sobre la escuela nueva, 37.
123. Ibid., 40.
124. See for example, Bases para la organización de la escuela primaria conforme al principio de la acción," 10.
125. Moisés Sáenz, "Extracto de la conferencia que el profesor Moisés Sáenz, sub-secretario de Educación Pública, sustentó en la Convención de Maestros del Estado de Texas, reunida en Dallas, Tex., en noviembre de 1925" *Boletín de la Secretaría de Educación Pública* 3, vol. V March 1926 (México: Talleres Gráficos de la Nación, Publicaciones de la Secretaría de Educación Pública 2, vol. VIII,1926), 32.
126. See Sáenz's report in Dr. J. M. Casauranc, *El Esfuerzo educativo en México*, 194.
127. See Ibid., 195.
128. Moisés Sáenz, *Escuelas Federales en San Luis Potosí: Informe de la visita practicada por el sub-secretario de educación pública en noviembre de 1927* (México: Talleres Gráficos de la Nación, 1928), 131.
129. Ibid., 18, 19, 26, 27, 29, 31, 36, 39, 64, 65.
130. Ibid., 126.
131. See Ibid., 50–51.
132. As for example in the town of *La villa de Guadalupe*. Moisés Sáenz, *Escuelas Federales en San Luis Potosí*, 43.
133. Moisés Sáenz, *Escuelas Federales en San Luis Potosí*, 17.
134. Ibid., 80.
135. Ibid., 126.
136. Ibid., 106. *Piloncillo* refers to a cone of raw sugar or molasses, which in Mexico was used profusely in the Day of the Dead to prepare pumpkin or *calabaza en tacha*.
137. Moisés Sáenz, *Escuelas Federales en San Luis Potosí*, 127.
138. Ibid., 128.
139. Ibid., 130.
140. See Moisés Sáenz, *Carapan: Bosquejo de una experiencia* (Lima: Librería e Imprenta Gil, 1936), 1–2, 16, 32, 295.
141. Ibid., 2.
142. Ibid.,146, 148, 152.
143. Ibid., 245.
144. Ibid., 325.
145. Ibid.
146. Ibid., 60.
147. Ibid., 160.
148. Ibid., 189.
149. Ibid., 261.
150. Ibid., 330. Here Sáenz could have been embracing a less-transparent approach to pedagogy by favoring "substitutions" where the substituted value would not be explicitly apparent during learning.
151. Moisés Sáenz, *Carapan*, 47, 48.
152. Ibid., 305.

153. Saénz elaborated on the differences between Western society and Mexican Native people as he imagined the transition to civilization for the Indian in ways analogous to European orientalism. "Let's recognize once and for all that the Indian is an oriental, opposed in this respect by the European." Within this framework, Indians represented "spiritual values" whereas Westerners represented a "material" culture. On the Indian, he said, "his reality is spiritual . . . while his culture is symbolical and allegorical, the white (European) is literal and instrumental." Echoing the cultural framework of his political rivals, Saénz called for the integration of the Indian "within a criteria of appreciation of the cultural and spiritual values of the Indian, respecting human personality and the full interpretation of the Mexican ideal." In other words, within the cultural parameters of state appropriation. See Moisés Saénz, *Carapan*, 35–37; 328.
154. Ibid., 317.
155. Ibid., 298.
156. By the end of the Carapan project, he rethought his faith in social science after having observed how some teachers only wanted to do the science whereas others did not care. Unable to harmonize "scientific speculation with social action," he abandoned his goal of having all teachers apply "general principles to specific applications." Invoking unconsciously perhaps the language of his rival Vasconcelos, he had failed in his attempt to fuse the Latin and the Anglo-Saxon spirits together. See Moisés Saénz, *Carapan*, 301–302.
157. Ibid., 248, 249, 250.
158. Ibid., 329.
159. Ibid., 308.
160. Ibid., 308–309.
161. Ibid., 251.
162. Ibid., 318.
163. Moisés Saénz, "México Indio: Conferencia de 1934 ante el Comité sobre Relaciones Culturales con América Latina," 136.
164. See for example, José Macías Padilla, "Informe del Inspector Federal de la Zona Sureste del estado de Chihuahua, correspondiente al año escolar de 1927" *Boletín de la Secretaría de Educación Pública* 1, vol. VII (México: January 1928), 164.
165. See for example, Juan B. Salazar, "Informe del director de educación federal en el estado de Chihuahua, relativo a las visitas practicadas a las escuelas primarias federales de aquella capital y de la zona de Juárez y Parral" *Boletín de la Secretaría de Educación Pública* 1, vol. VII (México: January 1928), 163.
166. See for example, Ibid., 153.
167. José Macías Padilla, "Informe del Inspector Federal de la Zona Sureste," 164.
168. See for example, Juan B. Salazar, "Informe del director de educación federal," 152.
169. See for example, A. Bautista Reyes, "Informe del inspector instructor de la primera zona del estado de Guerrero, relative al funcionamiento de las escuelas primarias federales, durante el año de 1927" *Boletín de la Secretaría de Educación Pública* 1, vol. VII (México: January 1928), 176.
170. Rafael Ramírez, *La escuela proletaria (cuatro pláticas acerca de educación socialista). Conferencia dada a los maestros del distrito federal* (Mexico, 1935), 54–56.
171. Huevos (eggs) being a euphemism for the men's genitalia.

5 Dangerous Dewey
The Critique of the Dewey Project in Mexico (and Dewey's Critique of Mexico)

> *The method of occasional improvisation better accommodates itself to the empirical temperament of the Anglo-Saxon; traditionally, their philosophy is inductive and their science is accumulative rather than generalizing. The Latin man, on the other hand, is more advanced in his spiritual development; he proceeds always from the general to the particular; his logic is deductive and his science is a system that must encompass all details no matter how minor or it falls apart.*
> (Jose Vasconcelos, *De Robinsón a Odiseo*)

> *It is a scientific or perverse lie that one can educate without imposing one or several ideas.*
> (Vicente Lombardo Toledano, *El problema de la educación en México*)

Introduction

The Dewey project in Mexico prompted passionate responses from Mexico's intellectual elite. The critique of Dewey owes its intensity to the ways in which this project challenged sacrosanct notions of the nation and intellectual legitimacy. Most critiques of Dewey metamorphosed into a critique of America. The challenge for Deweyan historians consists in understanding not only how but why Dewey's ideas prompted such virulent responses and to what extent the Mexican critique exposed, as it intended, radical weaknesses in America's own idea of itself. As opposed to other importations of American know-how, the appropriation of Dewey in Mexico led to an examination of sacred moments of Mexico's past invoked to define some authentic core of the nation eroded by Dewey's (and Protestant Sáenz's) intrusion into the national scene.

I will focus on the critiques of José Vasconcelos, Vicente Lombardo Toledano and Antonio Caso, intellectuals who, along with Sáenz, headed at one time Mexico's *Preparatoria*, the nation's foremost preparatory school, and who led the challenge against Sáenz. José Vasconcelos gained fame as Mexico's most important intellectual of the twentieth century and as Sáenz's bitterest rival. His book *De Robinsón a Odiseo—From Robinson to Odysseus*—offered a formal critique of Deweyan pedagogy exposing the deep cultural divide that separated Catholic-educated Mexican nationalists from Deweyan followers and their competing visions of a future Mexican state, the structure and legitimization of such a state and the role that intellectuals should play in the construction of a new nation.[1] Vicente Lombardo Toledano, one of Mexico's most salient Marxist intellectuals, educators and labor leaders in modern Mexican history, as director of Mexico's *Preparatoria*, grounded school learning on a progressive platform and activity-based pedagogy in order to create a social consciousness for social change.[2] Yet he was no friend of the Protestant-inspired movements of Mexico and the initiatives of Moisés Sáenz in modern education specifically. In 1924, he published a book entitled *El problema de la educación en México* or *The Problem of Education in Mexico*, where he criticized Sáenz's philosophy of education because it had ignored Mexico's "social tragedy."[3] Antonio Caso formed, along with José Vasconcelos, part of the *Ateneo de la juventud*, a coterie of elite reformist young intellectuals who at the turn of the century responded to the erosion of hemispheric sovereignty brought about by America's victory in the War of 1898. Caso became a bitter rival of Sáenz during the era of the Vasconcelos' administration at the helm of the Secretariat of Education in the early 1920s. As an academic, he formulated a critique of Sáenz and American pragmatism as a critique of progress, a concept that he did not reject, but believed could not fully be accommodated to Mexico because of Mexico's tragic history. Caso did not entirely reject pragmatism—he had read Dewey and James and found the latter praiseworthy—arguing that James' philosophy proved that scientific truths could be reduced to what was useful to thought.[4] As head of a *Preparatoria* rival to Sáenz's, Caso advocated an education with a pragmatic orientation, and like Toledano, who succeeded him as head of the same institution, he embraced many aspects of American pedagogy.

I end with a coda on Dewey's visit to Mexico. Although brief and in many ways inconclusive, the record does suggest that Dewey accepted the use of force to establish a basis whereby a shared set of values could serve as a foundation for democratic inquiry. Thus he seemed to align himself with the policies of the Calles administration and the educational project of Sáenz that it made possible. Yet, I conclude that the relationship between revolution and Deweyan philosophy remains open to discussion.

El Peligro Dewey: José Vasconcelos' Critique of Dewey as a Critique of America

The trauma of the war of 1898 and the penetration of American pedagogical ideas in its wake form an inseparable bond in Vasconcelos' critique of Dewey. As Julio Ramos claims, the year of "1898 and the reconfiguration of the hemispheric domain at the turn of the century marks a decisive moment in the history of Latin-Americanism."[5] America's victory in the war against Spain acquired the dimensions of a civilizational challenge, signaling for these thinkers that an expanding capitalist America portended the end of Mexican sovereignty.[6] America's power threatened to displace these intellectuals from their self-appointed sacrosanct mission to unify the continent. The intellectual's dream of hemispheric unification now seemed to be an American project rather than a Latin American mission.[7]

This humiliation produced contradictory responses in Vasconcelos. As a child, living in the border regions of the North of Mexico, he crossed the border a great number of times to attend American schools, which he came to see as reflecting a superior society. According to John Skirius, although Vasconcelos regarded "Mexicans and North Americans [as] historical enemies,"[8] he nevertheless "envied the prosperity and the superior schools of the United States during [the] decades of the 1890s."[9] On the other hand, Vasconcelos understood the United States as historically aligned with Mexico by a common history of discovery and conquest interpreting, for example, their war against the Apaches as an important bond uniting both nations.[10] As a member of the *Ateneo*, he supported the mission to save the nation by democratizing culture through education in order to close the gap between the nation as a political entity and the nation as a fragmented human entity identifying as the main goal the incorporation of the Native Mexican or *indio* into civilization and creation of one "national soul" through the diffusion of the Western canon among peasants and Indians. This national soul would provide the basis for the appropriation and efficient practice of the American values of empirical observation and scientific practice that structured America's rise to power and which they sought to foster in Mexico.[11]

The publication of José Enrique Rodó's *Ariel* deeply shaped Vasconcelos' understanding of American power and his critique of Dewey. *Ariel* revealed deep anxieties among Latin American intellectuals since the economic decline of Latin American nations vis-à-vis the United States tacitly disproved the innate racial superiority of the intelligentsia.[12] This most influential work addressed the crisis of the hemisphere in response to the war of 1898 by providing a sense of historical legibility to America's rise. It did so in two ways: first, by racializing the differences between the United States—representing the practical dimensions of the human experience—and Latin America—representing the spiritual dimensions. According to Walter L. Bernecker, in Latin America "a crucial aspect of turn-of-the-century ideas consisted in a vision of combat in racial terms . . . by the last quarter of the century, it was common for Hispanic Americans to use racial categories to explain their own failures and the success of the foreign . . . the war of 1898 could be interpreted as one more signal of the decadence of the Latin race."[13]

Second, it provided a historical explanation for the exceptional power of the pragmatic character of American civilization. *Ariel* aimed to define the "spirit of Americanism," a power, Rodó argued, bent not just on a material conquest, but on a "moral conquest."[14] Providing a cosmology of modern times, *Ariel* addressed the tensions between technology and morality that modernity engendered, positing that the modern world consisted of two spheres: one global where the United States and capital reigned supreme, and one private and national where Latin culture resided. The first sphere belonged to the technological and the mediatory qualities of capital, labor and science. The second sphere belonged to the spiritual, that is, the cultural, and the aesthetic production that defined the Latin spirit. The first realm predictably ruled according to interest, whereas the second only admitted disinterested action.

In this sense, Rodó's nationalism paralleled anti-colonial nationalist discourses in the colonized world. According to Partha Chatterjee,

> anti-colonial nationalism creates its own domain of sovereignty within colonial society well before it begins its political battle with the imperial power. It does this by dividing the world of social institutions and practices into two domains—the material and the spiritual. The material is the domain of the "outside," of the economy and of statecraft, of science and technology, a domain where the West had proved its superiority and the East had succumbed. In this domain, then, Western superiority had to be acknowledged . . . the spiritual, on the other hand, is an "inner" domain bearing the "essential" marks of cultural identity. The greater one's success in imitating Western skills in the material domain, therefore, the greater the need to preserve the distinctness of one's spiritual culture.[15]

Yet, as opposed to postcolonial intellectuals in India, Rodó's dichotomy constituted a defense of European empire. Whereas anti-colonial figures in India critiqued the modern as an import from the West, intellectuals such as Rodó, who articulated their authority and identity on the basis of their European lineage, did not, invoking older narrative of Anglo-Saxon and Latin imperial rivalry to articulate the significance of the American challenge. The split in the modern world alluded by Rodó corresponded within the nation to the relationship of labor to ideas and technology and culture. Within this cosmology, the highest value could not be the technological because it involved "interested" action and the "immediate." The higher use of the intellect involved "disinterested" action, the use of the mind removed from politics. Only within the realm of "disinterested" action could the nation be imagined. There the practical would be subordinated to the aesthetic. The practical-technological character of American society could not be a model for this society. America's admirable efficiency, directed "practically to realize an immediate end," could not "incorporate to the discoveries of science one single general law, one single principle,"[16] argued Rodó.

Rodó's reasoning on the practical's subordination to the aesthetic did not deny their relational quality and necessity for each other. Rodó claimed that ideal aspects of the human spirit have historically depended on the technological and "mercantile" activities of men. He provided an example: "the most precious and fundamental acquisition of the spirit—the alphabet, which gives wings of immortality to the word—is born in the bosom of Cananaean factories and is the exclusive find of mercenaries, who ignored that the genius of superior races would transfigure it, transforming it into the means for the propagation of its pure and luminous essence."[17] The quality that provided intellectual labor with its superior status resided in the ability of reason to imagine higher uses with no other purposes than pure reproduction. The spiritual realm situated itself at a higher end in the historical process not only because of its inherent superiority, but also because of the self-consciousness—"the genius"—of its mission. This self-consciousness, as an attribute of the spiritual, belonged to the Latin. The United States, on the other hand, with its republican government, its federation, its work ethic, the centrality it gave to work, its applied sciences, its preoccupation with sports and the body and individual liberty of conscience, constituted pure interested action. America was a nation without imagination because it could not possess the necessary "high and disinterested concept of the future."[18] "Its prosperity is so great," argued Rodó, "just as the impossibility of satisfying any mediocre conception of human destiny."[19]

Yet, how did America came to embody the spirit of the practical? Here Rodó advanced the idea that America constituted a "distillation" of one single social trait of the Anglo-Saxon people, their utilitarian spirit. This spirit had spread without being compromised by other cultural groups. The practical character of the American was not exactly a copy or a pure imitation of the British character, but a product of the dissemination of an Anglo-Saxon *geist*—in this case the utilitarian spirit—which, unencumbered by any obstacle, spread evenly throughout North America. "Democracy in America," stated Rodó, "does not find before itself any inaccessible obstacles . . . [thus] it extends and reproduces itself over a flat plain as that of an infinite *pampa*."[20] The utilitarian character of America's English ancestors had evolved into something akin to a pure state, unencumbered by any social obstacle. Rodó asserted that if "utilitarianism was the verb of the English spirit," then the United States should be considered "the incarnation of [that] utilitarian verb."[21]

In Rodó's own words:

> the genial positivism of the Metropolis has suffered, as it was transmitted to its emancipated children in America, a distillation that deprives them of all the elements of idealism that tempered it, reducing them, in reality, to the crudity that, in the exaggerations of passion or satire, has been possible to attribute to the positivism of England. The English spirit, under the rough bark of utilitarianism, under the indifference of commerce, under the severity of the Puritan, hides, without any doubt, a chosen poetic virtue, and a profound spring of sensibility, which reveals . . . the primitive depth, the Germanic depth of that race, modified then by the pressure of conquest and the habit of commercial activity . . . an extraordinary exaltation of sentiment. The American spirit

has not received as its heritage that ancestral poetic instinct that sprouts as limpid current from the bosom of the British rock when touched by the Moses of a delicate art. The English people have, in the institution of its aristocracy . . . a high and inexpugnable pillar to oppose mercantilism . . . in the environment of American democracy, the spirit of vulgarity does not find in its path an inaccessible relief to stop its ascending force, and thus it extends and propagates over the flatness of an infinite *pampa*.[22]

America represented the "ontologization of a useful trait, the practical, which it expressed through its total dedication to work and the expansion of its material circumstances."[23] This realization of its spirit through work only obsessed itself with the present and as we have seen before, "subordinate[d] all activity to the egotism of personal and collective welfare."[24] It was only the contingency of the dissemination of Anglo-Saxons over the continent—in obvious contrast to the Spanish, who had compromised their spirit (and racial purity) in their efforts to evangelize and incorporate the Natives into civilization, that explained how a lesser trait—and thus a subordinate political principle—could rise to define a people. He conceded the superiority of the American in the public domain (the world). As he famously said, "*No los amo, pero los admiro,*" or "I do not love them, but I do admire them." Yet he conceived of a future world where a "law of harmony . . . between the progress of utilitarian activity and the ideal"[25] would allow the Latin's spirit to ascend to world power.[26] Thus the work of *Calibán*—the United States—"will serve the cause of Ariel at the end."[27]

Rodó's critique profoundly shaped José Vasconcelos' response to American supremacy, which he began to theorize in his most famous book of the 1920s, *La Raza Cósmica* (*The Cosmic Race*) where he translated the narrative of Rodó's *Ariel* into a new epic of Mexican nationalism, a blueprint for the education of the Mexican citizen and a plan to protect the Mexican people from the Saxon and Protestant influences whose ends, according to him, were none other than to take possession of what Spain was able to gather.[28] For Vasconcelos, Mexico's arrested modernity could only be understood in terms of historical divide between Anglo-Saxons and Latin people and their common history of empire.[29] Historically, he argued, "from the earliest times, from the discovery and the conquest, it was Castilians and British, or Latins and Saxons . . . who consummated the task of initiating a new period of History, conquering and populating the new Hemisphere."[30] According to Vasconcelos, the Latin was destined for great achievements within the aesthetic realm where racial miscegenation would overcome a divided historical consciousness. He argued that "the white man has made possible for the world the fusion of all types and kinds. The civilizations conquered by the white men . . . has set the material and moral basis for the union of all men . . . fruit of all the previous ones and overcoming of all that was past."[31] According to Vasconcelos "they [the North Americans] do not bear in their blood the contradictory instincts of the mixture of dissimilar races, but have committed the sin of the destruction of other races, while we assimilate, and this gives us new rights and hopes of a mission without precedent in History."[32]

Vasconcelos' narrative did not just focus on the racial structure of a new society but on the cognitive abilities of its subjects. Vasconcelos had aligned himself with a great number of post-colonial thinkers who saw the power of the United States as closely connected with the empirical, non-dogmatic mind of the Anglo-Saxon people; these were people who exhibited in their societies a free and spontaneous competition among individuals with no loss of unity.[33] During his tenure as Secretary of Education during the presidency of General Alvaro Obregón from 1920 to 1923, Vasconcelos maintained that only a practical and useful education could assist Mexico to achieve that modernity,[34] advocating for the "fusion of utilitarian knowledge and social morality,"[35] and calling for a new era, the era of *el técnico*.[36] Vasconcelos had published *La Raza Cósmica* after his tenure at the helm of Mexico's Secretariat of Education, where he had implemented a national educational project to create new Mexican citizens through a series of educational missions to rural and Indigenous areas. His state project reflected the belief that the transition of Mexico to modernity could be expressed as the historical translation of the Latin *hombre abstracto* to a not-yet-realized New Man, *hombre técnico* or technical man. Vasconcelos believed Latin societies had produced what he termed a *hombre teórico*—a theoretical man—an individual rich in abstraction but unable to think in practical terms. To the Latin man the deductive method of reasoning applied; to the American, the deductive method. The Latin was mired in dogma, whereas the American or Saxon basked in experience. As we have seen, he ascertained that, "God Himself assists the Saxon, while we ourselves kill each other over dogma."[37]

Vasconcelos had initially valued American pragmatism highly because it synthesized the two most desired traits of American modernity: science and learning. He had read Emerson, James, and Dewey (along with Edgar Allan Poe) because they represented a scientific spirit that he desired for Mexico and offered a vision of how an empirical mind finds the truth.[38] Yet he insisted that truth existed outside of the individual, preferring to think of pragmatism as a method for the discovery of final truths or the "entrail of things,"[39] as he called it. This interpretation guided his national crusade to democratize culture with the understanding that culture occupied some place outside the individual and that an empirical mind should approach cultural artifacts the way a scientist approached nature. Decades before the Chinese Revolution and the Russian Revolution, Mexico embarked on a state-sponsored program to modernize the nation by way of mass education. As part of this mission, Vasconcelos created new public libraries, some of them mobile, to teach peasants how to read the great books of the West. He established the Western canon as the repository of "condensed experiences" that offered the peasant the possibility of moving up the social scale and into a more refined world and the Mexican Indian the opportunity of incorporating himself or herself into world civilization, and thus into the history of the nation. He proposed models for the edification of the masses, giving them the opportunity, as Claude Fell remarks, to "read Dante and Euripides."[40] The Iliad, the Odyssey, the Divine Comedy, the Platonic Dialogues, Faust and Cervantes' Quijote became obligatory reading for teachers and students alike. Faithful to his pragmatic principles, though, he defended the scientific and anti-dogmatic character of the experiment because it allowed the student to approach the truths of the great books through careful observation and guidance. He urged teachers to allow the child to develop his "natural tendencies," stressing the importance of work and "action" in the pursuit of truth.[41] Mexico became for Vasconcelos a "laboratory" for the creation of a new race.

Its most important vehicles were the cultural missions or *misiones culturales*, which consisted of groups of educated youth, many of them teachers and pedagogues from urban areas, sent to the countryside to establish schools, promote literacy and spread modern standards of hygiene. The state produced history textbooks for these teachers, reproducing in them simple Europe-centered histories that invoked the state as heir to the Spanish missionaries' civilizing mission to the Indian. Thus one of the cornerstones of his vision was the Europeanized intellectual offering civilization to the Indian as a "gift" where Native Mexican freedom could only be conceived within the European civilizational domain. He emphasized that a "true culture" for Mexico could only mean the "flowering of the native within the domain of the universal (*el florecimiento de lo nativo dentro de un ambiente universal*) . . . the union of our soul with all the vibrations of the universe in a jubilant rhythm similar to that of music and with such a joyous fusion as the one we will experiment within moments, when in our conscience the innocent sounds of popular song of thousands of voices of children's choruses will link with the profound melodies of classical music revived and bewitched by our symphonic orchestra."[42] He defended the intellectuals' (and missionary teachers') mission to rural Mexico as a form of "disinterested action."

Vasconcelos' project met with resistance by Marxists and Deweyan activists working in the SEP or Secretariat of Public Education. Marxists denounced his use of socialist language for purposes that were not revolutionary. Diego Rivera, one of Mexico's most famous muralists, castigated Vasconcelos' manipulation of work as a pedagogical instrument, his romanticization of peasant labor and his use of agricultural practices as the basis for the educational labor of the *misiones culturales*. Rivera asserted that "in the actions of any constructive administration . . . the creation of possibilities to develop good taste must occupy a very important place . . . [but] for taste to be true and thus favorable to the economy of the nation, the means used must favor the expansion and flowering of all of that is productive of the soil . . . it is needed for the peasant to cultivate that which is nutritive fruit given by the land he works."[43] Rivera conceded that labor and industry were signs of the modern, but not in the reductive sense given to them by Vasconcelos. Radical teachers in the SEP, advancing the vision of the *escuelas activas* project, seconded Rivera's ideas in the Secretariat of Education (SEP), in a sharp departure from Vasconcelos' aesthetic version of progressive education. For these teachers, as well as for Rivera, although the final goal of revolution meant peasant freedom, the exact shape of that future always had to remain open: the social contours of modern society were always in the making. Rallying around the notion of the *principio de la acción*, they challenged the totalizing vision of the state implied in Vasconcelos' project. Professors Salvador M. Lima and Marcelino Rentería, who openly supported the Deweyan faction, published in *Educación* a manifesto entitled *La escuela de la acción* in which they denounced the traditional school as a "true regimen of oppression," breeding "passivity and immobility," which denied the need for an "interior practical life."[44] These teachers opposed not only Vasconcelos but also conservative politicians who rejected the new school precisely because it openly associated pedagogical discourse with political life, especially the way teachers' discourse suggested that the relations between teachers and students and the curriculum were but mere reflections of the political order.[45] Moisés Sáenz and the teachers' project emerged triumphant from that struggle, and the *escuelas activas* were adopted into law in 1923. Vasconcelos left his post with bitterness toward Sáenz, the teachers and the administration of President Calles. He then turned his critique of America into a critique of Dewey and the project of the *escuelas activas*.

The Pedagogy of Robinson Crusoe

In 1924, Vasconcelos went into exile and returned in 1928 to run for president, losing in a bitterly contested election. He returned to Spain, where he published in 1935 an anti-Dewey tract entitled *De Robinsón a Odiseo* (*From Robinson to Odysseus*), in which he established a formal critique of the philosophy of Dewey as a critique of America, especially in its second chapter entitled *El peligro Dewey* ("The Dewey Danger"). There it linked the origins of Dewey's ideas to the logic of America's expansionism, which, having been accepted voluntarily by Mexicans such as Sáenz, had facilitated a spiritual invasion of the nation fostering Mexico's "spiritual subordination"[46] to Anglo-Saxons and launching a form of "spiritual colonialism" of the Mexican soul, an intrusion of the foreign into the consciousness of the nation. He warned that "the penetration is so advanced that it is being consummated by second-rate North-American [thinkers] like Dewey and anonymous *pochos*, their allies among ourselves."[47] This crisis was aggravated by the fact that *pochos* such as Moisés Sáenz, Dewey's disciple, and his brother, ex- presidential candidate Aaron Sáenz, were Presbyterians.[48] "The *escuela nueva* is Protestantism taken into pedagogy,"[49] he declared.

Within this intellectual platform, Vasconcelos' main goal consisted in reimagining Mexico's origins as part of the genealogy of Greek and Latin history and separate the values of Deweyan pragmatism from those of Europe transforming American culture into a non-Western domain. In reference to Sáenz's focus on inquiry, Vasconcelos located American barbarism in Americans' modes of thought and ways of thinking. Their inability to think in abstract terms meant they could not imagine themselves as a "true nation" or a "true culture." The United States, rather than a step forward in the history of humankind, was, as Robinson Crusoe, like a man "thrown in an island and born in an island, without any full concept of the extension of the continents and the content of culture."[50] "The notion of system," Vasconcelos stated, "which is inseparable from the Latin mind and all true culture, demands of us to prepare against certain ways of personal initiative, which are nothing else but primitivism."[51] Pragmatism, as a primitivist cultural product, valued the particular and the immediate, running counter to the abilities of "any true culture" to systematize, theorize and produce knowledge but merely "wisdom" of the past. It reduced "the general content of culture" to reproduce the ethos of the golden mean, a kind of American "pedagogical babbittism."[52] It had placed "the soul" of Mexicans "in the hands of the technical, such monstrosity," Vasconcelos cried out. "In a pragmatic nation," he added, "a vast anthill of experience, moving towards the utilization of the environment, the Dewey school, is the end point of a logical development ... Dewey confusionism, so much fashionable in ... nations thirsty for idols!"[53]

In his own words,

> we find ourselves in this case confronting a question of temperament. The method of occasional improvisation better accommodates itself to the empirical temperament of the Anglo-Saxon; traditionally, their philosophy is inductive and their science is accumulative rather than generalizing. The Latin man, on the other hand, is more advanced in his spiritual development; he proceeds always from the general to the particular; his logic is deductive and his science is a system that must encompass all details no matter how minor or it falls apart.[54]

Robinson, standing for the United States, exemplified the American spirit: simple, astute, improvising and strictly technical. Through Dewey's pedagogy in Mexico, it had now vanquished the European spirit of Mexico, exemplified by Odysseus, an expansive and conquering man, who was spiritually and materially, according to Vasconcelos, the counterpart of the Spanish conquistador Hernán Cortés.[55] He called the Spanish imperial soldier the creator of the Mexican nationality.[56] He virilized Mexican history at the same time it claimed America's most valuable trait—its practical character—for itself. Cortés was a doer: a conqueror, romantic and impulsive, "moved always by the impulse of a spiritual passion, by decisions of the moment, violent . . . sentimental in a great manner . . . because he knew and lived for the Christian purpose of bettering life, mending [life's] roots and transforming its character."[57] He was heroic, a creator, an artist and most importantly, a true practical man.

The book's claims relied on well-known narratives of European cognitive superiority. According to J.M. Blaut, in European narratives of progress, "the basic cause of European progress is some intellectual or spiritual factor, something characteristic of the 'European mind' . . . something that lead to creativity, imagination, invention, innovation, rationality, and a sense of honor or ethics . . . the reason for non-Europe's non-progress is a lack of this same intellectual or spiritual factor . . . the landscape of the non-European world is empty . . . of 'rationality.'"[58] Thus the primitive cannot conceive of abstract principles such as "private property" or suffers from what Blaut calls an "emptiness of intellectual creativity and spiritual values, sometimes described by Europeans . . . as an absence of rationality."[59] In Vasconcelos' narrative, American practicality occupied the sphere of the barbarian. Furthermore, Vasconcelos' fears of America also echoed similar European fears of counter-diffusion, such as those associated with magic, vampires, plagues or the 'bogeyman.' Blaut states that, "there is the possibility that these ancient, atavistic . . . traits will counterdiffuse back into the civilized core, in the form of ancient, magical, evil things like black magic, Dracula."[60] Dewey's philosophy performed that role, constituting, as it did for Vasconcelos, a "radical divorce" from civilized values, which "from the beginning assimilates us to the beast."[61]

Vasconcelos extended his right-wing demonization of American culture to those specifics of Deweyan philosophy he considered to be most salient to the character of the United States and the very source of its power: the values of commerce, the market and the perceived ability of those involved in commerce to profit from opportunities regardless of ideological commitment. He dramatized the notion that pragmatic values in Deweyan education attached themselves to money, to "accumulation," to "the subordination of quality to quantity," "Wall Street and Moscow." They formed part of both "the capitalist system" as well as the "economy of the Soviet State."[62] This vocabulary will not surprise scholars of Vasconcelos. After the Third Reich surged to power, Vasconcelos continued his critique of America as a defense of Hitler. Writing in the pro-fascist journal *Timón*, which he edited in Spain, Vasconcelos accused Dewey, "the one from Columbia," of being an "intermediary like all Anglo-Saxons" and an "agent of Moscow for the intellectual penetration of Hispanic America."[63]

Vasconcelos suggested that Dewey's philosophy expressed an end-point in American history, more specifically the formative experiences of Anglo-Saxon migration to the American west. He entertained the idea that the contingencies of history, especially the migration to the American west, had intensified the Americans' sense of practicality. He argued that "the desire to discover something by oneself in the order of the technical, which is a characteristic concern of the pedagogy of Dewey, must seem like an echo of the epic of the 'pioneers' . . . Today, when studying the reflections of the pragmatic pedagogue, we evoke the reality of the camping ground."[64] In the move to the American west, "each person made a discovery, others hunted, and the 'city evolved' by the accumulation of small discoveries . . . in the theoretical world of our reality, the method of our adaptation does not look anymore to those methods the 'pioneer' established in the jungle," he said. Mexicans did not live in the "desert of the Robinson pioneers that eighty years ago improvised" and " 'learned by doing,' "[65] he cried out. "We evoke the reality of the camping ground when one analyzes today the reflections of the pragmatic pedagogue,"[66] he continued.

America's history was a "regime of exception" or *régimen de excepción*:

> there is that one person that goes to the woods and jubilantly cries out when a thick and tall wood tree is discovered for the *pilastra*; another one has gone to search for water and another one yet is hunting the *liebre* that secures the mid-day meal; each one has contributed to their discovery and the *settlement* evolves in the city by the accumulation of those small discoveries in the desert. The labor of the explorer in such situations surpasses that of the wise man. But one lives within a regime of exception (*régimen de excepción*) that cannot be normative for an already established society. Similarly, our tactical moves change fully when we are dedicated to the study of the theory of our being and the environment within which we move. For example, the science of numbers is theoretical, no matter how much we may insert in each case its laws within the body of reality. It is known that high mathematics cannot any longer incarnate in physical objects and instead becomes a relation among fictitious entities . . . and this mathematical theory and the theory of language and in general the theories of every science are objects of scholarly investigation. Besides, they form part of the environment within which he [the scholar] would labor and live; they exercise in this environment an effective influence as that of the objects. In this theoretical world of our reality the method of our adaptation does not look anymore to the method the 'pioneer' established in the jungle. It is infantile to suppose that the child will discover how to add. In fact, the distinction that Dewey establishes between the academic activity of the spirit and the manual activity or manipulation is not that rigorous. In both cases the subject . . . is the same . . . the data changes and according to the datum the method varies. But the subject is one theoretical-active unit.[67]

Instead of the Dewey ideal, Vasconcelos proposed the discoverer as hero as the true subject of education. "The conditions of the modern era claim an Odysseus," he claimed, and "not just an international, but a universal one: a traveler that explores and acts, that discovers and creates, not only with his hands and never only with his hands; one that neither wants nor will surrender the inheritance that widens the soul, the ingenuity, and the treasures of a millenarian culture."[68] This was a very different subject from the "taylorized Robinsons of the Ford factory"![69] "Dewey it does seem," Vasconcelos concluded, "would like to annihilate in us our capacity to appreciate great things, instead having us invent anew the way to tie our necktie or the way to clear our room . . . with the pretext of awakening the curiosity of the pupil in relation to the world that surrounds him, the Dewey system wastes away the attention of the class in detail . . . the personal attention to detail, the desire to revolve the quotidian petty cases . . . [produces] the middle type so happily accomplished by Sinclair Lewis in his Babbitt, and naturally, I rebel against [it] . . . it has confused training with reason."[70] The point consisted in reiterating the idea that Dewey's anti-civilizational values reflect an anti-Christian ethos, meaning Dewey denied the "Christian thesis of original sin," replacing it with the "thesis of original perfection,"[71] a concept, according to Vasconcelos, "dogmatized by Dewey."

Vasconcelos oscillated between conceding that the values of "Caliban" (the United States) might be necessary to the cause of Latin America to the outright rejection of all values American. "Even if tomorrow it were to be demonstrated that the inductive temperament is the best," argued Vasconcelos, "we should not adopt it for its own sake and it will always be better to cultivate ourselves within the law of our own natural development."[72] "If the child of North America overcomes the Mexican," he concluded, "perhaps, in applied science, ours on the other hand will shine in art and musical sensibility."[73] This reconciliation was beneficial because the capacities for imagining the nation were to be found in the aesthetic and spiritual capabilities of man, not its practical orientation. If Robinson—the American subject—did not possess, "any full concept of the extension of the continents and the content of culture,"[74] Vasconcelos' subject, heir to Odysseus, could.

Vasconcelos' critique of Dewey stood for a critique of American values. These values represented the values of the market and of the corporate man for whom ideological commitment did not matter. The mediatory character of Deweyan pedagogy and the instrumental nature of social values that it represented constituted a form of primitivism, which threatened the "national soul." Vasconcelos argued that it was only a contingency in the historical evolution of humankind that allowed for a nation such as the United States to be ruled by values and instincts usually subordinated to politics. As an exception to history, in America the politico-moral substance of the nation was subordinated to the market. Vasconcelos' critique also exemplified how the defense of the nation structured the definition of Latin values. The necessity of defending identity consumed the rhetoric of nationality, thereby cementing the role that America played as the implicit and generative model in this discourse. Within this paradigm, Vasconcelos reproduced several of the features of Rodó's *Ariel*. Latin identity defined itself in terms of its cultural/spiritual dimensions, which were opposed to the instrumental values of America now clearly identified as embodied in the Deweyan philosophy of education.

Progress and Sacrifice: Vicente Lombardo Toledano, Antonio Caso and the Critique of Dewey as a Critique of American Progress

The Critique from the Left: Lombardo Toledano and the Problem of Revolution

Vicente Lombardo Toledano became a radical as a university student while studying law at the Autonomous University of Mexico in the early 1920s. In 1923, he joined CROM (Mexican Workers' Regional Confederation or *Confederación Regional Obrera Mexicana*), a confederation of labor unions faithful to the governments of General Alvaro Obregón (1920–1924) and General Plutarco Elías Calles (1924–1928). Although Toledano never became its leader, as its most important intellectual, it offered him a platform as a *pensador* or public intellectual. In the 1930s, he formed his own labor union, a chief ally of the leftist government of Lázaro Cárdenas del Río (1932–1940), whose educational platform invoked as its rationale the establishment of socialist education and the end to the bourgeois experiment of the *escuelas activas* project in Mexico.[75] His most important critique of Dewey in Mexico originated in his book *El Problema de la educación en México* (*The Problem of Education in Mexico*) of 1924.

There Lombardo Toledano expressed sympathy with Dewey's pedagogy, which in his mind offered the West hope for a "transformation" of human experience after the devastation of WWI. Dewey's schools, according to Toledano, were "based on a rapprochement of man to nature," he argued, "and to [the desire for] an honest and simple life." In grounding education on work, it sought "to make instincts fructiferous . . . [and] oriented all pedagogy towards socially useful production."[76] Yet its Mexican appropriation had taken the purely technocratic aspects of Dewey's pedagogy, which pertained to the disciplinary regime of an industrialized nation, and transplanted them to Mexico while ignoring the nation's "social tragedy," its incompleteness as a nation. Pedagogues had imported techniques to measure "the time employed in teaching lessons . . . the persistence of students' attention spans, the relative capacity, artistic intuition, physical resistance and other qualities of other nations," he argued,[77] but what Mexico needed first was national union. Toledano challenged the validity of pragmatism in times of revolution, especially because the democratic practices that Sáenz had attempted to foment in Mexican schools presupposed a social consensus that only violent change could produce.

For Toledano, Mexico did not possess such foundation or social cohesion. Schools could not leave instruction open, he said, to *"libre examen"*[78] nor to "the occasional inspiration that illuminates the conscience of men."[79]

Toledano rejected the notion of democratic debate implied in Protestant education as an open-ended system. Anticipating the critique of C. Wright Mills in America,[80] Toledano argued instead that "the confrontation with social injustice requires an education that accepts "dogma," and that could teach "man to produce and defend its product." "Experience [is] war," he proclaimed, adding that, "the proletarian conceives experience as a war for defensive purposes and for love."[81] "It is a scientific or perverse lie," Toledano stated, that "one can educate without imposing one or several ideas." He added, "we need a Mexican dogma, a truth that will facilitate the coming of love and justice among ourselves and that will convert us to optimists in life, into believers in our own power, that will wash away our hatreds and inferior appetites and that will reveal ourselves to the world as . . . humans."[82] Toledano did not abandon the progressive instrumentalism that he had embraced earlier in his life when helming the *Preparatoria*. He accepted the progressives' ideal that "only what is useful is true," adding that ideas are true only if they "serve men to attain a good life."[83] He concurred with Dewey that truth did not preexist human experience, but that all truth, as he said, "is a moment . . . within the development of human knowledge."[84] He advocated dogma as a tool for raising consciousness, teaching and leading the proletarian. Dogma could be accommodated to a practical and instrumentalist view of the struggle. He defended the view that it was consequent with pragmatism to use dogma as a tool when *la lucha* (the struggle) was revolutionary. He coined the phrase "Tequila Marxism" (rather than vodka Marxism) to denominate his own brand of Marxist thought. Toledano produced a critique that rejected the idea that communication could or should always be transparent and that, in turn, accepted certain kinds of authority over the subject on the grounds that Mexico did not possess the social conditions for the kind of communicative democracy that Sáenz advocated.

The Issue of Social Intelligence

But what did Toledano mean by Mexico's "social tragedy"? Toledano's understanding of Mexico's social tragedy explains his rejection of democracy and embrace of dogma. The tragic aspect of Mexico's social problems consisted in the inability of Mexicans to constitute themselves as a nation-state. The Spanish conquest had legated an incomplete modernity to the nation. According to Toledano, if the Spanish colonies had achieved any kind of national unity, it was mostly "in a negative and barbaric, cruel and unjust manner." Only "tragically the notion of national unity first appears in our history,"[85] he averred. When it came to social justice, the "integration of [Mexico's] nationality" came first. He identified the contemporary manifestation of Mexico's tragedy as a problem of the "social intelligence" of the nation because Indian heterogeneity constituted an obstacle to its unification and because it reflected multiple contradictory historical consciousness. He argued that, "the fundamental problem of the nation is the problem of intelligence among the diverse ethnic groups that make the Mexican region."[86] In order to raise the consciousness of the masses, the state needed to transform the Indians' social world by raising its consciousness and homogenizing the material circumstances of their world. Whereas the first goal could conceivably be democratic, the second goal—as necessary as the first one—had to be imposed. Its rival, the pragmatic experiment of the *escuelas activas*, did not recognize that possibility, moved, as it was, by an unshakable faith in human communication and by its own blindness to the state's historical violence against Indigenous people. In this sense, he defended an educational revolution to bring about economic and structural change. "The educational problem will resolve the economic problem [and] will become the base for its resolution," he argued.[87] Although in his address to the *Universidad Obrera* in 1961, he had stated that it was not "the conscience of men that determines their existence, but the existence that determines their conscience,"[88] his views on education contradicted that idea.

What could be the proper model for Mexico instead of Dewey's? Lombardo Toledano found the answer in the civilizing mission of Spanish friar Vasco de Quiroga, which he argued had already advanced important principles found in Mexico's Deweyan experiment. Vasco de Quiroga, a Spanish nobleman's son and bishop of Michoacán in 1537, undertook in colonial Mexico a series of utopian experiments inspired by the model of Sir Thomas Moore, using his own funds to build hospital-towns in Santa Fe, Mexico City, where he assembled Native Mexicans to convert them to Christianity and offer them refuge from the ravages of the *conquistadores*. As bishop of the new province of Michoacán, he promoted the cause of the Spanish empire by establishing communities where Indians received religious instruction in the Catholic faith and received instruction in arts and crafts production and the fundamentals of political organization. These communities were organized around hospitals, schools and churches, all interconnected, giving the community an organic character. Each community became the focus of one industry, each Native person working six hours a day to contribute to the welfare of the community. Quiroga called these communities hospital-towns or *pueblos-hospitales*. The organic quality of the community, the discipline implied in the surveillance of the model town, the transparency and uniformity of the subject, the emphasis on work and production and the figure of Vasco himself (a colonizer yet defender of the Indian) all lent themselves to the appropriation of this narrative by Lombardo Toledano's nationalist imagination.

In the colonial schools of the hospital-towns, the product of students' work constituted not only an aspect of common labor but was marketed to the community by Indians themselves. Thus production served to create the continuum between school and society, cementing the grounds for the production of social life. The organization of the social world was mirrored in the schools. Toledano valued positively how Quiroga's schools contained the agricultural life of the community within, with orchards, plots of land and animal care areas where, according to Toledano, "don Vasco emphasized that children were to work the land in common (in plots annexed to the school which today are called experimental schooling) and in the form of play, enjoyment" but also as "doctrine."[89] Even more importantly, these schools produced in the Indian "the need for social organization" and established the basis for consent, a process facilitated by the organicism of Vasco de Quiroga's colonial towns where the church, the hospital and the school were part of one single unity.[90] For Toledano, Vasco de Quiroga's *escuelas de indios* affirmed the centrality of production as the basis of instruction and the groundwork of social solidarity. Similarly to Dewey, "the program of studies strictly related to schooling [was] minimal: writing and reading on the Spanish language and religion; but [with] added communal work of the land and individual teaching of a profession and plain song."[91] Work made Indians useful to each other when it fostered bonds of love among them.[92] It socialized them as one people. Toledano argued that Quiroga's schools were historically aligned with the modern progressive command to conform the school to society because, as he argued, they functioned "in relation to the economic and moral needs of the milieu wherein they were founded."[93]

The experiment demonstrated the power of a project to create one single social consciousness among a diversity of people already identified as one by the state. It also showed the power of a logic that categorized cultural difference as "social disorganization" and in its stead proposed a state project of unification. Indians felt the "bonds" of solidarity because they had been forced to move into specially configured towns where these "bonds" made sense. With this purpose in mind, Toledano favored Vasco de Quiroga's reconfiguration of Indian social organization whereby the state moved the population into specially created spaces called *reducción* (or reduction), wherein "dispersed indigenous groups in vast territories [were relocated] in populations of greater importance . . . to make them feel the fraternal bond through the community of work, translating them [*conviertiéndolos*] in necessary factors of production for the locality, unifying them [socially] and bestowing upon them an economic value, as we say today."[94] In other words, Indians were converted into workers, the symbol of modernity and the most advanced figure in the historical course of humanity. "The worker," said Toledano, "is the representative of modern social organization even if he is now more subject economically to the tyranny of capital than most peasants in the region . . . because of the homogeneous character as far as his conditions of life, race and aspirations."[95] Whereas the *mestizo* or *métisse* was a symbol of the reconciliation of historical memory in the eyes of the Revolution, and for Sáenz the practical man was the man of modernity, for the Marxist Toledano, the worker represented the symbol of the modern; it occupied the realm of the universal.

Lombardo Toledano's ideas demonstrate how the essential features of Dewey's project were oftentimes understood in explicit comparison with the European civilizational mission to the Native Mexican because Mexican intellectuals understood Dewey's philosophy of education as part of a long lineage of projects of conversion tied to imperial conquest whose modern incarnation was the creation of a "national soul." For Lombardo Toledano, crucial features of the Dewey project invoked the imperial pedagogy, among them the centrality of production in education, the establishment of a continuum between school and community, the emphasis on the practical as the grounds for knowledge and the use of art as a technique of education. These had all been important features of the Spanish project to convert Indians to civilization through socialization and were central features of the rationale of the national state's project of education. Vasco de Quiroga offered a model of the state in which Indian life could be translated into new categories of identity without the loss of Indian values seemingly preserved in the product of their work. The techniques to erase Indian historical consciousness as well as transform the environment that supported Indian life (as exemplified in the historical narrative of the conversion of the Tarascos in Michoacán under Vasco de Quiroga's leadership) solved for Lombardo Toledano the problem of social intelligence (a key Deweyan idea raised by Sáenz) and set the grounds for the rise of the worker as the modern category that could perform in the present what the "Christian" and the "Indian" performed for Vasco de Quiroga and Spanish colonialism. His critique did not reject the concept of "social intelligence," but reconstituted it as a problem of historical consciousness that the Dewey project did not seem to solve at least in his mind. He castigated Sáenz for ignoring the conditions of Indian communities and for categorizing all Natives as uncivilized. He argued that "the belief that to educate the Indian means to translate (*convertir*) an inferior marked in his spirit neither by tradition nor history into a European is to commit a profound error."[96]

Antonio Caso and the Problem of Historical Tragedy

By the time José Vasconcelos became Secretary of Education in 1920, two rival systems competed for control of Mexico's *Preparatoria*, the symbol of Mexican education in the capital city: one headed by Sáenz and another by Antonio Caso. Sáenz directed the official *Preparatoria*, where he pioneered experiments on pragmatic pedagogy. Student activists opposed Sáenz within the school by branding his methods as anti-Mexican and for violating the tenets of traditional Mexican liberalism.[97] On the outside, he was bitterly opposed by Caso, who headed a rival *Preparatoria* that based its schooling on a system of "Christian idealism" whose core formed part of the classical European curriculum. These two systems opposed each other on the basis of pedagogical theory and intensified that contest by accusations of foreignness hurled against Sáenz. After his resignation as head of the second *Preparatoria*, Caso went on to direct the National University, where he obtained tenure as a professor of philosophy.

It was imperative for intellectuals like Caso, who had accused Sáenz and his supporters of anti-Mexican sentiment and ignorance of the history of Mexico, to articulate a true view of Mexican history and Mexico's place in world history to defend their system against Sáenz's. For Caso, a true Mexican understood Mexico's history as tragic: on the one hand blessed by Spain's gift of civilization; on the other, compromised by the necessary dissemination of Spanish culture through the destruction of Indian life. Caso's version of history centralized the Spanish role in the history of human progress (which meant that civilization possessed a Spanish lineage) at the same time that it identified the Indian world as central to the question of Mexico's incomplete modernity. He proclaimed that "Spain and England had assured their immortality. Rome succumbed . . . England and Spain will also succumb," there was "another thriving England—Mexicans, we know this well—and many *Españas*, heroic, in this land of Columbus."[98]

Caso's basic vision drew inspiration from William James, Henri Bergson and Herbert Spencer. From Spencer, he learned that there were two economic domains for human action: one vulgar and prosaic (the domain of the common man) and another beautiful and sublime (the domain of the artist). In the first domain, the practical and the scientific occupied the first domain. Selfishness sets the basis for the evolution of the species, a process ruled by the equation "a maximum of yield for a minimum of effort."[99] Modern science should be located within that domain because it constituted a purely descriptive process: "by virtue of selfishness, which counts with a surplus of forces to engender new and similar beings, new species are constituted and disappear . . . the struggle, the adaptation and heredity sustain the immense grid of living beings. *The maximum of yield with the minimum of effort*: such is the universal economy of the universe. Adaptation . . . is the only motivation for action in life."[100] The only purpose of science, as part of the economic domain, was the making things efficient. But this efficiency, Caso argued, derived purely from the ability of the sciences for imitating facts. "It is purely descriptive,"[101] he affirmed. In *La Definición del Progreso* or The Definition of Progress, he argued that American greatness reflected the "scientific and practical spirit [which] had covered with laboratories that face of the planet; the . . . ruler . . . of our utilitarian, industrial, and scientific civilization."[102]

Caso located the common man within the domain of the practical. Finding support in Henri Bergson, Caso cited the French philosopher as saying that,

> the vulgar man, that product of nature's wholesale production, created by the millions every day is, as we have stated, incapable, at least in a constant way, of a complete disinterested apperception, of a true contemplation. He cannot direct his attention towards things unless they have some kind of relation, even if indirect, with his will . . . the notion of the thing is enough and even preferable in the majority of cases . . . the vulgar man does not stop to intuit, does not fix his sight for a long

time over an object, but instead looks quickly for such a concept within which he can include all of that that appears to him, the same way the lazy man looks for a chair, after which he does not worry about it anymore.[103]

This described Sáenz's practical man. "How could one more eloquently register the utilitarian, economic, selfish and biological essence of that concept?" he asked.[104] This concept of the common man spoke to what Vasconcelos termed the American "Babbitt." The American model of "a judicious, too judicious people; disciplined and uniform, too uniform, but happy within their genial monotony,"[105] which did not apply to Mexicans awash in tragedy, a sad people, "whose popular songs are awash in tears, as in the real life of the fatherland."[106]

Caso's vision of a future Mexican state could not accommodate the Deweyan idea that practical knowledge or local practices could be the foundation of society let alone a modern nation-state. As Rodó, he became convinced that the practical aspects of life could not be other than a platform for another social domain where good will (the social action of the state) could be justified beyond the political as "disinterested" action. He believed that this domain of pure good will was made possible by the labor of society that enabled intellectuals to perform their task of producing culture. He drew inspiration from William James' observation on heroism, noting how "James has observed [that] vital energy produces a surplus that engenders its fertility and abundance . . . the surplus of human energy makes of man a possible instrument of disinterested action and heroism."[107] The heroic and disinterested subject was Caso's future citizen, one with "an attitude . . . of renunciation having contemplation for its sacred dedication",[108] a member of an aesthetic state ruling through cultural instrumentalities demonstrating not interested but disinterested action: it was beyond the political.[109]

Another target for Caso was the idea of progress, castigating American models such as Dewey's for disseminating "the belief in the betterment of humanity," which was "a truly modern superstition."[110] He warned that, "the intellectualist dimensions of this great illusion remains, then, manifest; and the problem of the philosophy of history, its only problem."[111] Any vision of progress had to contend with the great tragedy of empire that created the western hemisphere. He affirmed that "from the point of view of civilization, it is clear that the Conquest was an immense good. Europe, thanks to Spain, realized in America the most extraordinary amplification of its possibilities for cultural developments. But, from the point of view of human happiness (which is the highest and the best for judging the acts of a human group), the Conquest was evil, an immense evil for the aboriginal people of Anáhuac."[112] The solution to the problem posed to the world by American progress he termed *progreso filosófico* or philosophical progress. Philosophical progress, as opposed to indubitably real and useful scientific and practical progress, was superior because it had as its object what Caso called the "concrete universal," and not, as in the American example, "the generic, the uniform."[113] This *progreso filosófico* reversed the civilizational equation of Spencer: "maximum of effort with a minimum of yield,"[114] the principle of the sacrificial subject.

The Incomplete Nation

Caso's ideal citizen—the future Mexican modern subject—was defined by tragedy because progress in the American continent rested on a history of loss. Yet the subject needed a nation. This led Caso to reconsider the salience of the Spanish conquest to the social question of Mexico's lack of modernity. The Spanish conquest, Caso argued, created an incomplete nation due to "the adaptation of two human groups with very diverse cultural levels."[115] Secular Mexico had not resolved the problem of the unification of the race posed by imperial conquest, a "fatality of history" that had prevented Mexico from developing a "uniformity" of treatment, the unity that had "never existed" in the nation."[116] According to Caso, "the collective soul of the Mexican has not coalesced yet in definite and characteristic forms; and it is very difficult for a proper and adequate scientific study of anything to exist if the object itself of research has not yet realized itself in its integrity and plenitude."[117] Heterogeneity signified a lack of unified consciousness, which led the citizen to act on his own, as an individualist, for his or her own gain, without comprehension of a greater good. Racial heterogeneity had produced an alienated self in Mexico, which made it different from the United States since the Mexican self degenerated into "exalted individualism."[118] Lacking a homogeneous consciousness, Mexico was incapable of "true patriotism."[119] The United States, on the other hand, was able to generate patriotism and love, and for that they were open to the world because they were "conscious of themselves, and therefore open . . . to immigrants from the world, who reached New York in order to collaborate and feel themselves, as soon, citizens of the country as if it were theirs."[120] México could not produce such a legible polity.

The narrative of empire assisted Caso in reaffirming the major goal of education: the civilization of the Indian as a civilizational gift. The calculating logic of the American Dewey could not accommodate such a concept, a notion crucial for the self-articulation of the identity of the intellectual who bestow such gifts. It also permitted Caso to redefine the meaning of the teacher away from the Deweyan ideal to that of the teacher-artist who brought the gift of culture to the masses and democratized it in the first place. This form of self-representation separated elite intellectuals like Caso from Deweyans such as Sáenz.

The differing histories of European expansion were a useful point for separating American and Mexican history precisely on this point: how they dealt with the tragedy of the plurality of Indian life. The "Indian" figured as an "obstacle to the progress of the fatherland" because, as another contemporary of Caso put it, Mexicans had not been able to "annihilate them, as the English colonists did with the redskins or the buffalos."[121] For Caso, the full assimilation of the Native Indian was necessary[122] because only a homogenous consciousness could create a modern nation by erasing the memory of the conquest, a consciousness that impeded progress in everyday matters and in face-to-face interaction. As Ezequiel Chávez, an intellectual who preceded Caso's generation, noted in this regard, it is "the memory of Native oppression and exploitation and not the benevolent dissemination of European culture [that becomes the] constant preoccupations when diagnosing the Indian's character."[123] American style segregation could not be the solution because it would only intensify heterogeneity.[124]

Coda: Dewey's Visit (and Critique) to Mexico

The record speaks for itself: China was Dewey's most cherished foreign land. Yet Mexico—just as Turkey and the Soviet Union—still occupied an important place in his imagination and the issues that Dewey encountered in those nations as he traveled there fully speak to the centrality of violence in the constitution of a nation-state as the crucial issue in the dissemination of his pedagogy. More specifically, his views on the Mexican revolution and its projects indicate that the China-Dewey and the Mexico-Dewey did not think alike. I argue that the reasons lie in the fact that in witnessing Mexico's revolution, Dewey inevitably read American history. The comparative process thus affected the outcomes of his vision of Mexico in ways different from China, Soviet Russia and Turkey. Would Dewey stay silent when a state utilized violence to produce a world he recognized as fundamental for democracy, where the political had been separated from the social as he had claimed a few years earlier was the case in the United States? Or would he defend the victims of state violence (church and peasants) even if they represented a worldview he understood as antagonistic or "primitive" with regard to free inquiry and progress?

Dewey and the Mexican Revolution

In the essay *War and a Code of Law* of 1923, Dewey opposed an American war with Mexico to protect US oil interests instead defending the feasibility of an international court to settle the dispute.[125] The essay underscored Dewey's unwavering conviction that violence could not give birth to a democratic society, perhaps the only principle of his social theory that Dewey refused to reconsider.[126] Mexico would provide him with a striking contrast to his experience in China. Whereas in China the hopes for a democratic uprising rested on the shoulders of the May Fourth Movement, in Mexico the transition to modernity was a state-directed top-down project already in progress. Just as in China, Dewey serendipitously found himself in the midst of the May Fourth revolutionary movement, in Mexico—for a brief month-long speaking and teaching tour in 1926—he arrived at a moment of a violent confrontation between the modernizing state and a rebellious religious peasantry and Catholic Church.

This historic and monumental confrontation—known in Mexican history as the *cristero* rebellion—reached a crescendo at the time of Dewey's arrival, when the Mexican clergy went on "strike" to refuse Mexican believers the sacraments of the church as retaliation against the state's attempt to control it by "registering" all priests with the state and have them state in writing the parishes and churches where they would officiate. The state campaign to modernize minds—undertaken as the Dewey project reached its heights—targeted the Catholic Church as an enemy of society and as the historical culprit for the "under-development" of Mexico. Churches were closed, priests were murdered and the state took over all education in the country. In 1926, supporters of the Catholic Church called *cristeros* (for Christ) rose in revolt against the state.[127] The Mexican state's revolutionary anti-clericals of the 1920s initiated a grand campaign for what was called the "mental emancipation" of Mexicans Indians and peasants. The state sought to create a "new Mexican": secular, scientific, rationalist and progressive. According to Alan Knight, the Mexican intelligentsia believed that "peasants needed to know . . . that drought must be countered by prudent public works, not parading saints around parched fields . . . they also needed to know that fonts, like coughs and sneezes, spread disease."[128]

The church-state conflict shaped Dewey's responses to Mexico. His responses to the struggle he witnessed conformed to the historicist worldview he shared with Sáenz. Mexico, in his view, was passing through an earlier stage in the history of humankind. He praised the modern constitution of Mexico (the constitution of 1917), writing that it "marked a 'stadium' in the struggle of church and state which has been going on for several centuries in all modern nations, and which has ended in all European states in the definite subordination of the church to civil authority. What was distinctive in the Mexican laws was the extreme thoroughness with which anti-clerical legislation has been carried out."[129] Dewey himself acknowledged that although the legislation had been extreme, Mexico's struggle had to be seen as a "belated chapter in the secular struggle of church and state for superior political authority."[130] The spectacle of a revolutionary government battling what must have seemed like a medieval institution conformed to his long-standing view that it was necessary to remove "primitive" or authoritarian structures for modern democratic inquiry to prevail. Dewey conceded that Calles' tactics—"dissolution of monastic orders," "exclusion of all foreigners from the right to exercise religious functions and to teach religion in schools," "denial of the right to wear a distinctive religious garb or emblems outside the church," for example—were drastic, but he refused to condemn them, since it all depended "upon one's social and political philosophy and one's view of the nature of religion, and its connection with organized political life."[131] He thus prophesized "the victory of the state," remarking that

"Catholics as a whole will in the end, though the end may be remote in Mexico, be better off than when they had too easy and too monopolistic a possession of the field."[132]

His refusal to cast a critical eye on the Calles project must be related to his personal views on American history and the distinction between the social (and he mentioned religion specifically) from the political that made democracy possible. Dewey warned progressives in the United States not to judge Mexico through Western or American standards, but to understand its local conditions. He cautioned them that "the revolution in Mexico [was] not completed. There is not a single manifesto which does not refer to the Principles of the Revolution; it is from the standpoint of completing the revolution that events in Mexico must be judged, not from that of legalities and methods of countries where political and social institutions are stabilized."[133] This was a revolution he approved. Given the incompleteness of the revolution and the enduring power of the Catholic Church in Mexico, Dewey concluded that Mexico was not a nation in the modern sense because it had "no organized public opinion." He blamed the Catholic Church for the arrested development of the nation, arguing that "the church can hardly escape paying the penalty for the continued ignorance and lack of initiative it has tolerated if not cultivated" and for the "attitude of the mass of inert and ignorant peasants" that it produced.[134] He praised the Calles' project, calling it "a revolution rather than a renaissance." "It is not only a revolution for Mexico," Dewey affirmed, "but in some respects one of the most important social experiments undertaken anywhere in the world. For it marks a deliberate and systematic attempt to incorporate in the social body the Indians who form 80 percent of the total population."[135] Dewey never doubted that in "incorporating" native Indians into the nation, the Mexican state would further the spread of civilization. "The policy of incorporating Indians into modern life," said Dewey comparing Mexico with the United States, "is of such extraordinary difficulty, its execution demands so much time, peace and tranquility, that any action on our part which puts added obstacles in its way is simply criminal. One can sympathize with foreigners in Mexico who find that their legal rights are not assured; yet from the standpoint of business in the long run as well as from that of human development, vested legalities are secondary to the creation of an integrated people."[136] Social integration into nationhood was essential, and for Americans to disturb this process in Mexico would result in a "deliberate cultivation of all seeds of turbulence, confusion and chaos." Dewey fully aligned himself with the official rhetoric of the Calles regime and thus tacitly agreed that the conditions for democracy in Mexico rested on the homogenization of its population.

Thus Dewey assented to the state nation-building project of the Calles government, whereas in China he had strongly condemned the imposition of national forms by the state. His statements contradicted the Dewey who castigated state nationalism in Japan and China for its use of violence and myth to control its citizens. He identified and seemed willing to accept the displacement of local culture (mostly of religious nature) in Mexico if it would foster ways for democratic inquiry to bloom. Why would Dewey accept violence now? Part of the reason lies with an exceptionalist chord in Dewey's philosophy that erased violence as a historical condition of possibility for the emergence of the American nation and as the potential source of the shared set of values he always assumed Americans shared. American exceptionalism provided a powerful and productive matrix to his social theorizing overseas. Witness his comments on the historical parallels between Mexico and the United States. In thinking of the Mexican Indian, he claimed that "one most readily pictures the general state of the country by thinking of early colonial days in the United States."[137] According to Dewey, America's Eden consisted of "a comparatively small number of settlements of a high civilization surrounded by Indian peoples with whom they have but superficial contact."[138] The erasure of colonial violence in this statement—consistent with his previous historical commentary on the history of the United States—provided Dewey with a benevolent historical narrative to justify native assimilation and imagine the incorporation of Native Americans into "Anglo-Saxon" culture—as he spoke of the United States—as an incorporation into the nation.[139] There were times when Dewey seemed to simply absorb and iterate Mexican state rhetoric on the Indian. For example, he continually praised "the aesthetic temperament of the Indian." On a visit to a school, he observed that Indian schools' "vegetable sections" were neglected at the expense of the "flower garden," which was always "gay and well cared for."[140] These were identical to words used by Moisés Sáenz and Rafael Ramírez, who deployed an orientalist language popular among the intelligentsia that appropriated the Indian for the nation on aesthetic grounds: their musical spirit, their talent for painting and arts and crafts or simply the "beauty" of the female Indian. These perspectives mirrored the language of the Calles regime and that of his "disciple" Moisés Sáenz.

Historical difference (and Mexican uniqueness) rested on something else. In Mexico, integrating the Indian looked like an almost insurmountable enterprise. Why was Mexico different from the United States? Dewey pointed to Indian diversity. "The fact," said Dewey, "that the Mexican Indians have a settled agricultural life, a much higher culture and greater resistance than our own Indians increases the difficulty of the situation. Add to this fact that the Indians are anything but homogeneous among themselves, divided into some thirty different tribes, intensely self-centered, jealous of their autonomy, prizing an isolation which is accentuated by geographical conditions, and we begin to have a faint idea of the problem which the revolutionary government is facing as systematically as all previous régimes dodged it."[141] Such diversity, rather than being an asset, constituted an obstacle for Mexico. This was not the China-Dewey. The Mexico-Dewey concurred with the idea that nationalizing the spirit of the Mexican village justified displacing local cultural practices and languages.

Exonerating Dewey?

How could he not see the violence at the heart of nation-building? It might be possible that for Dewey Mexico, in spite of his very concrete statement on the revolution, seemed an inscrutable society. In his private letters to his wife, Alice Chipman Dewey, Dewey confessed that Mexico seemed to him a "mess of contradictions." On the church-state conflict, Dewey told his wife: "Well, thats [sic] all a mess, but the country comme landscape is certainly beautiful."[142] He noted how on the one hand, Mexico sought secular scientific thought; one the other it succumbed to the American "new thought" movement. He observed with fascination how Mexican "bookstores [were] filled with translations of different types of occult literature." He puzzled over "a reference to Emerson" in a Mexican daily that associated the American author with "Orison Swett Marden," the founder of the new thought movement. He wondered how Nick Carter—actually a fictional character from Mitchell Wilson's dime novels—could be named the best-selling American author in Mexico.[143] "Mexico," proclaimed Dewey, "is the land of contradictions." "This fact," insisted Dewey, "is so baffling it keeps the visitor in an unrelieved state of foggy confusion."[144]

At one point he overheard rumors of an "underground revolt" by priests and peasants; at another, a priest assured him that "the church hasnt (sic) been in politics since 1910, and always wants religious freedom."[145] The officials at the Secretariat of Education, Dewey told Alice, "profess to make light of the present conflict [and] say the American papers are much more excited about it than anybody in this country,"[146] whereas his own Mexican translator "thinks the govt is right in the church matter for its objects; raw economic at bottom, and the church schools and preists [sic] inculcate the young with hatred to the republic and the revolution."[147] On a train in Guadalajara, he heard people "shouting Romas for the next governor" and then, with that governor still "on the train," "the walls [were] covered with hand bills telling how he stole 250,000 pesos while a deputy."[148] It seemed impossible for Dewey to define clearly where allegiances resided in Mexico.

Yet, in spite of his difficulties in processing the conservatism of the peasantry, his opposition to the Catholic Church and his own misgivings about religion in general, his private letters conveyed a Dewey touched by the traditional religious devotion of the poor in Mexico. While visiting a cathedral near Guadalajara, he writes that a Mexican, a "nice grey haired woman," once she found out Dewey and his "girls" were American, "began pouring out her woes—causa terribile," wrote Dewey, crying out how "the Catholics were suffering; the Americans were the only ones who could help them with their own govt; we should go back & tell everybody so the American govt would interfere; Cooleege [sic] have great influence, we should get his ear & c."[149] Moved by an unexpected act of trust and spiritual militancy, Dewey confessed to Alice that Mexico was "quite a religious place,"[150] adding that "the churches are well attended, and they have prayers & singing etc, everything but mass in fact, conducted by laymen."[151] His encounter with Mexican Indians prompted him to comment on their syncretism with wonder and at times some confusion. On a visit to a rural school in mountains close to Mexico City, the mayor of the town, a Native Mexican, responded to one of Dewey's questions by stating that he was a "socialist [but] was also taking part in the ceremony of the adoration of the Virgin which was going on." When Dewey asked him to explain the "anomaly," the native responded that "he was a socialist because the government had made the village a pueblo—that is, granted it self-government—while he was adoring the Virgin because the charter arrived on the saint's day." The significance of the comment rested on the serendipitous intersection of two calendars, one secular and one religious, neither one displacing the other. Dewey wondered how could Catholic "rites have been superimposed upon pre-conquest creeds and cults."[152] This brief encounter suggested how Dewey, as well as Mexican officials, did not understand syncretism as a rational response to change.

In spite of confusions and doubts, the record strongly suggests that Dewey supported the Mexican state project, specifically in its homogenizing aspects with respect to culture and language, the displacement of native modes of organization and the imposition of state ideologies to substitute for the religious and superstitious ideas of the peasant. In spite of his sincere admiration for Indian life and his appreciation for their deeply held religious beliefs, Dewey did not identify these Indian customs as the source of democratic life as he did with village life in China. Perhaps there was not enough time for him—as there was in China—to absorb the idiosyncrasies of Mexican daily life and culture. Another factor in exonerating Dewey from complicity with the violence of Mexico's state project resides in his belief that the Calles experiment was not necessarily displacing local practices. When visiting Tlaxcala, as well as in Mexico City, Dewey praised the Mexican education movement for financing schooling at the rural level "without cost to the nation by the people of the locality."[153] He praised the participation of the rural areas in the building of schools, observing that in Sáenz's Indian school in Mexico City, the school facilities were "adobe dwelling-houses offered by the parents in lieu of any available buildings."[154] He even bought into the state's project to "protect" the Indian artistic heritage, arguing that the survival of the Indian's "marked genius" for the arts rested on whether the "rural schools can succeed in preserving the native arts, aesthetic traditions and patterns, [thus] protecting them from the influence of machine-made industry."[155]

Conclusion

The Mexican critique of the Dewey project (and of Dewey's pedagogy) asked us to locate Mexico's possibilities in its own past: the possibilities to create a new subject rested on understanding how the past had prevented the realization of a full modern subject, whether the subject be Vasconcelos' Cosmic Race, Lombardo Toledano's proletarian man or Caso's disinterested subject. Second, They fully inscribed their critique of Dewey (and the critique of America) within a colonial comparative framework whereby Dewey's pragmatic education was understood in terms of Mexico's colonial history. Third, and perhaps most importantly, this critique fully inserted race in the discussion of Deweyan (and American), education asserting on the one hand the value of the Native Mexican to national culture and at the same time, the necessity of circumscribing—if not eradicating—the immensity of Mexico's native pluralities in order to create a nation-state as the only political form that could give expression to Mexico's historical possibilities. Thus Dewey's means-ends philosophy and open-ended world of possibilities was eventually rejected not simply as mistaken educational avenues, but as historically incompatible with the meaning of Mexico.

Dewey, on the other hand, struggled with the ways violence seemed necessary to advance the conditions of possibility of democratic societies. Yet, rather than turning his eyes fully to his own assumptions on America's own social foundations, he for the most part persisted in defending the necessity of a shared set of values as conditions for democratic inquiry and thus aligned himself with the oppressive aspects of Calles' and Sáenz's educational policies. Although Dewey did not have much contact with Sáenz himself—they met only once—the record suggests he did form a strong perspective on the Mexican revolution and for the most part agreed that some form of force would be needed to generate the basis for modernity in Mexico. Given the brief time Dewey remained in Mexico and the fact that this nation did not hold a grip on his imagination as China and perhaps Russia, the judgment on Dewey and revolution remains open to further scrutiny.

Notes

1. Jose Vasconcelos, *De Robinsón a Odiseo: Pedagogía estructurativa* (México: Editorial Constancia 1952). The critical works on Vasconcelos are too numerous to mention. Among recent notable monographs see, Itzhak Bar-Lewaw M., *La Revista "Timón" y José Vasconcelos* (México: Casa Edimex, 1971); Mario Aguirre Beltrán, *Revista El Maestro, 1921–1923: raíces y vuelos de la propuesta vasconcelista* (México: Universidad Pedagógica Nacional, 2002); Joaquín Cárdenas, *José Vasconcelos: Caudillo cultural* (Oaxaca: Universidad José Vasconcelos de Oaxaca, 2002); Regina Aída Crespo, *Itinerarios Intelectuales: Vasconcelos, Lobata y sus proyectos para la nación* (México: Universidad Autónoma de México, 2005); Claude Fell, *José Vasconcelos: Los años del águila*; Luis A. Marentes, *José Vasconcelos and the Writing of the Mexican Revolution* (New York: Twayne Publishers, 2000).
2. On Lombardo Toledano as a teacher, see Michael E. Burke, "The University of Mexico and the Revolution, 1910–1940" *The Americas* 2, vol. 34 (October 1977).
3. On Toledano's life see Francie R. Chassen de López, *Lombardo Toledano y el movimiento obrero de México, 1917–1940* (México: Extemporáneos, 1977); Rosendo Bolívar Meza, *Vicente Lombardo: Vida, pensamiento y obra* (Puebla:

Secretaría de Cultura, 1998); Robert Paul Millon, *Vicente Lombardo Toledano: Mexican Marxist* (Chapel Hill: University of North Carolina Press, 1966); Martín Tavira Urióstegui, *Vicente Lombardo Toledano: acción y pensamiento* (México: Fondo de Cultura Económica, 1999); Martín Tavira Urióstegui, *Vicente Lombardo Toledano: rasgos de su lucha proletaria* (México: Partido Popular Socialista, 1990).

4. Antonio Caso, *La existencia como economía y como caridad* (México: Librería Porrúa Hermanos, MCMXVI, 1916), 8.
5. Julio Ramos, "Hemispheric Domains: 1898 and the Origins of Latin Americanism" *Journal of Latin American Cultural Studies* 3, vol. 10 (2001).
6. The literature on the impact of the war of 1898 on Spanish-speaking nations other than Cuba and Puerto Rico is scarce. Some notable works are Rodrigo Quesada Monge, *El legado de la guerra hispano-antillana-norteamericana* (San José: Editorial Universidad Estatal a Distancia, 2001); Octavio Ruiz Manjón, *Los significados del 98: la sociedad española en la génesis del siglo XX* (Madrid: Fundación ICO, Biblioteca Nueva, Universidad Complutense, 1999); Leopoldo Zea & Mario Magallón, *98, desastre o reconciliación?* (México: Instituto Panamericano de Geografía e Historia, 2000); Leopoldo Zea & Adalberto Santana, eds., *El 98 y su impacto en Latinoamérica* (México: Instituto Panamericano de Geografía e Historia, Fondo de Cultura Económica, 2001).
7. Ramos identifies a process of "hemispheric compression" through the promotion of agreements in commerce and industry, the construction of railways and telegraphic networks and the "ideal of a common currency [to] at long last unite the American nations." See Julio Ramos, "Hemispheric Domains," 244.
8. John Skirius, *José Vasconcelos y la cruzada del 1929* (México: Siglo Veintiuno Editores 1978), 14.
9. Ibid.
10. See José Vasconcelos, *Ulises Criollo* (México: Ediciones Botas, 1935).
11. On the *Ateneo de la juventud*, see Fernando Curiel Defossé, "Ambición sin límites. La Intelectualidad Mexicana del siglo XX" *Historia y Grafía*, 23 (2004): 55–94; Fernando Curiel, *La Revuelta: interpretación del Ateneo de la juventud* (México: Universidad Autónoma de México, 1998); Gabriella de Beer, "El Ateneo y los Ateneístas: un examen retrospectivo" *Revista Iberoamericana* 148–149, vol. 55 (July-December, 1989): 737–749; Horacio Legrás, "El Ateneo y los orígenes del estado ético en México" *Latin American Research Review* 2, vol. 38 (June 2003): 34–60; Salvador Mendez Reyes, "El Ateneo de la Juventud y el Primer Congreso Nacional de Estudiantes" *Anuario Latinoamérica* 24 (1991); Serge Ivan Zaïtzeff, "Hacia el concepto de una generación perdida mexicana" *Revista Iberoamericana*, 148–149, vol. 55 (July-December, 1989): 751–757.
12. See Lily Litvak, *Latinos y anglosajones: orígenes de una polémica* (Barcelona: Puvill, 1980); Mónica Quijada, "La generación hispanoamericana del 98" in *Perspectivas del 98, un siglo después*, ed. Juan Velarde Fuertes (Junta de Castilla y León: Consejería de Educación y Cultura, 1997).
13. Walter L. Bernecker, "El fin de siglo en el Río de la Plata: Intereses internacionales y reacciones latinoamericanas" *José Enrique Rodó y su tiempo: cien años de Ariel*, edited by Ottmar Ette and Titus Heydenreich (Vervuert: Iberoamericana, 2000), 37.
14. José Antonio Rodó, *Ariel* (Madrid: Cátedra, Letras Hispánicas, 2nd edition, 2003), 195.
15. Partha Chatterjee, *The Nation and its Fragments: Colonial and Postcolonial Histories* (Princeton, NJ: Princeton University Press, 1993), 6.
16. José Antonio Rodó, *Ariel*, 201.

17. Ibid., 217.
18. Ibid., 205.
19. Ibid.
20. Ibid., 207.
21. Ibid., 196.
22. Ibid., 206–207.
23. Ibid., 204.
24. Ibid., 206.
25. Ibid., 216.
26. Ibid.
27. Ibid.
28. Aguirre Beltrán, Mario. *Revista El Maestro*, 63.
29. Ibid., 52.
30. Ibid., 49–50.
31. Ibid., 49.
32. José Vasconcelos, *La Raza Cósmica*, 57.
33. See Borghi, L., "The Influence of American Thought on Italian Education" (lecture at the Rockefeller Foundation, October 13, 1960), Rockefeller Archives, Collection RF, Record Group 1.2, Series 700R, Box 17, folder 149. See also, W.H. Burston, "The Influence of American Educational Thought upon English Educational Thought and Practice" (lecture at the Rockefeller Foundation, October 13, 1960), Rockefeller Archive Center, Collection RF, Record Group RG 1.2, Series 700R, Box 17, Folder 149.
34. José Vasconcelos, "Programa para las escuelas de educación primaria" *Boletín de la Secretaría de Educación Pública* (1922), 127–131.
35. See Claude Fell, *José Vasconcelos*, 121. See also, Jose Vasconcelos, *De Robinsón a Odiseo*.
36. Claude Fell, *José Vasconcelos*, 121.
37. José Vasconcelos, *La Raza* Cósmica, 57.
38. José Vasconcelos, *Ulises Criollo*, 155.
39. Ibid., 156.
40. Claude Fell, *José Vasconcelos*, 549.
41. See for example, José Vasconcelos, "Programa para las escuelas de educación primaria," 127–131; also the curriculum for the schools in the same document, 131–149.
42. José Vasconcelos, "Discurso inaugural del edificio de la secretaría" José Vasconcelos, *Obras Completas*, vol. II (México: Libreros Mexicanos Unidos, 1957), 800.
43. Diego Rivera, "Diego Rivera diserta sobre su extraño arte pictórico," *El Demócrata* (March 2, 1924).
44. See Salvador M. Lima and Marcelino Rentería, "La escuela de la acción," *Educación* 4, vol. II (August 1923), 244–250; and Salvador M. Lima and Marcelino Rentería, "La escuela de la acción," *Educación* 5, vol. II (September 1923), 294–310.
45. "Diferencias de criterio en los grupos de los educadores," *El Demócrata*, June 22 1923.
46. José Vasconcelos, *De Robinsón a Odiseo*, 3.
47. Ibid., 132.
48. See John Skirius, *José Vasconcelos y la cruzada del 1929*, 93.
49. José Vasconcelos, *De Robinsón a Odiseo*, 37.
50. Ibid., 7.
51. Ibid., 28.
52. Ibid., 17.

130 *Dangerous Dewey*

53. Ibid., 19.
54. Ibid., 28.
55. Ibid., 7.
56. Vasconcelos, *Hernán Cortés: creador de la nacionalidad* (México: Ediciones Xochitl, 1941), 171.
57. Vasconcelos, opus cit., 171.
58. J.M. Blaut, *The Colonizer's Model of the World: Geographical Diffusionism and Eurocentric History* (New York: The Guildford Press, 1993), 15.
59. Ibid.
60. Ibid., 17.
61. José Vasconcelos, *De Robinsón a Odiseo*, 28.
61. Ibid., 8.
62. Ibid., 28.
62. Ibid., 18, 19, 32.
63. José Vasconcelos, "Rousseau, Maestro" *Timón* 19, vol. 1 (April 20, 1940); reproduced in Itzhak Bar-Lewaw M., *La revista "Timón" y José Vasconcelos* (México: Casa Edimex, 1971), 132.
64. José Vasconcelos, *De Robinsón a Odiseo*, 33.
65. Ibid.
66. Ibid.
67. Ibid., 33–34.
68. Ibid., 41.
69. Ibid.
70. Ibid., 17–18; 19.
71. The idea is that the child is born free and it is society that corrupts him. José Vasconcelos, *De Robinsón a Odiseo*, 7–11.
72. José Vasconcelos, *De Robinsón a Odiseo*, 28.
73. Ibid., 39.
74. Ibid., 7.
75. On Toledano's life see Francie R. Chassen de López, *Lombardo Toledano y el movimiento obrero de México, 1917–1940* (México: Extemporáneos, 1977); Rosendo Bolívar Meza, *Vicente Lombardo: Vida, pensamiento y obra* (Puebla: Secretaría de Cultura, 1998); Robert Paul Millon, *Vicente Lombardo Toledano: Mexican Marxist* (Chapel Hill: University of North Carolina Press, 1966); Martín Tavira Urióstegui, *Vicente Lombardo Toledano: acción y pensamiento* (México: Fondo de Cultura Económica, 1999); Martín Tavira Urióstegui, *Vicente Lombardo Toledano: rasgos de su lucha proletaria* (México: Partido Popular Socialista, 1990).
76. Vicente Lombardo Toledano, *El problema de la educación en México: Puntos de vista y Proposiciones del Comité de Educación de la C.R.O.M., presentados por el Presidente del Comité VICENTE LOMBARDO TOLEDANO Ante la 6a. Convención de la Confederación Regional Obrera Mexicana, celebrada en Ciudad Juárez, Chih., en el mes de noviembre de 1924* (México: Editorial "CVLTVRA", 1924), 23.
77. Vicente Lombardo Toledano, *El problema de la educación en México*, 10.
78. The Protestant doctrine of individual freedom of inquiry and "self-examination" was an important basis of the educational paradigm of Moisés Sáenz. Here Lombardo Toledano defines the Protestant character of Mexican education in terms of individual choice.
79. Vicente Lombardo Toledano, *El problema de la educación en México*, 24.
80. In the 1960s, C. Wright Mills would attempt to disprove the validity of Dewey's pragmatism and his theory of communicative democracy by claiming that social inquiry as Dewey imagined did not work in times of rapid mobilization or within large corporate structures. For Mills, organizations need to dogmatize

their theory of actions "not only to insure, in a time of quick mass communication, uniformity among party workers, but because they are organizations. Some party workers become functionaries, hence it is not permitted that they think through independently problems in a 'free' and 'intelligent' manner." Ironically, Mills argued that for that reason Dewey's inquiry could only work in agricultural and rural societies where face-to-face encounters defined the social world. In a complex industrial society, the progressive aspects of Dewey worked to the detriment of the survival of the corporate body. Thus Dewey's key aspects of schooling were inapplicable to complex technological societies such as the United States and by inference would not produce the modern world that Toledano would struggle for in his life. See C. Wright Mills, *Sociology and Pragmatism* (New York: Oxford University Press, 1966), 394, 381. Larry Hickman notes that Dewey understood better than anybody the complex technological fabric of American society and had specifically addressed his philosophy to the American moment in which he lived in order to produce a philosophy antithetical to the "uniformity, mediocrity, and domination" of industrial life. Hickman, like Westbrook, remind us that Dewey was born in Vermont, which was a diverse society. Diversity—especially through immigration—was considered a threat by many of his contemporaries who longed for rural communities long gone. Dewey, states Hickman, asserted that technological forces lead to consolidation, not to fragmentation, and thus there was nothing to fear. Hickman's analysis reveals that behind most critiques of Dewey—especially those that decried his innocence and naïve faith in progress—resides the fear that Dewey's philosophy leads to pluralization rather than the unity of the body public. As in the case of Mills, only rural small communities can afford to be radically democratic without loss of identity. See Hickman, *John Dewey's Pragmatic Technology* (Bloomingston: Indiana University Press, 1990), 167, 175–177.
81. Vicente Lombardo Toledano, *El problema de la educación en México*, 24.
82. Ibid., 24–25.
83. Ibid., 25.
84. Ibid.
85. Vicente Lombardo Toledano, "La integración de la nacionalidad" Vicente Lombardo Toledano, *Textos Políticos y Sindicales* (México: Consejo Nacional para la Cultura y las Artes, 1994), 174.
86. Vicente Lombardo Toledano, *El problema de la educación en México*, 7.
87. Ibid., 8.
88. Vicente Lombardo Toledano, "La educación obrera Mexicana" *Textos políticos y sindicales* (México: Consejo Nacional para la Cultura y las Artes, 1994), 234–235.
89. Vicente Lombardo Toledano, *El problema de la educación en México*, 21.
90. Ibid.
91. Ibid., 17.
92. Ibid., 19–20.
93. Ibid., 17.
94. Ibid., 18.
95. Ibid., 11.
96. Ibid., 9.
97. 47.
98. Antonio Caso, "Problemas Nacionales," 218.
99. Antonio Caso, *La existencia como economía y caridad* (México: Librería Porrúa Hermanos, MCMXVI), 5.
100. Ibid., 6–7.
101. Ibid., 7.

132   *Dangerous Dewey*

102. Antonio Caso, "La definición del progreso" *Antología filosófica* (México: Ediciones de la Universidad Autónoma, 1957), 139.
103. Antonio Caso, *La existencia como economía y caridad*, 17.
104. Ibid.
105. Antonio Caso, *El problema de México y la ideología nacional* vol. 22 (México: Ediciones Libro-Mex. Biblioteca Mínima Mexicana, 1955), 87.
106. Ibid.
107. Antonio Caso, *La existencia como economía y caridad*, 13–14.
108. Ibid., 18.
109. Once again, this idea would later become useful to the Mexican state, reason why scholars argue that it "pre-figures" not only the hegemonic or Gramscian use of culture as a unifying ideology, but also the national space occupied by the intellectual: a space that is seen as apolitical yet affirming of state policy. See Horacio Legrás, "El Ateneo y los orígenes del estado ético en México," 44–49.
110. Antonio Caso, "La definición del progreso," 133.
111. Ibid., 139.
112. Antonio Caso, *El problema de México y la ideología nacional*, 56.
113. Antonio Caso, "La definición del progreso," 130.
114. Antonio Caso, *La existencia como economía y caridad*, 26.
115. Antonio Caso, *El problema de México y la ideología nacional*, 56.
116. Ibid.
117. Antonio Caso, "Problemas Nacionales," 214.
118. Antonio Caso, *El problema de México y la ideología nacional*, 80.
119. Ibid., 80–81.
120. Ibid.
121. Salvador Alvarado, "El problema del indio" in *Antología Ideológica*, ed. Antonio Pompa y Pompa, 1st edition (México: Secretaría de Educación Pública, 1976), 102–103.
122. This is a very important point for later appropriations of Dewey. Dewey's pedagogy, when understood as being predicated on the idea that school and society should not be alienated from each other, would be used by those who sought full assimilation and Indian segregation. The Indian, whether understood as part of society or as part of nature, had perforce to fully assimilate for modernity to have a chance on a scale such as that of the United States. Dewey's pedagogy would be used solely for the latter purpose, and not the former.
123. Prasenjit Duara, *Rescuing History from the Nation: Questioning Narratives of Modern China* (Chicago: The University of Chicago Press 1997), 61.
124. America could be a model only if its social solutions approximated the Spanish model of the *república de indios*, when Spanish authorities set aside *pueblos* through legislation intended to separate and protect Indians from total extermination. This was an ideal that Caso rejected, but it demonstrated the prevalent view that America's efficiency had been possible for the homogeneity of its social life.
125. Dewey, John. *War and a Code of Law*, MW 15: 122–127.
126. Witness the case of Dewey and Soviet Russia, for example. See for example, David C. Engerman, "John Dewey and the Soviet Union: Pragmatism meets Revolution."
127. The *cristiada* and the history of the Mexican anti-Catholic movement in general is too vast to list here. For some useful works see, Adrian Bantjes, *As if Jesus Walked on Earth: Cardenismo, Sonora and the Mexican Revolution* (Wilmington Del: Scholarly Resources, 1998); Marjorie Becker, *Setting the Virgin on Fire: Lázaro Cárdenas, Michoacán Campesinos, and the*

Redemption of the Mexican Revolution (Berkeley, CA: University of California Press, 1995); Mathew Butler, *Popular Piety and Political Identity in Mexico's Cristero Rebellion: Michoacán, 1927–1929* (Oxford: Oxford University Press, 2004); Alan Knight, *The Mexican Revolution*, vol. 1 & 2 (Lincoln: University of Nebraska Press, 1990); Enrique Krauze, *Reformar desde el Origen: Plutarco Elias Calles* (Mexico City: Fondo de Cultural Económica, 1987); Jean Meyer, *La Cristiada*, vol. 1& 2 (México City: Siglo XXI, 1973–1974). Also see the essays in *Faith and Impiety in Revolutionary Mexico*, edited by Matthew Butler.
128. Alan Knight, "The Mentality and Modus Operandi of Revolutionary Anticlericalism," *Faith and Impiety in Revolutionary Mexico*, edited by Matthew Butler (New York: Palgrave Macmillan, 2007), 30.
129. John Dewey, "Church and State in Mexico," *Impressions of Soviet Russia and the Revolutionary World: Mexico, China, Turkey, 1929* (New York: Bureau of Publications, Teachers College, 1964), 115. Also published in his collected works, LW 2:194.
130. John Dewey, "Church and State in Mexico," 119.
131. Ibid., 115.
132. Ibid., 119.
133. Ibid., 118–119.
134. Ibid., 117.
135. Dewey, John. *Mexico's Educational Renaissance*. In *John Dewey's Impressions*, opus cit., 121–121. Also published in *What Mr. John Dewey Thinks of the Educational Policies of Mexico* (México City: Publicaciones de la Secretaría de Educación Pública, vol. XI, no. 13, Talleres Gráficos de la Nación, 1926).
136. Dewey, opus cit., 129.
137. Ibid.
138. Ibid.
139. Dewey's statement also demonstrates that his assumptions about American history only surfaced when pressed by circumstances that spoke to the origins of nations or to projects to integrate nations.
140. Dewey, *Mexico's Educational Renaissance*, opus cit., 125.
141. Dewey, opus cit., 123.
142. John Dewey to Alice Chipman Dewey, 1926, 08.22-26 (04012), in the electronic edition of *The Correspondence of John Dewey, 1871–1952* (Charlottesville, VA: InteLex Corporation, 1999–2005).
143. Dewey, *From a Mexican Notebook*, in *John Dewey's Impressions of Soviet Russia*, 131.
144. Ibid.
145. John Dewey to Alice Chipman Dewey, 1926, 08.17 (04011) in the electronic edition of *The Correspondence of John Dewey, 1871–1952* (Charlottesville, VA: InteLex Corporation, 1999–2005).
146. Ibid.
147. Ibid.
148. Ibid.
149. Ibid.
150. Ibid.
151. Ibid.
152. Dewey, *From a Mexican Notebook*, in *John Dewey's Impressions of Soviet Russia*, 132.
153. Ibid., 125.
154. Ibid.
155. Ibid., 126.

Bibliography

Archives—USA

Archives of the Presbyterian Church of the United States, Philadelphia, Pennsylvania
The Bancroft Library, UC Berkeley, Berkeley, California
The Center for John Dewey Studies, Carbondale, Illinois
The Doe & Moffitt Libraries, UC Berkeley, Berkeley, California
The Gottesman Library at Teachers College, New York, New York
The Hoover Library and Archives, Hoover Institution, Stanford, California
The Joseph Regenstein Library Special Collections Research Center, Chicago, Illinois
Special Collections Research Center, The Morris Library, Carbondale, Illinois
Young Research Library Special Collections, UCLA, Los Angeles, California
Young Research Library, UCLA, Los Angeles, California

Archives—México

AGN—*Archivos Generales de la Nación*, Mexico City, México
A-SEP—*Archivos de la Secretaría de Educación Pública*, Mexico City, México

Newspapers & Journals—México

Educación
El Abogado Cristiano
El Abogado Cristiano Ilustrado
El Demócrata
El Testigo
La Antorcha Evangélica
La Prensa
Mundo Cristiano

Works Cited

Agamben, Giorgio. *Homo Sacer: Sovereign Power and Bare Life*. Stanford: Stanford University Press, 1998.
Aguilar Camín, Héctor. *La Frontera Nómada: Sonora y la Revolución Mexicana*. México City: Secretaría de Educación Pública, 1985.

Aguirre Beltrán, Gonzalo. "Introdución: El hombre y su obra." In *La escuela rural mexicana*, edited by Rafael Ramírez. México: Fondo de Cultural Económica, SE/80, 1981.

Aguirre Beltrán, Mario. *Revista El Maestro, 1921–1923: raíces y vuelos de la propuesta vasconcelista*. México: Universidad Pedagógica Nacional, 2002.

Alvarado, Salvador. "El Problema del indio." In *Antología Ideológica*, edited by Antonio Pompa y Pompa, 1st edition. México: Secretaría de Educación Pública, 1976.

Alvarado, Salvador. "El Problema de la educación." In *Antología Ideológica*, edited by Antonio Pompa y Pompa, 1st edition. México: Secretaría de Educación Pública, 1976.

Anderson, Benedict. *Imagined Communities: Reflections on the Origins and Spread of Nationalism*. Revised edition. London: Verso, 1991.

Arreguine, Víctor. *En que consiste la superioridad de los latinos sobre los anglosajones*. Buenos Aires: La Enseñanza Argentina, 1900.

Avrich, Paul. *The Modern School Movement: Anarchism and Education in the United States*. Princeton, NJ: Princeton University Press, 1980.

Baldwin, Deborah J. *Protestants and the Mexican Revolution: Missionaries, Ministers, and Social Change*. Urbana and Chicago: University of Illinois Press, 1990.

Bar-Lewaw, Itzhak M. *La Revista "Timón" y José Vasconcelos*. México: Casa Edimex, 1971.

Barranco, Manuel. "La Escuela Primaria del Futuro." *Mundo Cristiano*, July 6, 1919.

Basauri, Carlos. "La etnología de México." *Boletín de la Secretaría de Educación Pública* 7, Vol. IV. México: Talleres Gráficos de la Nación, Publicaciones de la Secretaría de Educación Pública, October 1925.

Basave Benítez, Agustín. *México mestizo: Análisis del nacionalismo mexicano en torno a la mestizofilia de Andrés Molina Enríquez*. México: Fondo de Cultura Económica, 1992.

"Bases para la organización de la escuela primaria conforme al principio de la acción." *Publicaciones de la Secretaría de Educación Pública*, Vol. X, no. 8. México: Talleres Gráficos de la Nación, 1926.

Bastian, Jean-Pierre. *Protestantismo y sociedad en México*. México: CUPSA (Casa Unidad de Publicaciones), 1983.

Bastian, Jean-Pierre. "Las sociedades protestantes y la oposición a Porfirio Díaz en México, 1877–1911." In *Protestantes, liberales y francmasones: Sociedades de ideas y modernidad en América Latina, siglo XIX*. México, edited by Jean-Pierre Bastian. Fondo de Cultura Económica, 1990.

Bastian, Jean-Pierre. *Protestantismos y modernidad latinoamericana: Historia de unas minorías religiosas activas en América Latina*. México: Fondo de Cultura Económica, 1994.

Bautista Reyes, A. "Informe del inspector instructor de la primera zona del estado de Guerrero, relative al funcionamiento de las escuelas primarias federales, durante el año de 1927." *Boletín de la Secretaría de Educación Pública*, Vol. VII, no. 1. México, January 1928.

Bernecker, Walter L. "El fin de siglo en el Río de la Plata: Intereses internacionales y reacciones latinoamericanas." In *José Enrique Rodó y su tiempo: cien años de Ariel*, edited by Ottmar Ette and Titus Heydenreich. Vervuert: Iberoamericana, 2000.

Blaut, J.M. *The Colonizer's Model of the World: Geographical Diffusionism and Eurocentric History*. New York: The Guildford Press, 1993.
Bolívar Meza, Rosendo. *Vicente Lombardo: Vida, pensamiento y obra*. Puebla: Secretaría de Cultura, 1998.
Bookchin, Murray. *The Spanish Anarchists: The Heroic Years, 1868–1936*. Oakland: AK Press, 1997.
Borghi, L. "The Influence of American Thought on Italian Education." Lecture at the Rockefeller Foundation, October 13 1960. Rockefeller Archives, Collection RF, Record Group 1.2, Series 700R, Box 17, Folder 149.
Boyd, Carolyn P. "The Anarchists and Education in Spain, 1868–1909." *The Journal of Modern History*, Vol. 48, no. 4 (December 1976): 125–170.
Brickman, William W. "Soviet Attitudes toward John Dewey as an Educator." *John Dewey and the World View*, edited by Douglas E. Lawson and Arthur E. Lean. Carbondale: Southern Illinois University Press, 1964.
Bruno-Jofré, Rosa and Jürgen Schriewer, eds. *The Global Reception of John Dewey's Thought: Multiple Refractions through Time and Space*. New York: Routledge, 2012.
Bruno-Jofré, Rosa and Carlos Martínez Valle. "Ruralizing Dewey: The American Friend, Internal Colonization, and the Action School in Post-Revolutionary Mexico (1921–1940)." In *The Global Reception of John Dewey's Thought: Multiple Refractions through Time and Space*, edited by Rosa Bruno-Jofré and Jürgen Schriewer. New York: Routledge, 2012.
Buenfil Burgos, Rosa N. "Discursive Inscriptions in the Fabrication of a Modern Self: Mexican Educational Appropriations of Dewey's Writings." In *Inventing the Modern Self and John Dewey: Modernities and the Traveling of Pragmatism in Education*, edited by Thomas S. Popkewitz. New York: Palgrave MacMillan, 2005.
Bulnes, Francisco. *Juárez y las revoluciones de Ayutla y de Reforma*. México: Antigua Imprenta de Murguía, 1905.
Burke, Michael E. "The University of Mexico and the Revolution, 1910–1940." *The Americas* 2, Vol. 34 (October 1977): 252–273.
Burston, W.H. "The Influence of American Educational Thought upon English Educational Thought and Practice." Lecture at the Rockefeller Foundation, October 13, 1960. Rockefeller Archive Center, Collection RF, Record Group RG 1.2, Series 700R, Box 17, Folder 149.
Calles, General Plutarco Elías. "Speech at the Opening of the Ordinary Sessions of Congress. (September 1st of 1927)," In *México a través de los informes presidenciales, Volume II, La Educación Pública*. México: Secretaría de Educación Pública, Secretaría de la Presidencia, 1976.
Cárdenas, Joaquín. *José Vasconcelos: Caudillo Cultural*. Oaxaca: Universidad José Vasconcelos de Oaxaca, 2002.
Casauranc, Dr. J.M. "Plática que sobre asuntos educativos y en respuesta a preguntas concretas de algunos señores profesores, sustentó el ciudadano secretario de educación pública, Doctor J. M. Puig Casauranc, el día dos de abril del presente año en la primera session del Congreso de Directores Federales." *Boletín de la Secretaría de Educación Pública*, Vol. 4, no. 1. México, April 1925.
Casauranc, Dr. J.M. *El Esfuerzo educativo en México: la obra del gobierno federal en el ramo de educación pública durante la administración del Presidente Plutarco Elías Calles (1924–1928). Memoria analítico-crítica de la organización actual*

de la Secretaría de Educación Pública sus éxitos, sus fracasos, los derroteros que la experiencia señala. Presentada al H. Congreso de la Unión por el Dr. J. M. Puig Casauranc, Secretario del Ramo en obediencia al artículo 93 constitucional, Tomo 1. México: Publicaciones de la Secretaría de Educación Pública, 1928.

Caso, Antonio. *La existencia como economía y como caridad.* México: Librería Porrúa Hermanos, MCMXVI, 1916.

Caso, Antonio. *El problema de México y la ideología nacional.* Vol. 22. México: Ediciones Libro-Mex. Biblioteca Mínima Mexicana, 1955.

Caso, Antonio. "La definición del progreso." In *Antología filosófica.* México: Ediciones de la Universidad Nacional Autónoma, 1957.

Caso, Antonio. "Problemas Nacionales." In *Antología filosófica.* México: Ediciones de la Universidad Nacional Autónoma, México, 1957.

Chakrabarti, Dipesh. *Provincializing Europe: Postcolonial Thought and Historical Difference.* Princeton, NJ: Princeton University Press, 2000.

Chakrabarty, Dipesh. "The Names and Repetitions of Postcolonial History." In *The Ambiguous Allure of the West: Traces of the Colonial in Thailand*, edited by Rachel V. Harrison and Peter A. Jackson. Hong Kong: Hong Kong University Press, 2010. Kindle edition.

Chassen de López, Francie R. *Lombardo Toledano y el movimiento obrero de México, 1917–1940.* México: Extemporáneos, 1977.

Chatterjee, Partha. *Nationalist Thought and the Colonial World.* Minneapolis, MN: University of Minnesota Press, 1986.

Chatterjee, Partha. *The Nation and its Fragments: Colonial and Postcolonial Histories.* Princeton, NJ: Princeton University Press, 1993.

Chávez, José María. *Censura e impugnación del folleto del C. Juan Amador, titulado El Apocalipsis o revelación de un sans culotte.* Guadalajara: Tipografía de Rodríguez, 1856.

Childs, John L. "The Civilizational Functions of Philosophy and Education." In *John Dewey and the World View*, edited by Douglas E. Lawson and Arthur E. Lean. Carbondale: Southern Illinois University Press, 1964.

"Código de Moralidad de los niños que concurren a las escuelas primarias." *Boletín de la Secretaría de Educación Pública* 7, Vol. IV. México: Talleres Gráficos de la Nación, Publicaciones de la Secretaría de Educación Pública no. illegible, Vol. VI, October 1925.

Crespo, Regina Aída. *Itinerarios Intelectuales: Vasconcelos, Lobata y sus proyectos para la nación.* México: Universidad Autónoma de México, 2005.

Curiel Defosse, Fernando. *La Revuelta: interpretación del Ateneo de la juventud.* México: Universidad Autónoma de México, 1998.

Curiel Defossé, Fernando. "Ambición sin límites: La Intelectualidad Mexicana del siglo XX." *Historia y Grafía*, Vol. 23(2004): 55–94.

Da Cunha, Vinicius. "John Dewey, the Other Face of the Brazilian New School." *Studies in Philosophy and Education*, Vol. 24(2005): 455–470.

Dávila, Jerry. *Diploma of Whiteness: Race and Social Policy in Brazil, 1917–1945.* Durham, NC: Duke University Press, 2003.

Dawson, Alexander S. *Indian and Nation in Revolutionary Mexico.* Tucson: University of Arizona Press, 2004.

de Beer, Gabriella. "El Ateneo y los Ateneístas: un examen retrospectivo." *Revista Iberoamericana*, 148–149, Vol. 55 (July-December, 1989): 737–749.

de la Luz Mena, José. *La escuela socialista, su desorientación y fracaso.* México: El verdadero derrotero, 1941.
de la Vega, José. "Informe de José de la Vega: El método de proyectos aplicado a las escuelas normales rurales." *Boletín de la Secretaría de Educación Pública*, Vol. VII, no. 5. Mexico, May 1928.
DePencier, Ida B. *The History of the Laboratory Schools: The University of Chicago, 1896–1965.* Chicago: Quadrangle Books, 1967.
Derrida, Jacques. *Of Grammatology.* Trans. Gayatri Chakravorti Spivak. Baltimore: The John Hopkins University Press, 1998.
Desmolins, Edmond. *A quoi tient la superiorité des anglo-saxons.* Paris: Firmin-Didot et cie, 1898.
Desmolins, Edmond. *La science sociale depuis F. Le Play, 1882–1905: Classification sociale resultant des observations faites d'après la methode de la science sociale par Edmond Desmolines.* Paris, 1905.
Dewey, John. *The School and Society and the Child and the Curriculum.* Chicago: The University of Chicago Press, 1900, 1991.
Dewey, John. *Introduction to Essays in Experimental Logic.* Chicago: The University of Chicago Press, 1916.
Dewey, John. *Art as Experience.* New York: Minton, Balch and Co., 1934.
Dewey, John. *Experience and Nature.* La Salle: Open Court Publishing, 1965.
Dewey, John. *Experience and Nature.* In *The Collected Works of John Dewey, 1882–1953*, edited by Jo Ann Boydston. Carbondale and Edwardsville: Southern Illinois University Press, 1967–1991.
Dewey, John. *Collected Works*, edited by Ann Boydston. Carbondale: Southern Illinois University Press, 1972–1985.
Duara, Prasenjit. *Rescuing History from the Nation: Questioning Narratives of Modern China.* Chicago: The University of Chicago Press, 1997.
El Primer Congreso Feminista de Yucatán, convocado por el C. gobernador y comandante militar del estado, Gral: Don Salvador Alvarado. Mérida: Talleres Tipográficos del "Ateneo Peninsular," 1916.
Engerman, David C. "John Dewey and the Soviet Union: Pragmatism meets Revolution," *Modern Intellectual History*, Vol. 3, no. 1 (2006): 33–63.
Fell, Claude. *José Vasconcelos: Los años del águila.* México: Universidad Nacional Autónoma de México, 1989.
Ferrer, Francisco. *The Origins and Ideals of the Modern School.* Trans. Joseph McCabe. New York: G.P. Putnam's Sons, 1913.
French, William E. *A Peaceful and Working People: Manners, Morals, and Class Formation in Northern Mexico.* Albuquerque: University of New Mexico Press, 1996.
Gellner, Ernest. *Nations and Nationalism.* 2nd edition. Ithaca, NY: Cornell University Press, 2009.
Gónzalez, Michael J. *The Mexican Revolution, 1910–1940.* Albuquerque: University of New Mexico Press, 2002.
González Navarro, Moisés. *Raya y tierra: la Guerra de castas y el henequen.* México: Colegio de México, 1970.
Grange, Joseph. *John Dewey, Confucius, and Global Philosophy.* Albany: State University of New York Press, 2004.
Guzmán, Eulalia. *La escuela nueva o de la acción.* México, 1923.

Hale, Charles A. "The Civil Law Tradition and Constitutionalism in Twentieth-Century Mexico: The Legacy of Emilio Rabasa," *Law and History Review*, Vol. 18, no. 2 (Summer 2000): 257–280.

Hall, David A. *The Democracy of the Dead: Dewey, Confucius, and the Hope of Democracy for China*. New York: Open Court Publishing Company, 1999.

Hickman, Larry. *John Dewey's Pragmatic Technology*. Bloomington: Indiana University Press, 1990.

Hickman, Larry. "Dewey's Theory of Inquiry." In *Reading Dewey: Interpretations for a Postmodern Generation*, edited by Larry A. Hickman. Bloomington: Indiana University Press, 1998.

Hofstadter, Richard. *Anti-Intellectualism in American Life*. New York: Vintage Books, 1962, 1963.

Iglesia Metodista Episcopal de México. *Actas de las conferencias anuales de la Iglesia Metodista Episcopal de México*. México: Imprenta Metodista, 1885–1911, 1889, 1902.

"Informe del director de educación federal en el estado de Tamaulipas, con relación a las escuelas primarias, correspondientes a los meses de noviembre y diciembre de 1927." *Boletín de la Secretaría de Educación Pública*, Vol. VII, no. 3. México: Talleres Gráficos de la Nación, March 1928).

Keenan, Barry. *The Dewey Experiment in China: Educational Reform and Political Power in the Early Republic*. Cambridge, MA: Harvard University Press, 1977.

Kilpatrick, William Heard. "The Project Method: Child Centeredness in Progressive Education." *History Matters*, 1918. http://historymatters.gmu.edu/d/4954/

Kilpatrick, William Heard. "Danger and Difficulties of the Project Method and How to Overcome Them: Introductory Statement, Definition of Terms." *Teachers College* Record 4, Vol. 22 (1921): 297–305.

Kilpatrick, William Heard. *Foundations of Method: Informal Talks on Teaching*. New York: Macmillan, 1925.

Knight, Alan. *The Mexican Revolution, Vol.2: Counter-Revolution and Reconstruction*. Lincoln: University of Nebraska Press, 1990.

Kobayashi, Victor N. *John Dewey in Japanese Educational Thought*. Ann Arbor: University of Michigan, Comparative Education Series, no. 2, 1964.

Legrás, Horacio. "El Ateneo y los orígenes del estado ético en México." *Latin American Research Review* 2, Vol. 38 (June 2003): 34–60.

Lewis, Stephen E. *The Ambivalent Revolution: Forging State and Nation in Chiapas, 1910–1945*. Albuquerque: University of New Mexico Press, 2005.

Ley de educación primaria. Mérida: Departamento de Educación Pública de Yucatán, 1918.

Lima, Salvador M. and Marcelino Rentería. "La escuela nueva de la acción: los errores de la vieja escuela." *Educación*, Vol. 2, no. 4 (August 1923): 244–250.

Litvak, Lily. *Latinos y anglosajones: orígenes de una polémica*. Barcelona: Biblioteca Universitaria Puvill, 1980.

Lombardo Toledano, Vicente. *El problema de la educación en México. Puntos de vista y Proposiciones del Comité de Educación de la C.R.O.M., presentados por el Presidente del Comité VICENTE LOMBARDO TOLEDANO Ante la 6a. Convención de la Confederación Regional Obrera Mexicana, celebrada en Ciudad Juárez, Chih., en el mes de noviembre de 1924*. México: Editorial "CVLTVRA", 1924.

Bibliography 141

Lombardo Toledano, Vicente. "La educación obrera Mexicana." In *Textos políticos y sindicales. Vicente Lombardo Toledano*. México: Consejo Nacional para la Cultura y las Artes, 1994.

Lombardo Toledano, Vicente. "La integración de la nacionalidad." In *Textos políticos y sindicales. Vicente Lombardo Toledano*. México: Consejo Nacional para la Cultura y las Artes, 1994.

Lomnitz-Adler, Claudio. *Exits from the Labyrinth: Culture and Ideology in the Mexican National Space*. Berkeley, CA: University of California Press, 1992.

Lomnitz-Adler, Claudio. *Deep Mexico, Silent Mexico: An Anthropology of Nationalism*. Minneapolis, MN: University of Minnesota Press, 2001.

Marentes, Luis A. *José Vasconcelos and the Writing of the Mexican Revolution*. New York: Twayne Publishers, 2000.

Martin, Jay. *The Education of John Dewey: A Biography*. New York: Columbia University Press, 2003.

Martínez Assad, Carlos, ed. *Los Lunes Rojos: la educación racionalista en México*, 1st edition. México: Secretaría de Educación Pública. Ediciones El Caballito, 1986.

Meisner, Maurice. *Li Ta-Chao and the Origins of Chinese Marxism*. New York: Atheneum, 1974.

Mendez Reyes, Salvador. "El Ateneo de la Juventud y el Primer Congreso Nacional de Estudiantes." *Anuario Latinoamérica*, Vol. 24 (1991).

Millon, Robert Paul. *Vicente Lombardo Toledano: Mexican Marxist*. Chapel Hill: University of North Carolina Press, 1966.

Memoria del primer congreso mexicano del niño patrocinado por "El Universal." México, 1921.

Mendieta y Núñez, Lucio. "Importancia Científica y práctica de los estudios etnológicos y etnográficos." *Boletín de la Secretaría de Educación Pública* 1, Vol. IV. México: Talleres Gráficos de la Nación, Publicaciones de la Secretaría de Educación Pública, 1925.

Mills, C. Wright. *Sociology and Pragmatism*. New York: Oxford University Press, 1966.

Molina Enríquez, Andrés. *Los grandes problemas nacionales*. México: Impresora de A. Carranza e Hijos, 1909.

Moore, Aaron Stephen. *Constructing East Asia: Technology, Ideology, and Empire in Japan's Wartime Era, 1931–1945*. Stanford: Stanford University Press, 2013.

Müller, Detlef, Fritz Ringer and Brian Simon, ed. *The Rise of the Modern Educational System: Structural Change and Social Reproduction 1870–1920*. Cambridge: Cambridge University Press, 1990.

Nolte, Sharon H. "Industrial Democracy for Japan: Tanaka Odo and John Dewey." *Journal of the History of Ideas*, Vol. 45, no. 2 (April-June 1984): 277–294.

Nubiola, Jaime. "The Reception of John Dewey in the Hispanic World." *Studies in Philosophy and Education* (November 1, 2005): 437–453.

Núñez Mata, Efrén. "Salvador Alvarado y la educación nacional." *Historia Mexicana*, Vol. 11 (1962): 422–436.

Obregón, General Álvaro. "Speech at the Opening of the 30th Congress in its Second Year of Sessions. (September 1st 1923)." In *México a través de los informes presidenciales, Volume II, La Educación Pública*. México: Secretaría de Educación Pública, Secretaría de la Presidencia, 1976.

142 Bibliography

Obregón, General Álvaro. "Speech on September 1st of 1924 at the Opening of the 3rd Congress on its First Year of Sessions. (September 1st 1924)." In *México a través de los informes presidenciales, Volume II, La Educación Pública*. Mexico: Secretaría de Educación Pública, Secretaría de la Presidencia, 1976.

O'Gorman, Edmundo. *México: El trauma de su historia*. 1st edition. México: Ciudad Universitaria: Universidad Nacional Autónoma de México, 1977.

Osuna, Andrés. *Elementos de Psicología Pedagógica*. México y París: Librería de la Vda. De Ch. Bouret, 4a. edición, 1917.

Padilla, José Macías. "Informe del Inspector Federal de la Zona Sureste del estado de Chihuahua, correspondiente al año escolar de 1927." *Boletín de la Secretaría de Educación Pública*, Vol. VII, no. 1. México: Talleres Gráficos de la Nación, Publicaciones de la Secretaría de Educación Pública, January 1928.

Paoli, Francisco and Montalvo. *El socialismo olvidado de Yucatán*. México: Siglo Veintiuno, 1974.

Pappas, Gregory Fernando and Jim Garrison. "Pragmatism as a Philosophy of Education in the Hispanic World: A Response." *Studies in Philosophy and Education*, Vol. 24, no. 6 (2005): 515–529.

Paulo, Ghiraldelli Jr. and Cody Carr. "What is Pragmatism in Brazil today?" *Studies in Philosophy and Education*, Vol. 24, no. 6 (2005): 499–514.

Planchet, Regis. *La Cuestión religiosa en México o sea la vida de Benito Juárez*. Roma: Librería Pontificia, 1906.

Pompa y Pompa, Antonio, ed. *Antología Ideológica*. México: Secretaría de Educación Pública. Primera edición, 1976.

Popkewitz, Thomas S. ed. *Inventing the Modern Self and John Dewey: Modernities and the Traveling of Pragmatism in Education*. New York: Palgrave MacMillan, 2005.

Porter, Glenn. *The Rise of Big Business, 1860–1920*. Wheeling, ILL: Harlan Davidson, Inc., 1973, 1992, 2006.

Programa de filosofía, Colegio de San Juan Nepomuceno, Saltillo, Coahuila. México: Saltillo: Tipografía La Perla Fronteriza.

Puig Casauranc, Dr. José Manuel. *Addresses delivered by Dr. J. M. Puig Casauranc, Secretary of Public Education of Mexico, the 23rd and 24th of March, 1926, at Columbia University, New York*. México: Talleres Gráficos de la Nación, Secretaría de Educación, 1926.

Puig Casauranc, Dr. José Manuel. "Speech at Teachers' College, Columbia University, New York. (23rd & 24th of March 1926)." *Boletín de la Secretaría de Educación Pública*, Vol. V, no. 4. México, Secretaría de Educación Pública, 1926.

Quesada Monge, Rodrigo. *El legado de la guerra hispano-antillana-norteamericana*. San José: Editorial Universidad Estatal a Distancia, 2001.

Quijada, Mónica. "La generación hispanoamericana del 98." In *Perspectivas del 98, un siglo después*, edited by Juan Velarde Fuertes. Junta de Castilla y León: Consejería de Educación y Cultura, 1997.

Rabasa, Emilio. *El juicio constitucional: orígenes, teoría y extensión*. Paris: Ch. Bouret, 1919.

Ramírez, Rafael. *La enseñanza por la acción dentro de la escuela rural*. Mexico: Ediciones de la Secretaría de Educación Pública, 1925, 1942.

Ramírez, Rafael. *La escuela proletaria (cuatro pláticas acerca de educación socialista): Conferencia dada a los maestros del distrito federal*. México, 1935.

Ramírez, Rafael. *La escuela rural mexicana*. México: Fondo de Cultura Económica, SE/80, 1981.

Ramos, Julio. "Hemispheric Domains: 1898 and the Origins of Latin Americanism." *Journal of Latin American Cultural Studies* 3, Vol. 10 (2001): 237–251.
"Reglas Generales de la Iglesia Metodista Episcopal del sur en México." *El Evangelista Mexicano*, August 1879.
Rockefeller, Steven. *John Dewey: Religious Faith and Democratic Humanism*. New York: Columbia University Press, 1994.
Rodó, José Enrique. *Ariel*. 2nd edition. Madrid: Cátedra, Letras Hispánicas, 2003.
Roma y el evangelio: estudios filosófico-religiosos, teórico-prácticos hechos por el círculo cristiano espiritista de Lérida y reimpreso por el círculo espiritista "Buena Esperanza" de Monterrey. Monterrey: A. Lagrange y Hermanos, 1876.
Ruiz Manjón, Octavio. *Los significados del 98: la sociedad española en la génesis del siglo XX*. Madrid: Fundación ICO, Biblioteca Nueva, Universidad Complutense, 1999.
Ryan, Alan. *John Dewey and the High Tide of American Liberalism*. New York: W. W. Norton and Company, Inc., 1997.
Sáenz, Moisés. "El cuatro de Julio," *El Abogado Cristiano*, July 8, 1915.
Sáenz, Moisés. *La escuela preparatoria: Estudios realizados por acuerdo del consejo de Educación Pública y llevados a cabo por los señores profesores Andrés Osuna, Moisés Sáenz, Galación Gómez, José Arturo Pichardo, Emilio Bustamante, y José Romano Muñoz*. México: Departamento Editorial de la Dirección General de Educación Pública, 1917. In *Folletos sobre educación en México 1917*. México, 1917–1938.
Sáenz, Moisés. "Editorial del 6 de Julio de 1919." *Mundo Cristiano*, July 6, 1919.
Sáenz, Moisés. "El Plan de Cincinati." *Mundo Cristiano*, July 10, 1919.
Sáenz, Moisés. "Lo esencial en la educación del estudiante." *Mundo Cristiano*, December 11, 1919.
Sáenz, Moisés. "¿Es la escuela una preparación para la vida?" *Mundo Cristiano*, December 18, 1919.
Sáenz, Moisés. "¿Quién es el verdadero agente de la educación?" *Mundo Cristiano*, December 25, 1919.
Sáenz, Moisés. "El Papel de la escuela de la acción en la República." *Boletín de la Secretaría de Educación Pública*, Vol. 4, no. 7. México: Talleres Gráficos de la Nación, Publicaciones de la Secretaría de Educación, México, 1925.
Sáenz, Moisés. "Una escuela socializada." *Boletín de la Secretaría de Educación Pública*, Vol. IV, no. 6, September 1925. México: Talleres Gráficos de la Nación, Publicaciones de la Secretaría de Educación Pública, Vol. V, no. 15, 1925.
Sáenz, Moisés. "Algunos aspectos sintéticos de la educación en México." *Boletín de la Secretaría de Educación Pública* 3, Vol. V. México: Talleres Gráficos de la Nación, Publicaciones de la Secretaría de Educación 8, Vol. VIII, México, 1926.
Sáenz, Moisés. "Discurso pronunciado por radio en Dallas, Texas, E.U.A. (November 26, 1925)." *Boletín de la Secretaría de Educación Pública*, Vol. V, no. 1. México: Talleres Gráficos de la Nación, Publicaciones de la Secretaría de Educación Pública, January 1926.
Sáenz, Moisés. "Extracto de la conferencia que el profesor Moisés Sáenz, subsecretario de Educación Pública, sustentó en la Convención de Maestros del Estado de Texas, reunida en Dallas, Tex., en noviembre de 1925." *Boletín de la Secretaría de Educación Pública*, Vol. V, no. 3. México: Talleres Gráficos de la Nación, Publicaciones de la Secretaría de Educación Pública 2, Vol. VIII, 1926.
Sáenz, Moisés. *Some Mexican Problems: Lectures on the Harris Foundation*. Chicago: University of Chicago Press, 1926.

Bibliography

Sáenz, Moisés. "Conferencia del Señor Moisés Sáenz, subsecretario de Educación Pública, dictada ante el Primer Congreso Nacional de Bibliotecarios, el día 18 de marzo de 1927." *Boletín de la Secretaría de Educación Pública*, Vol. VI, no. 4. México: Talleres Gráficos de la Nación, Publicaciones de la Secretaría de Educación Pública, 1927.

Sáenz, Moisés. *Reseña de la educación pública en México en 1927*. México: Publicaciones de la Secretaría de Educación Pública, 1927.

Sáenz, Moisés. *Escuelas Federales en San Luis Potosí: Informe de la visita practicada por el sub-secretario de educación pública en noviembre de 1927*. México: Talleres Gráficos de la Nación, 1928.

Sáenz, Moisés. *La educación rural en México*. México: Talleres Gráficos de la Nación, 1928.

Sáenz, Moisés. "Newer Aspects of Education in Mexico." *Bulletin of the Pan American Union*, Vol. XIII, no. 9 (September 1929): 861–877.

Sáenz, Moisés and Cristoph F. Steinke, *Segundo curso de inglés*. México: Herrero, 1930.

Sáenz, Moisés. *Carapan: Bosquejo de una experiencia*. Lima: Librería e Imprenta Gil, 1936.

Sáenz, Moisés. "México Indio: Conferencia de 1934 ante el Comité sobre Relaciones Culturales con América Latina" in *Renascent Mexico*, edited by Hubert Herring and Herbert Weinstock. New York: Covici-Friede Publications, 1935.

Saito, Naoko. "Education for Global Understanding: Learning from Dewey's Visit to Japan." *Teachers College Record*, Vol. 105, no. 9 (December 2003): 1758–1773.

Saito, Naoko. "Globalization and the understanding of other cultures: Beyond the Limits of Deweyan Democracy," presentation, Annual Meeting of the Philosophy of Education Society at Great Britain, Oxford, March 31, 2007.

Salazar, Juan B. "Informe del director de educación federal en el estado de Chihuahua, relativo a las visitas practicadas a las escuelas primarias federales de aquella capital y de la zona de Juárez y Parral." *Boletín de la Secretaría de Educación Pública*, Vol. VII, no. 1. México: January 1928.

Sánchez O. Alfredo. "Rectificaciones y aclaraciones sobre la escuela nueva. (Conclusión)." *Boletín de la Secretaría de Educación Pública*, Vol. V, no. 4. México: Talleres Gráficos de la Nación, Publicaciones de la Secretaría de Educación Pública 7, Vol. IX, 1926.

Scott, James C. *Seeing Like a State: How Certain Schemes to Improve the Human Condition Have Failed*. New Haven, CT: Yale University Press, 1999.

Segundo congreso nacional de maestros. Reunido en la capital de la República en los días del 15 al 28 del mes de diciembre de 1920. Obra escrita por el Profesor Higinio Vásquez Santa Ana, Srio. del referido Congreso y delegado de los estados de Jalisco, Michoacán y Chiapas Querétaro, Oficina Tipográfica del gobierno, 1923.

Silva Herzog, Jesús, ed. *La cuestión de la tierra, 1915–1917: Colección de folletos para la historia de la Revolución Mexicana*. México: Instituto Mexicana de Investigaciones Económicas, 1962.

Skirius, John. *José Vasconcelos y la cruzada del 1929*. México: Siglo Veintiuno Editores 1978.

Sordo y Cedeño, Reynaldo. "Las sociedades de socorros mutuos, 1867–1880" *Historia Mexicana*, Vol. 1, no. 129 (1983): 72–96.

Su, Zhixin. "A Critical Evaluation of John Dewey's Influence on Chinese Education." *American Journal of Education*, Vol. 103, no. 3 (May 1995): 302–325.

Tablada, José Juan. "El libro de un educador." *Boletín de la Secretaría de Educación Pública*, Vol. V, no. 5. México: Talleres Gráficos de la Nación, Publicaciones de la Secretaría de Educación Pública, May 1926.
Tan, Sor-Hoon. "China's Pragmatist Experiment in Democracy: Hi Shih's Pragmatism and Dewey's Influence in China." *Metaphilosophy*, Vol. 35, no. 1 & 2 (January 2004): 44–64.
Tan, Sor-Hoon. *Confucian Democracy: A Deweyan Reconstruction*. Albany: State University of New York, 2004. Tavira Urióstegui, Martín. *Vicente Lombardo Toledano: rasgos de su lucha proletaria*. México: Partido Popular Socialista, 1990.
Tavira Urióstegui, Martín. *Vicente Lombardo Toledano: acción y pensamiento*. México: Fondo de Cultura Económica, 1999.
Torres Quintero, Gregorio. "Coordinación de los programas de las escuelas federales con los de los gobiernos locales." In *Memorias de los trabajos realizados en la junta de directores de educación federal, verificada en la ciudad de México, del 24 de mayo al 2 de junio de 1926*. México: Publicaciones de la Secretaría de Educación, 1926.
Turan, Selahattin. "John Dewey's Report of 1924 and his recommendations on the Turkish Educational System." *History of Education*, Vol. 29, no. 6 (2000): 543–555.
Tyack, David B. *The One Best System: A History of American Urban Education*. Cambridge, MA: Harvard University Press, 1974.
Valderrama, Flores. "Educación y no solo instrucción." *El abogado cristiano ilustrado*, México, November 13, 1902.
Vasconcelos, José. "Por la unión Latino Americana. Discurso del 11 de octubre de 1922, ofreciendo el Banquete de los escritores Argentinos Imprenta Rafael Reyes, San Salvador, 1922." Box 25, file 104-B-21, Mexico: Obregón Calles Collection, Archivos Generales de la Nación.
Vasconcelos, José. "Programa para las escuelas de educación primaria." *Boletín de la Secretaría de Educación Pública*. México: Talleres Gráficos de la Nación, Publicaciones de la Secretaría de Educación, México, 1922.
Vasconcelos, José. "Conferencia dictada en el "Continental Memorial Hall de Washington, la noche del 9 de diciembre de 1922, a invitación de la 'Chataucua International Lecture Association' por el licenciado José Vasconcelos, Secretario de Educación Pública." *Educación* 1, Vol. 2 (May 1923).
Vasconcelos, José. *Ulises Criollo*. México: Ediciones Botas, 1935.
Vasconcelos, José. *Hernán Cortés: creador de la nacionalidad*. México: Ediciones Xochitl, 1941.
Vasconcelos, José. *De Robinsón a Odiseo: Pedagogía estructurativa*. México: Editorial Constancia, 1952.
Vasconcelos, José. "Discurso inaugural del edificio de la secretaría." *José Vasconcelos, Obras Completas*. Vol. II. México: Libreros Mexicanos Unidos, 1957.
Vasconcelos, José. *Obras Completas*, 1st edition, Vol. I-IV. México: Libreros Mexicanos Unidos, 1957–1961. Vasconcelos, José. "Rousseau, Maestro." *Timón* 19, Vol. 1 (April 20, 1940). In Itzhak Bar-Lewaw M. *La revista "Timón" y José Vasconcelos*. México: Casa Edimex, 1971.
Vasconcelos, José. *La Raza Cósmica*, Trans. Dider T. Jaén. Baltimore: The John Hopkins University Press, 1979.
Vaughan, Mary Kay. *The State, Education, and Social Class in Mexico, 1880–1928*. DeKalb: Northern Illinois Press, 1982.

Vaughan, Mary Kay. *Cultural Politics in Revolution: Teachers, Peasants, and Schools in Mexico, 1930–1940*. Tucson: University of Arizona Press, 1997.

Vaughan, Mary Kay. *The Eagle and the Virgin: Nation and Cultural Revolution in Mexico, 1920–1940*. Durham, NC: Duke University Press, 2006.

Waks, Leonard J. "The Project Method in Postindustrial Education." *Journal of Curriculum Studies* 4, Vol. 29 (1997): 391–406.

Waks, Leonard J. "John Dewey and Progressive Education, 1900–2000: The School and Society Revisted." In *John Dewey's Educational Philosophy in International Perspective: A New Democracy for the Twenty-First Century*, edited by Larry A. Hickman and Giuseppe Spadafora. Carbondale: Southern Illinois Press, 2009.

Waleska P.C. Ana, Mendoça, Libania Nacif Xavier, Vera Lucia Alves Breglia, Miriam Waidenfeld Chaves, Maria Teresa Cavalcanti De Oliveria, Cecilia Neves Lima and Pable S.M. Bispo Dos Santo. "Pragmatism and Developmentalism in Brazilian Educational Thought in the 1950s/1960s." *Studies in Philosophy and Education*, Vol. 24 (2005): 471–498.

Wallace, James M. *The Promise of Progressivism: Angelo Patri and Urban Education*. New York: Peter Lang Publishing, 2006.

Wang, Jessica Ching-Sze. "John Dewey as a Learner in China." *Education and Culture*, Vol. 21, no. 1 (2006): 59–73.

Wang, Jessica Ching-Sze. *John Dewey in China: To Teach and to Learn*. Albany: State University of New York Press, 2007.

West, Cornell. *The American Evasion of Philosophy: A Genealogy of Pragmatism*. Madison: The University of Wisconsin Press, 1989.

Westbrook, Robert. "Schools for Industrial Democrats: The Social Origins of John Dewey's Philosophy of Education." *American Journal of Education* 4, Vol. 100 (1992): 401–419.

Westbrook, Robert. *John Dewey and American Democracy*. Ithaca, NY: Cornell University Press, 1993.

Wolf-Gazo, Ernest. "John Dewey in Turkey: An Educational Mission." *Journal of American Studies of Turkey*, no. 3 (1996): 15–42.

Yao, Yusheng. "The Making of a National Hero: Tao Xingzhi's Legacies in the People's Republic of China." *Pedagogy and Cultural Studies*, Vol. 24, no. 3 (2002): 251–281.

Yao, Yusheng. "National Reconstruction through Education: Tao Xingzhi's Search for Individual and National Identity." *East-West Connections: Review of Asian Studies*, Vol. 1, no. 2 (2002): 129–148.

Yao, Yusheng. "Rediscovering Tao Xingzhi as an Educational and Social Revolutionary." *Twentieth Century China*, Vol. 27, no. 2 (2002): 79–120.

Zaid, Gabriel. *El Progreso Improductivo*. México: Siglo Veintiuno Editores, 1979.

Zaïtzeff, Serge Ivan. "Hacia el concepto de una generación perdida mexicana." *Revista Iberoamericana* 148–149, Vol. 55 (July–December, 1989): 751–757.

Zea, Leopoldo and Adalberto Santana, eds. *El 98 y su impacto en Latinoamérica*. México: Instituto Panamericano de Geografía e Historia, Fondo de Cultura Económica, 2001.

Zea, Leopoldo and Mario Magallón. *98, desastre o reconciliación?* México: Instituto Panamericano de Geografía e Historia, 2000.

Zhixin, Su. "Teaching, Learning and Reflective Acting: A Dewey Experiment in Chinese Teacher Education." *Teachers College Record* 1, Vol. 98 (Fall 1996): 126–152.

Zida, Zeng. "A Chinese View of the Educational Ideas of John Dewey." *Interchange*, Vol. 19, no. 3 and 4 (Fall/Winter, 1988): 85–91.

Index

Addams, Jane 43
Agamben, Giorgio 5
Aguirre Beltrán, Gonzalo 2, 75–6, 97
Alvarado, Salvador 19–21, 41, 56, 59, 62; and Dewey 20, 64
Americanization 12
American pragmatism 19, 48, 101, 106, 109, 113
American progressive education 10, 12, 15, 19–20, 22, 29, 45, 86
anarchists xi–xiv, 7–11, 19, 29, 40–1, 59; *see also escuela racionalistas*
Anderson, Benedict 51
Anglo-Saxon liberalism 20
Anglo-Saxons 17, 19, 21, 36, 59, 93, 99, 100, 103–6, 110, 124
Ariel xvii, 27, 102–5, 112, 128
Ariel see Rodó, José Antonio
Arreguine, Victor 17
associated child 60, 82
associated individual 38, 61
Ateneo de la Juventud xix, 101–2

Bakunin, Mikhail xi, 9
Baldwin, Deborah J. 42
Barranco, Manuel 17
Bases para la organización de la escuela primaria conforme al principio de la acción 17, 19, 28, 59, 64, 98
Bastian, Jean-Pierre 20 33, 38
Bergson, Henri 118
Bernecker, Walter L. 102
Blaut, J. M. 110
Bonilla, José 18
Bruno-Joffré, Rosa x, xxiv
Buenfil Burgos, Rosa N. x

Calderón, Lisandro 15–16, 27
Calles, Plutarco Elías 58, 61, 101, 108, 113, 122–4, 126–7

Carapan xx, 88–91
Cárdenas, Lázaro 58, 79, 91, 113
Carranza, Venustiano 40
Casa del Pueblo (Mexico City) 83
Casauranc 74, 96
Caso, Antonio xix, 18, 100, 101, 127; critique of Dewey and Sáenz 117–21; critique of progress 119–20; as head of the *Preparatoria* 117; *see also* Ateneo de la Juventud
Catholicism in Mexico xii–xiv, xvii, 20, 22–3, 40 47, 49, 62, 65, 66, 71, 72, 75, 85–6, 91, 101, 115, 122–3, 125; artificial order in Mexico xv, 9–10, 13, 19, 34, 49
Centro Anáhucac 82–3
Chakrabarti, Dipesh 5, 27, 76
Chatterjee, Partha 24, 30, 103, 128
Chávez, Ezequiel 122
Child and the Curriculum, The 94
Chuminópolis 8
Cincinnati Plan 42, 54
civilizing mission 19, 50, 74, 87, 120; ambivalence of 87, 90–1, 96, 117; futility of 89
cofradías 73
Confederación Regional Obrera Mexicana (CROM) 113
consummatory thought 22–3, 48–9, 55, 66
Cortés, Hernán 109; as a practical man 110
cristeros 85, 122, 132–3

de la Luz Mena, José 8, 10
de la Rosa, Guillermo 12
de la Vega, José 71, 80–1
DePencier, Ida B. 63
De Robinson a Odiseo 100, 108–13
Derrida, Jacques 2, 25

148 Index

Desmolins, Edmond 17
Dewey, John: American exceptionalism 124; Americanization of 8; as an American progressive 33; as anti-Christian 111; assumptions in his philosophy xvii; and child-centered education 68; and China 121, 123; and the civilizing mission 19, 117; critique of authoritarianism 92; and Indian assimilation 132; and the laboratory schools 21, 46, 63–5; Matamoros school (Tamaulipas) 80; means-ends philosophy 127; on Mexican Indian diversity 124; and the Mexican revolution 121–6; and modernity xiii, xv; as patron saint and prophet for Mexico 19–20, 29, 31, 45, 57; and practicality xiv; and productive inquiry xv, 22–3, 45, 47–9, 65; and race 2, 76, 127; reception by anarchists and socialists 7–11, 13–15, 17, 26; reception by Mexican Protestants 29; reception by the *escuelas activas* movement 12; on Sáenz's schools 126; tensions and contradictions in reception x–xi, xix, 16, 22, 73; vision of the United States of America 91; visit to Mexico 121–6; and workplace democracy 50
disinterested acts xix, 103–4, 107, 118–19, 127
Duara, Prasenjit 132

Educación (journal) xiii, 7–8, 14, 17–18, 22, 108
educational techniques: center of interest xvi, 17, 60–1, 69, 72–3, 80; *correlaciones* (correlations) xvi, 68–9, 81; *see also escuelas activas*; project method
ejidatarios 84
El Abogado Cristiano 36
El Faro 36
El Problema de las educación en México 113
Emerson, Ralph Waldo 106, 125
Engerman, David C. ix, 21
escuelas activas: as adversarial to Catholic education 72; ambivalences and tensions 5, 92; critique of as critique of America 100; critique of by Mexican intellectuals 100–27; as a Deweyan state project 1–2, 7, 58–61, 93; established by law 59; as a form of asynchronous substitution 1; as a movement in Mexican education xii, 11–12, 15, 40; opposite of vocational education xvi, 87; and *orientación para la vida* 58; racial underpinnings xx, 74–6, 88; school as corporation 82–3; as schools with no pedagogy 84; as a school with no tradition 74; as site of social engagement 86; as a supplement to Deweyan pragmatism 1–2, 75–6; supported by radical teachers in government 108
Escuelas Federales de San Luis Potosí 83
escuelas racionalistas 8, 24, 41
escuelas socialistas 91, 113; *see also* Cárdenas, Lázaro
escuelas tipos xv, 4, 59, 61–2, 80, 91
Estación Experimental de Incorporación del Indio 88; *see also* Carapan
Experience and Nature 23

Ferrer i Guàrdia, Francesc xi, 8–9, 11, 24; analogies to Dewey 9
First Mexican Congress on the Child of 1921 15
First Socialist Congress of Yucatán 10
Francisco I. Madero school 13

Gellner, Ernest 4, 36, 50, 69, 76
gente de razón 5
González, Michael J. 41
Guzmán, Eulalia 7–8, 11–13, 25

Hernán Cortés: creador de la nacionalidad 130
Hickman, Larry A. 22, 23, 47, 48, 49, 77, 131
Hofstadter, Richard 21–2
hombre teórico 18
homogeneity: as an aspect of American society xvii, 18; association with Deweyan education xii, xviii, 58; in consciousness 62, 86; Dewey on 123–4, 126; and industrial society 50; as integration of social contexts 58, 115; lack of in Mexican society 2, 49; as a necessary foundation for the nation xi, xvii, 60–1; and race xiii, xvi, 59, 61, 74, 96–7; and the socialized aspects of schooling xvii, 1
How to Think 8, 58

internal colonialism x
isolated individual xii, xvi, 12–13, 16, 49–50, 56, 60–1, 74, 90

James, William 101, 106, 118, 119
Juárez, Benito 32

Kilpatrick, William H. 17; and the American slave xv, 47; and the project method 17, 29, 31, 44–7, 50, 55, 66, 68, 80, 94, 97
Knight, Alan 122
Korea 82, 96
Kropotkin, Peter 9

laboratory schools: Chicago laboratory schools xvii, 63, 76, 1; Columbia University laboratory schools xvii, 1, 45, 76
La Concepción (San Luis Potosí) 85
La Escuela Nueva o de la acción 12–13
La Raza Cósmica 105–6
La Sierra de Puebla 87
La Villa de Guadalupe (San Luis Potosí) 98
Le Bon, Gustav 17
Legrás, Horacio 132
Lewis, Sinclair 111
Leyes de la Reforma 32
Lima, Marcelino M. 17, 108
Lo de Acosta (San Luis Potosí) 85
Lombardo Toledano, Vicente xviii, 100–1, 127, 13; as critic of Moisés Sáenz 101, 113–170; critique of Dewey 113–17; critique of Sáenz 130; and social intelligence 114–17; *see also* Confederación Regional Obrera Mexicana (CROM); *El Problema de las educación en México*
Lomnitz, Claudio 3, 58, 77, 94, 96, 97
López, Matías 61
Los Once Pueblos (Michoacán) 88–9

Marden, Orison Swett 125
Martínez Valle, Carlos x
Matamoros school (Tamaulipas, Mexico) 80–1
melancholia: and progress 16, 18
Mexican Indian: as "apathetic" and "passive" 65; as artistic 96; and Carapan project xx; and conception of Christianity 75; as a factor of production xviii, 18, 75; feminized 96–7; as ignorant 85–6, 123; location in Mexican history 96; as "mute" 77; as obstacle to progress 115, 120, 124; as the opposite of the entrepreneurial subject 18; as subject of state action 21, 50, 60, 73–5, 88–91; syncretism 86, 126; *see also Carapan*; Vasco de Quiroga
Mexico: arrested modernity 105; and fears of racial degeneration 16; as an incomplete nation 113, 114, 118, 123; as a laboratory for a new race 107; as lacking a homogeneous consciousness 120; as a nation of contradictions 125; need for a national character xiii, xv, 16, 49, 62; need for a national soul xi, xv, 30, 45, 50, 57–8, 102, 112, 117; as racially fragmented 15, 49; as a sad people 119; utopian vision of 60; as not white or Indian 90
Mexico Indio 91
modernity: as end of poverty 57, 77; and the *escuelas activas* movement xiv; and a homogeneous consciousness 122; and John Dewey xiii, 8; and the Mexican Indian 96–7; and Mexican society 2, 74; as modernization 96; as an object of desire 2; and practical inquiry 30, 93; and race 16; and science 106; and urban life 71; various meanings of xi, 11
Molina Enríquez, Andrés x, xxiv, 2; and the great national problems 3, 58, 60, 77, 84, 101
Moore, Aaron Stephen 4, 6
Mundo Cristiano 36

Normal de Jalapa 31

Obregón, Alvaro 40–1, 58, 106, 113
O'Gorman, Edmundo xviii, 53
Oropeza, Arturo 13–14
Osuna, Andrés 40

Padilla, José Macías 99
Pan-American Union 42, 44
Patri, Angelo 12
Paz Octavio 57
Pedagogic Congress of Mérida of 1915 10
Poe, Edgar Allan 106
Popkewitz, Thomas S. x
Porter, Glen 37
practicality: as an American trait 39, 110; as cognitive skills xvi, 58, 62,

88; as foundation for industrial growth 58; as a national trait 40, 49, 62; and Northern Mexicans 41
practical man: as an American character trait xvii–xviii, 19; as the American entrepreneur xiv, 20, 36; as an associated subject 60; as an enterprising subject 61, 66; as the eternal inquirer 36; as Mexico's future national subject 7; and practical inquiry 35, 58; as a Protestant minister 38; as a rational subject 5; and socialized schooling 75; as subject of indigenous modernity xiii, xvi, 17, 29, 31
Preparatoria 32, 100–1, 117
Presbyterians (American) 31
project method xiv, xvi, 44–6, 57, 59, 65–9, 76–7, 80–1, 83, 97; and Dewey 23, 46, 55; see also Kilpatrick, William H.
Protestantism in Mexico xiv, 20, 23, 29–33, 40; communities 34; in contradistinction to Catholicism 35; and education 34–5, 37; instrumentalism 39; and *orientación para la vida* 20, 31, 36, 37, 62; and practical inquiry 33; in relation to the *escuelas activas* 91, 108
Proudhon, Pierre-Joseph 9
Puig Casauranc, José Manuel 74

Ramírez, Rafael 68–9, 71, 92, 97, 124
Ramos, Julio 101, 128
Rentería, Marcelino 17, 108
Reyes, A. Bautista 99
Rivera, Diego 107–8, 129
Rodó, José Antonio xvii, 17, 102–5, 112, 119
rural schools xvi, 58–9, 61, 64, 65, 70, 77, 83, 87, 126

Sáenz, Aaron 108
Sáenz, Moisés ix, xiv, 2, 19, 29–30, 36, 41–3, 47, 50, 98, 108; accusations of being foreign 117; and the American corporate order xiv, 31, 37, 43–4, 58–9; anti-intellectualism 70–1; and the Carapan project 88–91, 99; as critic of Dewey xx; distinction between Mexican and Indian 96; duality of Deweyan project 30, 58, 61; and the high school 51, 73–4;

and John Dewey xiv, 30, 42, 47, 49, 58, 61, 63, 70, 72, 75, 79, 85, 122, 127; and the journal *Educación* 17; and the Mexican state Deweyan school project xvi, 57–8, 61–93; as ordained minister and Protestant 37, 92, 100; orientalism 99, 124; and practical inquiry 35, 39, 49–50, 58; as a practical man 91; and the project method 45, 47, 65–70; and race xx, 2; reconstruction of rural life 71; scientism 90; self-critique of *escuelas activas* project 88–90; as teacher of English 38; vision of community 39; vision of Mexico 49, 71
Salazar, Juan B. 99
Sánchez, Alfredo O. 74, 82–3, 96, 98
San Francisco Culhuacán school (Mexico City) 78–9; and the entrepreneurial ideal 79
School and Society, The 8, 58, 94
schools: as a community in miniature xii, 9, 18–21, 45, 59, 63–4, 85, 89; harmonious disorder xii, 13, 17, 61, 83; see also *escuelas activas*; project method
Schriewer, Jürgen x
Second National Teachers Congress of Mexico City of 1920 15
Secretariat of Public Education (SEP) 14, 59, 87–8, 101, 107–8, 125
Skirius, John 102
Smiles, Samuel 19
socialists xi–xii, xiv, 7–10, 19, 24, 29, 40–1, 107, 126
socialización (socialization): as an aspect of anarchist schools 11; as an aspect of Sáenz's Deweyan schools xvii, 1–2, 19, 31, 50, 58, 62, 75; and Carapan project 88; as a continuum between school and community 72; as different from American schools 86; and inquiry 60; as mutual change 90; as precondition for modernity 86; and race 71, 74; and Vasco de Quiroga's schools 117
Spencer, Herbert 118
spiritual colonialism 108

Tablada, José Juan 96
Tao Xingzhi 45
Tapia, Lucio 17–18
Taylorism 45

Teachers' College 32, 39, 45–6
Torres, Elena 10
Torres Quintero, Gregorio 41, 67
transition to modernity narrative 1, 5, 27, 40, 45, 92–3, 121

United States of America: as an Anglo-Saxon nation 104; as a barbarian nation 110; as a model of order and organization 12, 37, 59, 65, 76, 82; as a regime of exception 111; reliance on experience 37; as a scientific nation 118; standing for Mexico's future 92; as a teacher of good values 33; as a unified homogeneous nation 30, 132; as a utilitarian and practical nation 104–5
University of Chicago 19

Vasco de Quiroga xviii, 115–16; similarities to Dewey 116
Vasconcelos, José xviii, 15, 18, 26, 28, 37, 44, 58–9, 70, 71, 93, 100, 101, 105, 117, 119, 127, 130; critique of Dewey and *escuelas activas* project 101–13; *see also De Robinson a Odiseo*; *Hernán Cortés: creador de la nacionalidad*; *La Raza Cósmica*
Vaughan, Mary K. 24

Yucatán 7–8, 10, 19, 24, 41, 64, 67

Waks, Leonard J. 3, 55–6
Wang, Jessica Ching-Sze ix
Washington and Jefferson College 31
West, Cornell xi
Westbrook, Robert B. x, 50, 95, 131
Wright Mills, C. 114, 130–1